A Theory of International Organization

Transformations in Governance

Transformations in Governance is a major academic book series from Oxford University Press. It is designed to accommodate the impressive growth of research in comparative politics, international relations, public policy, federalism, and environmental and urban studies concerned with the dispersion of authority from central states to supranational institutions, subnational governments, and public–private networks. It brings together work that advances our understanding of the organization, causes, and consequences of multilevel and complex governance. The series is selective, containing annually a small number of books of exceptionally high quality by leading and emerging scholars.

The series is edited by Liesbet Hooghe and Gary Marks of the University of North Carolina, Chapel Hill, and Walter Mattli of the University of Oxford. The most recent publications include:

Managing Money and Discord in the UN: Budgeting and Bureaucracy
Ronny Patz, Klaus H. Goetz

Voluntary Disruptions: International Soft Law, Finance, and Power
Abraham L. Newman, Elliot Posner

Rules without Rights: Land, Labor, and Private Authority in the Global Economy
Tim Bartley

Measuring International Authority: A Postfunctionalist Theory of Governance, Volume III
Liesbet Hooghe, Gary Marks, Tobias Lenz, Jeanine Bezuijen, Besir Ceka, Svet Derderyan

Community, Scale, and Regional Governance: A Postfunctionalist Theory of Governance, Volume II
Liesbet Hooghe, Gary Marks

Territory and Ideology in Latin America: Policy Conflicts between National and Subnational Governments
Kent Eaton

With, Without, or Against the State? How European Regions Play the Brussels Game
Michaël Tatham

Constitutional Policy in Multilevel Government: The Art of Keeping the Balance
Arthur Benz

A Theory of International Organization

A Postfunctionalist Theory of Governance, Volume IV

Liesbet Hooghe, Tobias Lenz, and Gary Marks

OXFORD
UNIVERSITY PRESS

Great Clarendon Street, Oxford, OX2 6DP,
United Kingdom

Oxford University Press is a department of the University of Oxford.
It furthers the University's objective of excellence in research, scholarship,
and education by publishing worldwide. Oxford is a registered trade mark of
Oxford University Press in the UK and in certain other countries

© Liesbet Hooghe, Tobias Lenz, and Gary Marks 2019

The moral rights of the authors have been asserted

First Edition published in 2019

Impression: 1

All rights reserved. No part of this publication may be reproduced, stored in
a retrieval system, or transmitted, in any form or by any means, without the
prior permission in writing of Oxford University Press, or as expressly permitted
by law, by licence or under terms agreed with the appropriate reprographics
rights organization. Enquiries concerning reproduction outside the scope of the
above should be sent to the Rights Department, Oxford University Press, at the
address above

You must not circulate this work in any other form
and you must impose this same condition on any acquirer

Published in the United States of America by Oxford University Press
198 Madison Avenue, New York, NY 10016, United States of America

British Library Cataloguing in Publication Data
Data available

Library of Congress Control Number: 2019934006

ISBN 978–0–19–876698–8 (hbk.)
ISBN 978–0–19–884507–2 (pbk.)

Printed and bound by
CPI Group (UK) Ltd, Croydon, CR0 4YY

Links to third party websites are provided by Oxford in good faith and
for information only. Oxford disclaims any responsibility for the materials
contained in any third party website referenced in this work.

Acknowledgments

This book has had a long gestation. Liesbet and Gary's interest dates from the early 2000s when they were seeking to understand multilevel governance beyond the European Union. This motivated a European Research Council project on multilevel governance within and beyond states. Tobias' interest was piqued in Santiago de Chile, where he interned at the European Commission Delegation and the UN Economic Commission for Latin America and the Caribbean (CEPAL). He next moved to Oxford to write a dissertation on EU influence on global regionalism. Our paths crossed in Berlin in 2010, where all three of us were visiting fellows at the Kollegforschungsgruppe "The Transformative Power of Europe." We co-ran a reading group on regional IOs, and a few months later, Gary and Liesbet invited Tobias to join the ERC team.

Placing the EU among international organizations throws the diversity of international governance into sharp relief. Why is authority mostly thin beyond the national state, and why so dispersed? Why do some international organizations have just a few member states, and others span the globe? Why do many focus on a specific problem, alongside others that have policy portfolios almost as diverse as those of national states? In short, what drives variation in international organization?

The idea that governance is shaped by the tension between a functionalist impetus to tackle problems and a communal desire for self-rule began to take form from the early 2000s. This lies at the hard core of postfunctionalist theory, and motivates our work on European integration and subnational governance. We have found it useful for thinking about jurisdictional design in the international domain, and for IOs in particular. The intellectual breakthrough in this venture was to conceive an IO as a contract among member states. This allowed us to build a bridge between social contract theory in Western political thought and the economic theory of incomplete contracting. In this approach, the willingness of the participants to share incompletely contracted governance requires normative commitment as well as functional benefits. Rather than setting up a competition between constructivist and rationalist theory, we felt it was essential to draw on both.

Having an idea is one thing, making it tangible and disconfirmable is quite another. Our first step was to lay the groundwork that would allow us to test

Acknowledgments

our hunches, a project that took five years. We required reasonably accurate estimates of authority for a sizeable number of international organizations (IOs) over an extended period of time. The measure of international authority (MIA), which estimates the structure and decision making of seventy-six IOs on an annual basis from 1950 to 2010, was released in 2016 (Hooghe et al. 2017). We were immensely fortunate to work with a talented group of researchers and co-authors in Jeanine Bezuijen, Besir Ceka, and Svet Derderyan.

Conceptualization and measurement never venture far from theory, and we began writing this book soon after we produced the data. A first version of the book appeared in mid-2014, though it took several revisions before we felt that a draft was ready for circulation. In the end we managed to escape Jorge Luis Borges' library of Babel.

We have benefited from many people's advice and help. Special thanks go to Tanja Börzel and Thomas Risse who put the three of us in touch at the KFG, invited us back multiple times, and provided incisive comments on more drafts than they may care to remember! Participants at a conference on international design at UNC-Chapel Hill in spring 2013 discussed our early attempt to articulate a theory of IO design. Julia Gray and Yoram Haftel gave extensive comments on draft book chapters at the Wissenschaftskolleg in Delmenhorst in July 2014. Tanja Börzel, Matthias Ecker-Ehrhardt, Thomas Risse, Thomas Sommerer, Alex Tokhi, Lora Viola, and Michael Zürn provided invaluable feedback at a book workshop in Berlin in June 2018. We also wish to thank Brian Burgoon, Besir Ceka, Gary Goertz, and Marco Steenbergen for methodological advice. Emanuel Coman and Jeanine Bezuijen were terrific in developing the stata syntax for key variables. Kyle Chan, David Guevara, Benjamin Neudorfer, Annika Reinke, Elena Sandmann, Alexandre San Martim Portes, Rick Scholten, Kai Stern, and Emily Venturi provided research assistance.

We presented drafts of chapters at the American Political Science Association (2006, 2010, 2014, 2018); the Council of Europeanists (2016); the Dreiländertagung in Zürich (2019); the German Political Science Association Conference (2016); the International Studies Association (2013, 2014, 2019); Berlin Graduate School for Transnational Studies (2011); ETH Zürich (2011); the European University Institute, Florence (2014, 2015); the Free University of Berlin (2011, 2012, 2013, 2014, 2018); GIGA office in Berlin (2017); University of Göttingen (2014, 2017); the University of Hamburg (2019); the Hanse Wissenschaftskolleg in Delmenhorst (2011, 2014); Harvard (2018); the University of Lisbon (2018); the University of Munich (2011); New York University (2012); the Steiner seminar at the University of North Carolina (2012, 2013); Nuffield College, Oxford (2012, 2016); Salamanca University (2012); the Social Science Center in Berlin (2012, 2015); and VU Amsterdam (2010, 2012, 2016).

Acknowledgments

Many people have commented on papers and drafts, and we are deeply appreciative for their advice. We wish to thank, in particular, Karen Alter, Cameron Ballard-Rosa, Frank Biermann, Jeff Checkel, Eugenia Conceiçao-Heldt, Philipp Genschel, Edgar Grande, Jessica Green, Adrienne Héritier, Markus Jachtenfuchs, Bob Keohane, Hanspeter Kriesi, Barbara Koremenos, Steve Krasner, Brigid Laffan, David Lake, Juan Díez Medrano, Frank Schimmelfennig, Duncan Snidal, Theresa Squatrito, Jonas Tallberg, and Erik Voeten.

Graduate seminar participants David Attewell, Ann-Sophie Gast, Jacob Gunderson, Andreas Jozwiak, Jelle Koedam, Caroline Lancaster, Stephanie Shady, and Kai Stern read the entire final manuscript and provided valuable feedback. Both the argument and the book have been greatly helped by all those mentioned here, but the usual disclaimer applies—we alone are responsible for the result, errors included.

The University of North Carolina at Chapel Hill has been a wonderful home base for Gary and Liesbet. Thanks also to the VU Amsterdam, which administered this project through 2016. Tobias would like to thank the European University Institute in Florence for hosting him as a Max Weber Fellow in 2015–16, and Gary and Liesbet are very grateful to Brigid Laffan at the EUI for welcoming them as Robert Schuman Fellows from May through July each year. The Center for European Studies at UNC-Chapel Hill hosted a workshop on international organization in 2013, the Hanse-Wissenschaftskolleg in Delmenhorst an authors' workshop in 2014, and the KFG-Berlin a book workshop in June 2018. The project has been funded by Gary Marks' Advanced European Research Council grant # 249543 "Causes and Consequences of Multilevel Governance."

This is the last of four volumes that set out a theory of postfunctionalist governance. Previous volumes measure and theorize multilevel governance within states (Vols. I and II) and set out a measure of international authority (Vol. III). Over the years, Dominic Byatt has been a tremendously supportive editor at Oxford University Press. The editorial and production teams at OUP have been super.

We dedicate this book to our children and nephews and nieces—Joshua, Yessica, Ben, Thomas, Teddy, Tine, Norea, and Elias.

May 2019

Contents

Detailed Contents   xi
List of Figures   xv
List of Tables   xvii
List of Abbreviations   xix

1. Introduction   1
2. Philosophical Foundations of a Postfunctionalist Theory of International Organization   9
3. Measuring International Authority   26
4. The Basic Set-Up: How International Organizations Vary   44
5. Why Do Some IOs Expand their Policy Portfolio?   60
6. The Resistible Rise of International Authority   84
7. Why States Pool Authority   104
8. Five Theses on International Governance   121

Appendix   135
References   159
Index   187

Detailed Contents

List of Figures	xv
List of Tables	xvii
List of Abbreviations	xix

1. Introduction	1
Situating Postfunctionalism	3
Plan of the Book	6
2. Philosophical Foundations of a Postfunctionalist Theory of International Organization	9
Scale and Community in the Provision of Governance	12
The Sociality of Incomplete Contracting	14
The Constraint of National Community	18
The Puzzle of International Governance	20
Conclusion	24
3. Measuring International Authority	26
Defining Authority	28
Specifying the Concept	29
Unit of Analysis	29
Why Formal Rules?	30
Dimensions of International Authority	32
Developing Indicators	33
Scoring and Adjudicating Cases	37
A Bird's-Eye View	38
Conclusion	43
4. The Basic Set-Up: How International Organizations Vary	44
The Basic Set-Up	45
Theorizing Variation in the Basic Set-Up	46
Scale and Community	46
Types of Governance	47
Key Expectations	50
Key Variables	53
Results	53
Conclusion	59

Detailed Contents

5. Why Do Some IOs Expand their Policy Portfolio?	60
Incomplete Contracting and Policy Scope	60
Key Variables	62
Policy Scope	63
Contract	64
Community	65
Controls	66
Evidence	67
Community and Contract	67
Trade	70
Exceptional Cases	73
The Council of Europe	74
United Nations	75
The Commonwealth	78
The Organization of American States	79
The African Union	81
Conclusion	83
6. The Resistible Rise of International Authority	84
Policy Expansion	86
Politicization	88
Key Variables	91
Delegation	91
Pooling	94
Policy Scope	96
Politicization	97
Controls	97
Evidence	98
Illustrative Cases	100
Conclusion	103
7. Why States Pool Authority	104
The Scale Hypothesis	105
Evidence	108
Illustrative Cases	114
Conclusion	119
8. Five Theses on International Governance	121
International Governance is Formal and Informal	122
International Governance is Contractual	127
International Governance is Functional	128
International Governance is Social	130
International Governance is Politicized	132

Appendix		135
Part I:	Operationalization	135
Part II:	Variables	140
	International Authority	140
	Policy Scope	145
	Community	148
	IO Contract	151
	Politicization	153
	Trade Interdependence	156
References		159
Index		187

List of Figures

3.1	Measurement model	27
3.2	A model of IO decision making	34
3.3	Delegation and pooling over time	38
3.4	Boxplots for change in delegation	40
3.5	Boxplots for change in pooling	41
3.6	Delegation and pooling in 2010	42
4.1	The community versus scale trade-off	51
4.2	The trade-off between scale and community	54
4.3	Bimodal distribution of international organizations	56
5.1	A model of policy scope	62
5.2	Change in policy scope	63
5.3	Community and contract	68
6.1	A model of international authority	85
6.2	Change in delegation by IO	92
6.3	Change in delegation by IO body	93
6.4	Change in pooling by IO	95
6.5	Change in majority voting in 76 IOs	96
7.1	The risk of exploitation	106
7.2	The cost of decision making	106
7.3	The scale hypothesis	108
7.4	Scale and pooling	111
A.1	Policy scope over time	147
A.2	Average annual politicization by IO	155
A.3	Trends in politicization	156

List of Tables

3.1	Change in delegation and pooling compared	39
4.1	General purpose and task-specific governance	48
4.2	Predictions and findings	56
5.1	IOs by contract	65
5.2	Principal components analysis for *Community*	66
5.3	Community and contract, 1950–2010	67
5.4	Explaining policy scope with the community-contract model	69
5.5	Community, contract, and trade policy	71
5.6	IOs by trade interdependence and trade policy	72
5.7	Community, contract, and trade interdependence	73
6.1	Change in bindingness and ratification in 76 IOs	96
6.2	Explaining change in delegation and pooling	98
6.3	A two-stage model explaining change in delegation and pooling	100
7.1	Cross-sectional models for pooling	110
7.2	Epistemic community	113
7.3	Membership and majority rule	115
8.1	Formal and informal governance	123
A.1	Operationalization of variables	135
A.2	Descriptives	138
A.3	IO population in MIA	139
A.4	Principal components factor analysis of delegation and pooling	143
A.5	Correlation matrix of delegation and pooling	143
A.6	Descriptives for delegation	144
A.7	Descriptives for pooling	144
A.8	Policy categories	145
A.9	Descriptives for policy scope, core, flanking policies	147

List of Tables

A.10	Correlation matrix of indicators of community	149
A.11	Historical ties among IO founding members	150
A.12	Descriptives for politicization	154
A.13	Incidence of politicization	155
A.14	Correlations among measures of trade interdependence	158
A.15	Descriptives for trade interdependence	158

List of Abbreviations

ALADI	Latin American Integration Association
AMU	Arab Maghreb Union
ASEAN	Association of Southeast Asian Nations
AU	African Union
BIS	Bank for International Settlements
CABI	Centre for Agriculture and Bioscience International
CARICOM	Caribbean Community
CARIFTA	Caribbean Free Trade Association
CCNR	Central Commission for the Navigation of the Rhine
CELAC	Community of Latin American and Caribbean States
CEMAC	Economic and Monetary Community of Central African States
CERN	European Organization for Nuclear Research
CoE	Council of Europe
COMECON	Council for Mutual Economic Assistance
COMESA	Common Market for Eastern and Southern Africa
ComSec	Commonwealth Secretariat
EAC	East African Community
ECB	European Central Bank
ECCAS	Economic Community of Central African States
ECOSOC	UN Economic and Social Council
ECOWAS	Economic Community of West African States
ECSC	European Coal and Steel Community
EEA	European Economic Area
EEC	European Economic Community
EU	European Union
GDP	gross domestic product
IACHR	Inter-American Court of Human Rights

List of Abbreviations

IADB	Inter-American Development Bank
IAEA	International Atomic Energy Agency
ICAO	International Civil Aviation Organization
ICC	International Criminal Court
ICPC	International Criminal Police Commission
IGAD	Intergovernmental Authority on Development
IMF	International Monetary Fund
Interpol	International Criminal Police Organization
IO	international organization
IOM	International Organization for Migration
IWhale	International Whaling Commission
Mercosur	Southern Common Market
MIA	Measure of International Authority
NAFTA	North American Free Trade Agreement
NATO	North Atlantic Treaty Organization
NGO	non-governmental organization
OAU	Organization of African Unity
OAS	Organization of American States
ODECA	Organization of Central American States
OECD	Organization for Economic Co-Operation and Development
OEEC	Organization for European Economic Cooperation
OIF	la Francophonie
OPEC	Organization of Petroleum-Exporting Countries
OSCE	Organization for Security and Cooperation in Europe
OTIF	Intergovernmental Organization for International Carriage by Rail
PCA	Permanent Court of Arbitration
PTA-ESA	Preferential Trade Area for Eastern and Southern Africa
SACU	Southern African Customs Union
SADC	Southern African Development Community
SELA	Latin American and Caribbean Economic System
SICA	Central American Integration System
SPÖ/ÖVP	Social-Democrat party/Christian-Democrat party in Austria
UDEAC	Central African Customs and Economic Union
UK	United Kingdom
UN	United Nations

List of Abbreviations

UNASUR	Union of South American Nations
UNESCO	UN Educational, Scientific and Cultural Organization
UNIDO	UN Industrial Development Organization
USMCA	United States–Mexico–Canada Agreement
WHO	World Health Organization
WTO	World Trade Organization

1

Introduction

How is governance organized among states? States remain by far the most powerful political actors on the planet, but only by cooperating can they handle the problems that arise when their populations interact. They do so chiefly by forming international organizations (IOs) with standing administrations that allow them to respond in real time to changing circumstances. This book seeks to explain the forms that institutionalized governance takes in the international domain.

The possibilities are diverse. Some international organizations have just a few member states, while others span the globe. Some are targeted at a specific problem, while others have policy portfolios almost as broad as national states. Some are member-state driven, while others have independent courts, secretariats, and parliaments. Some curb national sovereignty by making binding decisions by majority, while others use unanimity or provide opt-outs. Variation among international organizations appears as wide as that among states. The purpose of this book is to explain this variation, both across international organizations and over time.

Postfunctionalist theory draws on two ways of thinking about governance. The first considers governance—collective decision making in the expectation of obedience—as a rational response to the human condition. Governance allows individuals to provide themselves with security, law, knowledge, and civilization itself, and thereby escape "the state of nature." This functionalist approach to the provision of public goods transcends the ceiling of the state. It applies to the problems generated by human interaction, regardless of territorial scale. The level at which a public good should be provided depends on the costs and benefits of centralization, and these vary widely with the externalities and scale economies of the public good in question. Hence, from a functionalist perspective, governance should be multilevel. Where the externalities of human interaction extend beyond national borders, it is efficient to organize governance at the international level.

Functionalist theorizing about governance has been productive in both comparative politics and international relations. It has enriched our understanding of how the search for efficient solutions to the provision of public goods shapes governance in general and international organization in particular. In order to explain the conditions under which states empower IOs, we confirm and extend functionalist theory.

However, the premise of postfunctionalism is that this is not sufficient because it ignores the sociality of governance. Beyond its functionality, governance expresses the right of a people to determine its laws. Hence, to explain international governance one needs to engage a second way of thinking about governance that considers the *Who Question*—who claims a right to rule themselves? We need to consider how the participants feel about being bound together in collective rule.

This approach to governance draws attention to perceptions of community. Do the participants conceive themselves as a community with a shared history and norms, or as a group that has little in common beyond facing a collective problem? Do they perceive themselves as having some overarching identity, or do they conceive their national identities as exclusive and incompatible? Do they share religious, social, or political norms that can help them negotiate the ambiguities of cooperation and defection? Shared norms extend the possibilities of cooperation by assuaging fears of exploitation, by promoting diffuse rather than specific reciprocity, and by making it feasible for the participants to bind themselves in an incomplete contract for broad-ranging governance.

Community is double-edged. Communities can facilitate cooperation because they sustain diffuse reciprocity. However, communities are also settings for parochialism expressed in favoritism for one's own group, a readiness to draw a sharp boundary between one's in-group and out-groups, and a tendency to harbor grievances stemming from a Manichaean "us versus them" conception of the social world.[1] Those who understand their identity, and particularly their national identity, as exclusive are prone to regard international governance as foreign imposition. Shared rule, for all its functional benefits, limits the self-rule of those living in the participating states. We argue that the effect of this for international cooperation depends on the extent to which people(s) conceive themselves as members of a community.

Hence, the core claim of this book is that international governance is both functional and social. One must take up their interplay to explain the institutional set-up of an IO, its membership, contractual basis, policy portfolio, decision rules, and the extent to which an IO's member states delegate authority to non-state actors and pool authority in binding collective decision making.

---

[1] The idea that community is double-edged is expressed in the concept of parochial altruism.

This study is the fourth in a series of books that seek to explain multilevel governance.[2] The theory that guides this project applies to governance both within and among states. The first two volumes are concerned with subnational authority. The third volume conceptualizes and measures the authority of IOs with standing from 1950 to 2010. This book uses that information to evaluate postfunctionalist conjectures about the structure, competences, and authority of IOs. Doing so moves the analysis beyond the demarcation criterion, which posits that international and domestic governance are causally distinct spheres characterized by anarchy on the one side and hierarchy on the other. We conceive domestic and international politics as different contexts for a coherent set of generalizations rather than as two causally unique worlds.

Our focus is on institutionalized governance, i.e. governance in organizations having an ongoing capacity for problem solving. The diversity of such organizations on just about every dimension of interest is very wide, and to explain this it makes sense to frame this study broadly. This means that we include regional IOs, global IOs, and IOs that do not fall neatly into either category. Rather than having distinct theories for different subsets of IOs, we seek to generalize about the population of IOs as a whole.

Situating Postfunctionalism

Three streams of thought have been especially influential in the study of international governance, and this book relates to each.

Realism explains international governance as the result of strategic choices made by independent states which exist in the absence of overarching authority. We concur that states are the most powerful actors in international politics and they vary widely in their power capabilities. There is, indeed, no coercive authority above states capable of sustaining international organization. States exist in potential competition and conflict with each other. Hence, international governance must be self-sustaining for there is no external actor that can impose rules on states. However, conflict is just one possible outcome. If one assumes that states are (differentially) powerful, independent, and competitive, it would be perfectly rational for them to contract governance among themselves.

This is the point of departure for social contract theory. Hobbes, Locke, Kant, Rousseau, and Rawls conceive governance as contracted to avoid anarchy. This has profound implications for international governance. Whereas anarchy is a

---

[2] *Measuring Regional Authority* (Hooghe, Marks, Schakel, Niedzwiecki, Chapman Osterkatz, and Shair-Rosenfield 2016); *Community, Scale, and Regional Governance* (Hooghe and Marks 2016); *Measuring International Authority* (Hooghe, Marks, Lenz, Bezuijen, Ceka, and Derderyan 2017).

theoretical possibility among persons, it is an actual possibility among states. The contracts among individuals that produce states are imaginary, whereas the contracts among states that produce international organizations are real documents negotiated by real actors in real time.

This book is concerned with the character of these contracts and their effect on cooperation over time. Under what circumstances will states enter into an incomplete contract for general purpose government? Under what conditions will they conclude a relatively complete contract that specifies exactly what the IO can and cannot do? And what are the consequences of this for the institutional set-up of an IO and for its authority?

We conceive governance within states and among states as having a logic that can travel across scale. This takes issue with the realist premise that the causal underpinnings of international politics are unique (Waltz 1979: 88; Mearsheimer 1995: note 183). The characteristics that realists perceive as distinctive of the international system appear to be present in degree rather than kind (Milner 1991). This includes the claim that the international domain is populated by units that have survival as their chief goal. State survival and national independence are often highly valued, but they are not the only goals that motivate states. States can decide to sacrifice considerable independence for the benefits of shared rule, as the history of federalism reveals (Riker 1964).

Federalism is an extreme example of a more general phenomenon in which a state gives up some freedom of action for the benefits of collective governance. States find many ways short of federalism to share rule, from general purpose governance to leaner organizational forms targeted at specific problems. Hence it makes sense to regard the existence of independent states in the absence of coercive hierarchy as a point of departure for a theory of international governance rather than its outcome. One can then consider the conditions that would lead states to contract certain forms of governance. What these forms are and how to explain them is the subject of this study.

From *liberal institutionalism* we take the idea that states act rationally in dealing with the collective action problems produced by interdependence. This approach conceives IOs as means to reduce the transaction costs of cooperation in areas where states have overlapping interests, thereby facilitating international governance under the structural constraints imposed by anarchy. Functionalist theory is indispensable if one wishes to explain two puzzling features of international governance: Why do states delegate authority to independent IO bodies and why do states collectivize decision making in binding majoritarianism? The answer, we believe, has to do with the functional pressures arising from the complexity of decision making and the risk of decisional blockage. International authority in our account is a functional adaptation to the benefits of finessing the national veto as the number of member states increases and the benefits of empowering independent actors to set the agenda, provide information, and settle disputes as the policy portfolio of an IO expands.

However, a functionalist account can only take one so far. To explain how functionalist pressures play out in different contexts one must theorize the sociality of governance—how participants perceive themselves in relation to others. The extent to which the participants consider themselves to be a community conditions the contractual incompleteness of an IO, the course of its policy competences, and the size of its membership. Community comes into play in designing an IO, and so what appears to be a functionally determined process depends on the normative basis on which an organization is built.

This opens the door to a third stream of literature, *constructivism*, which explores how norms, identities, and discourse shape international cooperation. The character of international governance depends not only on its benefits, but on what the participants make of each other. Constructivism draws attention to the social fabric of international cooperation. To explain variation in international governance one needs to theorize the conditions under which the participants will be prepared to surrender some national self-rule for international shared rule.

We theorize the social character of international governance along two paths. The first concerns the extent to which the populations of the member states conceive themselves as having some overarching community. As Elinor Ostrom (1990) observes, community—expressed in overarching norms, a shared identity, and a common sense of fate—underpins diffuse reciprocity which can sustain incompletely contracted cooperation in a non-hierarchical setting. Community is generally weaker in the international domain than within states, but we find that the variation that exists in the international domain is decisive for explaining the diverse forms of governance that one can observe.

The second way in which the social nature of cooperation comes into play is through the politicization of international governance. The tension between shared rule and self-rule may intensify as an IO becomes more authoritative. This can play out in domestic political debate, which has seen growing opposition to international governance on the ground that it weakens national community and undermines national sovereignty. The mobilization of exclusive nationalism can constrain the willingness of a government to further empower an IO even in the face of functional pressures. We expect this to matter most for international organizations that are particularly salient and polarizing in domestic politics.

The objective of this study is to explain the institutionalization of IOs. How are they designed? What are their rules of decision making? How are they empowered to exercise authority? This leaves important topics unconsidered. How effective are IOs in implementing decisions on the ground? How is the governance of an IO related to its performance? How do increasingly numerous IOs interact within regions and at a global scale? While these questions lie beyond the present study, a theory that explains how IOs are institutionally structured may contribute to each of them. The institutional character of a jurisdiction is a useful place to start in investigating how it implements policy, how it interacts with other units, and how well it performs. In general, it usually makes sense to analyze the characteristics of the units in a network, and how they came to be, if one intends to explain the relative strength of their ties with other nodes, why some units are more central than others, and how effective they are.

Distributional struggles over international governance—the subject of an extensive political economy literature—are beyond the scope of this study. The benefits of international cooperation may be distributed unequally both between member states and across social groups within them. Rational actors anticipate the distributional consequences of alternative institutional choices and seek to influence them in order to gain a disproportionate share of the cooperative surplus. In the analyses that follow, we control for distributional factors, such as hegemony and asymmetric trade interdependence, but our focus is on the interaction between efficiency-related and social factors.

From a long historical perspective this is a study of a single case, the liberal world order following World War II. This world order has been sustained by factors that lie outside our theory, including American material and ideational dominance and an extended period devoid of world war. It is possible that the functional and cultural variables in our theory are time-bound in ways that are not yet evident. As postfunctionalism argues, the chief constraint on international governance today is nationalism. Whether this will remain so, we cannot yet tell.

Plan of the Book

Chapter 2 lays out the hard core of a postfunctionalist theory of international organization. The point of departure is to conceive governance as a social contract among rational actors to escape anarchy. It refines social contract theory by assuming that a contract for governance can concentrate authority or disperse it across jurisdictions at diverse scale. Postfunctionalism proposes that the willingness to conclude a highly incomplete contract depends on whether participants think of themselves as a community. The remainder of the book specifies and tests the theory's observational implications.

Introduction

Chapter 3 explains why we conceptualize international authority as delegation and pooling and demonstrates how these abstract qualities can be measured. Our model of IO decision making disaggregates agenda setting, final decision making, bindingness of decisions, ratification, and dispute settlement across six decision areas: policy making, constitutional reform, the budget, financial compliance, membership accession, and the suspension of members. The chapter concludes by summarizing variation in pooling and delegation for seventy-six major IOs cross-sectionally and over time (1950–2010).

Chapter 4 explains the basic set-up of an IO—its membership, contract, and policy portfolio—as resulting from the tension between the functional logic of public goods provision and the preference of exclusive communities for self-rule. The theory expects international organization to be bimodal. General purpose governance builds on transnational community to contract cooperation as an open-ended venture among peoples. Task-specific governance is more targeted. It contracts cooperation narrowly so that states, no matter how diverse, can come together to problem-solve. General purpose and task-specific IOs relate to their constituencies differently, and this shapes the scale of their membership, their openness to membership growth, and the breadth and dynamism of their policy portfolios.

Chapters 5, 6, and 7 test some observable implications of a postfunctionalist theory of international organization. Chapter 5 models an IO's policy portfolio in two steps. The first explains change in an IO's policy portfolio as a function of the incompleteness of its contract. The second explains the incompleteness of an IO's contract as conditioned by shared norms that allay fears of exploitation. A model that specifies an IO's contractual basis and its normative coherence accounts for more than half of the variance in the policy portfolio over time.

Chapter 6 examines how functional and non-functional pressures affect pooling and delegation in IOs. Functional pressures stem from the need to make decision making tractable under an expanding policy portfolio. This prompts an IO's member states to pool authority in majoritarian decision making and to delegate agenda setting to independent agents who can frame the agenda and mediate disputes. However, the politicization of exclusive national identity can constrain IO authority even in the presence of intense functional pressure.

Chapter 7 explains variation in pooling as a response to the number of potential veto players in the IO. The incentive to suspend the national veto is a function of an IO's decision costs, which depend on the number of member states an IO anticipates. This hypothesis is assessed in a cross-sectional analysis using a measure of pooling that distinguishes the mode, bindingness, and substantive area of decision making.

Chapter 8 summarizes the argument of the book in five theses. International governance has both a formal and an informal basis. Its foundation in IOs is explicitly contractual. To explain the basic set-up and authority of an IO one needs to theorize the functional pressures that arise in the provision of public goods, the social constraints in adapting to those pressures, and the consequent politicization of IO legitimacy.

2

Philosophical Foundations of a Postfunctionalist Theory of International Organization

"Are you prepared to part with any degree of national sovereignty in any circumstances for the sake of a larger synthesis?" The question was directed at Winston Churchill on the floor of the House of Commons in a debate about whether Britain should participate in negotiations to form a European Coal and Steel Community. Churchill's answer was yes:

> The whole movement of the world is towards an inter-dependence of nations. We feel all around us the belief that it is our best hope... We are prepared to consider and, if convinced, to accept the abrogation of national sovereignty, provided that we are satisfied with the conditions and the safeguards... national sovereignty is not inviolable, and it may be resolutely diminished for the sake of all men in all the lands finding their way home together.[1]

The prime minister, Clement Attlee, agreed in principle, though he believed that Britain's time to join a European Union had not come:

> There must be a common basis of moral values.... I have often spoken against the continuance of some absolute idea of sovereignty.... As a matter of fact, anyone entering into an alliance or a treaty does take away to an extent their absolute power to do as they will... In advocating Western Union, we are prepared with other Powers to pool some degree of authority. I am not prepared at the present to agree to all the propositions in the Motion as being immediately practicable, but as an ideal to work towards.[2]

"Men in all the lands finding their way home together," "a common basis of moral values"—these are appeals not just to the functional benefits of

---

[1] Parliamentary debates House of Commons, Vol. 476, June 27, 1950, cols. 2158–9.
[2] Parliamentary debates House of Commons, Vol. 450, May 5, 1949, cols. 1317–18.

international governance but to its social requisites. Both Churchill and Attlee recognized that the European Coal and Steel Community, the forerunner of the European Union, would have profound consequences for national self-rule. The 1951 Treaty was highly incomplete in its purpose, calling for the peoples of Europe to "lay the basis of institutions capable of giving direction to their future common destiny." Proponents stressed the benefits of cooperation with European countries that were finding their feet after the war. Opponents raised issues of sovereignty and community. They included the chair of the 22 Club of Conservative backbenchers, Harry Legge-Bourke, who "believe[d] that federation in Europe can never work because, although the geography is very often the same, there is not sufficient common ground in sympathy and characteristics to make it work."[3]

Sir Stafford Cripps, the Chancellor of the Exchequer in the Labour government, explained his refusal to participate in negotiations for a European Coal and Steel Community as follows:

> So far as the Schuman Plan is concerned, it seems to us that the French are looking at the proposals from a different angle from that which we adopt. The French Government...says this: 'By pooling basic production and by instituting a new higher authority, whose decisions will bind France, Germany and other member countries, these proposals will build the first concrete foundation of the European Federation which is indispensable to the preservation of peace.'...It does not, however, seem to us either necessary or appropriate, in order to achieve these purposes, to invest a supra-national authority of independent persons with powers for overriding Governmental and Parliamentary decisions in the participating countries. Indeed, it seems to us that, even if desirable, such a scheme could hardly prove to be workable in democratic communities, unless it were to be preceded by complete political federation.[4]

Governance—collective decision making in the expectation of obedience—allows humans to exert joint control over problems that they cannot handle independently. However, the kind of governance that people will consent to depends on more than the need to solve problems. It depends also on how the participants perceive each other. We reject the notion that governance is contracted among thinly rational actors who exist prior to society. Our premise is that governance arises out of social relations, and that the willingness to contract governance depends not only on its functional benefits but also on the way in which actors conceive themselves in relation to others.

A contract for international governance is no different from a constitution in that there is no external power to enforce it. An international organization

---

[3] Parliamentary debates House of Commons, Vol. 476, June 26, 1950, col. 1990.
[4] Parliamentary debates House of Commons, Vol. 476, June 26, 1950, cols. 1947–9.

can survive only if the participants want it to survive. A decisive challenge for international governance is therefore to harness the willingness of the participants to constrain themselves in the knowledge that this must be self-enforcing. Those subject to the authority of an international organization must be willing subjects even when obliged to implement decisions they do not like. Obedience in the international realm requires legitimacy (Lenz and Viola 2017; Lenz, Burilkov, and Viola 2019).

This problem has preoccupied constitutionalists over the ages. How should one design a political constitution so that it endures in the absence of an external authority? How can one frame rules for political engagement that will serve a people under conditions that cannot be predicted by those who write the constitution?

This book draws on two lessons from the history of constitution making. The first is that formal rules can play a vital role in coordinating expectations in the absence of an external authority. Written rules provide a record which anchors subsequent debate about how to interpret the agreement as conditions change. This is why it is worth paying close attention to the rules negotiated by states when they create and reform an international organization.

Second, no contract for governance stands on its own feet. The effects of a constitution depend on its informal setting, and in particular on the sociality of the persons it governs. To what extent do the participants conceive themselves as part of an overarching community? Are they willing to bind themselves in collective rule even if this means limiting self-rule?

These effects underpin variation. Contracts for international governance vary in how they specify the purpose of cooperation. Some seek to radically restrict the scope for subsequent interpretation by precisely specifying what the organization can and cannot do, while others seek flexibility by framing the IO's purpose in open-ended terms. General purpose governance—governance on a wide range of incompletely contracted policies—is akin to marriage, except that it is intended to outlast the lives of its founders. Like a marriage, this requires an informal basis of shared norms. Those who contract general purpose governance must expect that they can cooperate in the absence of immediate payoff and in circumstances they cannot predict. The alternative is to specify the purpose of cooperation as completely as possible around a particular problem so that diverse populations might cooperate while minimizing the costs of uncertainty.

The remainder of this chapter sets out a postfunctionalist theory of international governance in which sociality decisively conditions the effects of functionality. The foundations of the theory lie in classical social contract theory and contemporary contract theory as we now explain.

Scale and Community in the Provision of Governance

Governance is an exercise in human ingenuity under incentives and constraints. Our theory rests on the contention that the benefits of scale are a strong incentive for governance at diverse scale, while community, or its relative absence, explains the form that governance takes.

Why would rational individuals subject themselves to governance constraining their freedom of action? The classical approach to governance is to regard it as a solution to the dilemma of collective action. The discovery of this dilemma in the seventeenth century was the point of departure for modern political science, and it remains the core of political science to this day. The social contract in the philosophies of Hobbes, Locke, and Rawls is the form in which individuals escape anarchy by consenting to bind themselves in collective governance. Only by doing so can they provide themselves with public goods including economic exchange, security, and law.

Such goods are no less desirable among states than within them. By encompassing a greater number of people, larger jurisdictions—whether states, empires, or international organizations—expand trade, extend the division of labor, and facilitate economies of scale in production and distribution (Marks 2012). The larger a jurisdiction, the greater the benefit of standardization of weights and measures, of a single system of law regarding contracts, and of other jurisdiction-wide laws that reduce the transaction costs of exchange. An enormous range of public goods call for international cooperation, including climate change, migration, biodiversity management, nuclear proliferation, scientific research, disease control, communication, human rights, and environmental protection. Scale enhances efficiency in each of these endeavors because it makes sense to determine the policy for all those affected and because the cost of providing a public policy is lower if it is shared across a very large number of people.

Yet, the provision of governance does not just depend on its functional benefits. It hinges also on a willingness to be collectively governed. A major shortcoming of a functionalist theory of governance is that it takes for granted one of the most problematic features of governance—the *Who Question*: Who contracts governance? Hobbes and Locke assume that it does not really matter who agrees to the contract; what matters is the logic of the state of nature that impels rational persons to contract a state or "Commonwealth." Hobbes (2001 [1651]: ch. XXIX) goes further to conceive society not as the starting point for the social contract, but as its product: "For the sovereign is the public soul, giving life and motion to the Commonwealth."

Rawls (1971: 4) is concerned with how individuals in a given society, "a more or less self-sufficient association of persons," should choose to govern themselves. Rawls' normative commitment to liberal individualism allows him to sidestep the *Who Question* by assuming that states are societies, and societies are states. In his treatise on international justice, Rawls (1999: 24) takes as his unit the "people" within a state-society "united by common sympathies."[5] The identification of peoples with states is a simplification that allows Rawls to set out an elegant and humane vision of liberal international governance. However, the notion that a state has a people and a people has a state compresses the possibilities of governance both within and among states. What are the consequences for governance within a state when common sympathies divide as well as unite the groups within? And what might one conclude about governance among states if common sympathies spilled beyond national borders to neighboring countries? The world has never been compartmentalized into national peoples. In order to understand governance among, as within, states, it is vital to relax the assumption that structures of authority fix patterns of sociality.

Sociality is generally weaker among states than within them, but where it exists it opens up opportunities for governance that go beyond the liberal reciprocity that Rawls envisages in the "Law of Peoples." The principles that Rawls prescribes for relations among peoples—freedom, independence, equality, non-intervention, self-defense, human rights, restriction on the conduct of war, assistance to those living in unjust regimes—assume weak bonds among peoples and strong bonds within them. Each people in this schema is a clearly demarcated entity with corresponding limits on its toleration of overarching governance.

Because governance is fundamentally interpersonal, one must come to grips with the sociality of the participants as well as their functional needs. The *Who Question* is theoretically and empirically prior to the *How Question*, how governance should operate. A theory that tells us how authority should be contracted does not tell us for whom authority should be contracted. A veil of ignorance can usefully ask us to detach preferences over rules from our personal status, income, and capabilities. But can it strip away a person's conception of who she is and with whom she identifies? Who, then are the persons that contract governance? How do they form a community? Which sets of individuals are willing to commit themselves to the ultimate political act of sharing rule? Will they consider collective governance as legitimate rule or as an illegitimate imposition? These questions require that one probe beyond the

---

[5] Rawls (1999: 112) maintains that mutual assistance presupposes "a degree of affinity among peoples, that is, a sense of social cohesion and closeness that cannot be expected even in a society of liberal peoples...with their separate languages, religions, and culture. The members of a single domestic society share a common central government and political culture, and the moral learning of political concepts and principles works most effectively in the context of society-wide political and social institutions that are part of their shared daily life." At the same time, Rawls (1999: 113) recognizes that "as cooperation among peoples proceeds apace they may come to care about each other and affinity between them becomes stronger" (see this volume, Chapter 6).

functional benefits of governance to how individuals perceive themselves in relation to others.

This is where community comes in. *Sharing in common* is a literal translation of Aristotle's *koinōnia*, the root of the modern concept of community (Liddell and Scott 1940).[6] According to Sandel (1998: 172), "What marks community is not merely a spirit of benevolence, or the prevalence of communitarian values, or even certain 'shared final ends' alone, but a common vocabulary of discourse and a background of implicit practices and understandings within which the opacity of the participants is reduced if never finally dissolved." These characteristics of community facilitate general purpose governance because they nurture *diffuse reciprocity*—atemporal exchange over incommensurate values. Exchange that takes place over an unspecified time period—atemporal—escapes the constraint of sequentiality in which a person concedes something only on condition of payback at a later time. Incommensurate values refer to goods that cannot be priced and cannot be exchanged by calculating matching values. So diffuse reciprocity has the virtue of making cooperation possible in situations where the participants are unsure about the timeliness or the equivalence of their exchange. The participants may cooperate even if they receive no compensation for doing someone else a favor or for retaliating against an antisocial act (Brazys et al. 2017; Keohane 1986; Knack 2001; Ostrom 1998).

Community in the Aristotelian sense is generally thinner among than within countries. But it is far from absent among countries, and it can underpin thick international governance. The populations of some regions have overarching norms that may provide a foundation for general purpose governance based on highly incomplete contracting—as we now discuss.

The Sociality of Incomplete Contracting

An incomplete contract that commits states to general purpose governance can be far more flexible in responding to unforeseen events than a contract specifying exactly what should be done under all circumstances. However, incompleteness comes at the cost of ambiguity, and ambiguity can subvert cooperation unless the participants find common ground in their perceptions of what the contract implies for their behavior. Whether other participants are really cooperating, or just pretending to, involves judgment. No matter how extensive and effective the court system, the participants cannot rely on formal procedures to punish shading (Hart and Moore 2008). Incompleteness

---

[6] Liddell and Scott's (1940) dictionary, accessed online: http://perseus.uchicago.edu/cgi-bin/philologic/getobject.pl?c.40:3:19.LSJ.

enlarges the scope for perceptual ambiguity by increasing the importance of performance in the *spirit* of the contract in relation to performance in the *letter* of the contract (Hart and Moore 2008: 3; Williamson 1975: 69).[7] Performance in the spirit, unlike performance in the letter, cannot be judicially enforced. In order for states to make a highly incomplete contract for broad, open-ended governance they must expect not merely to be able to enforce the letter of the contract, but to share priors about its interpretation. And they must be willing to make a commitment not only to the current contract, but to their ability to collectively execute and adapt it. The participants are not merely making a bargain. They are also consenting to an iterated process of negotiation as circumstances change.

This, as Risse (2000) suggests, depends on the capacity of actors to transcend a logic of consequentiality and engage in argumentative discourse. Arguing implies that actors "are open to being persuaded by the better argument... Actors' interests, preferences, and the perceptions of the situation are no longer fixed, but subject to discursive challenges.... [Actors] are prepared to change their views of the world or even their interests in light of the better argument." "Argumentative and deliberative behavior is as goal oriented as strategic interaction, but the goal is not to attain one's fixed preferences, but to seek a reasoned consensus" (7). Drawing on Habermas (1981), Risse emphasizes that argumentative rationality requires *eine gemeinsame Lebenswelt*—a common life world, "a supply of collective interpretations of the world and of themselves, as provided by language, a common history, or culture.... [For] it provides arguing actors with a repertoire of collective understandings to which they can refer when making truth claims" (10–11).

Cooperation requires community when governance extends beyond the classic two-person prisoners' dilemma because uncertainty and ambiguity enter the picture (Ostrom 2005). Two players can spontaneously provide themselves with a public good by acting independently in a repeated prisoner's dilemma (Axelrod 1984; Snidal 1985; Zürn 1992). Mutual perceptions are irrelevant in this scenario. If both players adopt a tit-for-tat strategy they can cooperate without having any regard at all for the other player. This is an elegant and surprising finding, and it tells us that institutions are unnecessary for cooperation if the contract between the parties is complete. In this scenario, each participant has full knowledge of the rules of the game in the present and future, the past behavior of the other participant, the past and present distribution of gains, and knows that everyone has the same complete

---

[7] The distinction is made by Hume (1896 [1739]: 413): "[W]hen we praise any actions, we regard only the motives that produced them, and consider the actions as signs or indications of certain principles in the mind or temper... We must look within to find the moral quality... If we find, upon enquiry, that the virtuous motive was still powerful... tho' checked in its operation by some circumstances unknown to us, we retract our blame..."

information. Cooperation and defection are transparent as are the payoffs. The only thing that participants cannot predict is the future behavior of the other player.[8]

Sociality enters the picture as soon as one begins to relax these assumptions. Imagine that cooperation is broad in scope, flexible in content, incompletely contracted, and offers benefits that are difficult or impossible to quantify. Under these circumstances, whether a player cooperates or defects becomes a matter of judgment.[9] Cooperation and defection do not come clearly packaged, and judging whether a participant is really cooperating or really defecting requires that one interpret rules in relation to events and behavior. Is a specific behavior compatible with this rule or does it violate the rule? Consequently, the participants are continuously trying to figure out what motivates their partners (Chayes and Chayes 1993; McCabe et al. 2001; Smith 2010).[10] This suggests that mutual perceptions are vital for cooperation under real-world uncertainty.

Dense interaction in a bounded group with shared understandings—community, in short—facilitates the provision of public goods in the face of uncertainty. The greater the scope for contending perceptions of the same behavior, the greater the importance of shared mental models for interpreting contractually agreed rules (Ostrom 2005: 26–7).[11] "Interpretive communities set the parameters within the institution—the terms in which positions are explained, defended, and justified to others in what is fundamentally an intersubjective enterprise" (Johnstone 2005: 186). Ostrom (1990: 88–9) summarizes the lessons of dozens of case studies of effective management of common pool resource problems as follows:

> [T]he populations in these locations have remained stable over long periods of time. Individuals have shared a past and expect to share a future. It is important for individuals to maintain their reputations as reliable members of the community. These individuals live side by side and farm the same plots year after year. They expect their children and their grandchildren to inherit their land.... Extensive norms have evolved in all of these settings that narrowly define 'proper' behavior. Many of these norms make it feasible for individuals to live in close interdependence

---

[8] Based on known probability distributions of future payoffs, they can make only educated guesses (Koremenos 2005: 550; Koremenos, Lipson, and Snidal 2001; Rathbun 2007).

[9] Here one enters the realm of uncertainty in which it is not possible to calculate optimal strategies (on possible short-cuts) (Beckert 1996: 827–9; Beckert 2003; Nelson and Katzenstein 2014).

[10] Information about the preferences of others is incomplete, and, in mixed motives situations, information is a private good that can influence distributional outcomes (Laffont and Martimort 2002).

[11] Morrow (2014: 6) adopts the term "common conjecture" to describe how legal obligations can restrain the use of violence by states in war. Our argument is complementary in emphasizing the causal role of shared understandings and the norms that underpin them. Whereas Morrow estimates shared understandings by examining the ratification of international laws, we conceive shared understandings as embedded in norms of sociality that exist prior to agreements among states, but which shape the governance of an IO in the course of its existence.

on many fronts without excessive conflict. Further, a reputation for keeping promises, honest dealings, and reliability in one arena is a valuable asset. Prudent, long-term self-interest reinforces the acceptance of the norms of proper behavior.

Ostrom is describing cooperation in local communities, but it is worth entertaining the idea that the principles underlying cooperation are robust across scale (Keohane and Ostrom 1995). Bounded groups of individuals who share common understandings are settings for thick international governance because they lengthen time horizons and make it easier for people to identify mutual gains, negotiate rules for reaping them, and sanction freeriding. Sustained cooperation in large groups requires "strong reciprocity, which is a predisposition to cooperate with others, and to punish (at personal cost, if necessary) those who violate the norms of cooperation" (Tuomela 2007: 150).

Cooperation in the provision of public goods can be considered a group characteristic. Aristotle begins his *Politics* by saying that "every state is a community (*koinōnia*) of some kind, and every community is established with a view to some good." The greater the capacity of a group to provide itself with public goods, the more that group can be conceived as a *koinōnia*. In this conception, the property of being a community is intended "to characterize all social groups rather than to characterize one especially close and highly integrated form of social life" (Yack 1993: 26).

We wish to investigate the effect of community on the provision of international governance, so we conceive a community more narrowly as a bounded group of individuals who perceive that they share common understandings.

We take an Aristotelian approach to community which breaks with the notion that a community is an intergenerational phenomenon that moves through social space. Communities do not travel as objects through time but are sustained or dissolved as patterns of human interaction change (Deutsch 1966 [1953]). In the short term, the possibilities for governance are constrained by common understandings; in the long term, shared governance can feed back to shape identities (Marks 2012: 5). The world has never been divided into mutually exclusive communities. Territorial communities exist at different scales, and often their edges are blurred (Mann 1986: ch. 1). Patterns of social, economic, and political interaction almost never coincide even in autarkic states, and most persons consider themselves members of more than one territorial community. Hence, communities have nested and overlapping memberships. A community, in the Aristotelian sense, is a generic concept applied to a group by virtue of its capacity to produce public goods. Our notion of community is similarly non-categorical. Instead of classifying some groups as communities and others as non-communities, every social group can be considered a community to some degree.

The Constraint of National Community

Community is double-edged. The social solidarity that facilitates governance within a group can constrain governance among groups. Communities may exhibit intense parochial altruism, a combination of unselfish concern for the welfare of others within the group combined with resistance to the rule of those from outside. Communities are parochial when they divide the social world into us and them, into insiders and outsiders. Distinctive norms and perceptions may lead a group to demand self-rule as a matter of principle. Jurisdictional reform is potentially a conflictual process that can foment nationalism. As international governance reaches into society, one can expect to see politicized debate about the relative virtues of shared rule and self-rule.

David Mitrany, a leading functionalist in the decades around World War II, was acutely aware of the constraining force of national identity (1966: 151): "We are favored by the need and the habit of material cooperation; we are hampered by the general clinging to political segregation. How to reconcile these two trends, both of them natural and both of them active, is the main problem for political invention." The weakness of community in the international domain led Mitrany (1948: 353) to advocate cooperation in task-specific functional arrangements because "under present conditions of political nationalism an international federation is difficult to achieve, under present conditions... it would be difficult to maintain."

National sovereignty and self-rule have an emotional resonance rooted in the principle that "Every man, and every body of men on earth, possesses the right of self-government" (Jefferson 1790: 60). The demand for self-rule on behalf of minority groups within states comes from all parts of the political spectrum, but the politicization of national sovereignty in the face of international governance is strongest on the political right. Objecting to a UN Convention on the Rights of Persons with Disabilities, Senator Orrin Hatch stated the nationalist position: "Sovereignty certainly includes the authority to elect representatives and the authority of those representatives to enact laws. But it is much more than that. The American people also have authority to define our culture, express our values, set our priorities, and balance the many competing interests that exist in a free society. To put it simply, the American people must have the last word."[12]

The politicization of international governance—rising awareness, mobilization, and contestation—can foster transnational community (de Wilde et al. 2019; Zürn 2012: 50; also Zürn 2018). On human rights, for example, transnational coalitions of rooted cosmopolitans have identified problems,

---

[12] July 10, 2013. "Hatch: UN Disabilities Treaty a Threat to American Sovereignty and Self-Government": https://www.youtube.com/watch?v=sMwtEe7C5cI.

developed common understandings, and helped implement humanitarian norms in the international domain.[13] However, up to this point in time, politicization has chiefly mobilized nationalism and the defense of national sovereignty against international governance (Hooghe, Lenz, Marks 2018; Hooghe and Marks 2018; Kriesi et al. 2006; Zürn 2012: 47).

International governance and self-rule are perfectly compatible for a country that can impose its policies on other countries. In the absence of hegemony, the trade-off between self-rule and international governance depends on the politicization of national identity. A person who has an exclusive national identity will resent the rule of those they regard as "foreign," whereas a person who conceives their identity as multi-layered, as encompassing the overarching group as well as the nation, will be more willing to tolerate some loss of national self-rule in international governance (Hooghe and Marks 2005; Risse 2010).[14] Because feelings of community are much stronger within than among states, the dilemma for governance among states is to gain the benefits of scale while adjusting to the shallowness of transnational community. A majority of Europeans attest some European identity, yet a decisive constraint on European integration lies in the opposition of those with an exclusive national identity who reject rule by people they perceive as foreign (Hooghe and Marks 2009b).

This suggests that governance cannot be explained as an efficient response to collective problems. This line of argument is postfunctionalist in that it builds on the idea that governance is two-sided. It is the exercise of shared rule in the provision of public goods at diverse scale from the local to the global. But it is not only this. Governance is no less the exercise of self-rule, rule by and for a specific political collectivity. The first conception conceives governance as a functional response to the benefits of multilevel governance. The second conceives governance as an expression of human sociality. It stresses that humans are social beings who value self-rule for what it is as well as for what it does. The benefits of providing public goods at diverse scale can exert sustained functional pressure, but those who conceive their group identity in exclusive terms may exhibit intense parochial altruism leading to the rejection of international governance.

This is the hard core of the theory in this book.[15] In the next section we explore some of its implications for international governance.

---

[13] "Rooted cosmopolitans" is borrowed from Sidney Tarrow (2005: 183–200, 218). On human rights, see Keck and Sikkink 1998; Risse 1999; Risse, Ropp, and Sikkink 1999; Simmons 2009.
[14] For a related argument about the relationship between state identities and international governance, see Hebel and Lenz 2016.
[15] Volume II in this series applies this theory to multilevel governance within states (Hooghe and Marks 2016).

The Puzzle of International Governance

If rational individuals are impelled into collective governance, why not states? Why should states not heed the lesson of the social contract theorists that it is rational for individuals to exchange self-rule for the benefits of overarching governance? If governance is a contract among individuals who wish to provide themselves with goods that they cannot provide individually, it stands to reason that the contract should encompass all those who would benefit by provision of the good or who would suffer if they were excluded. If some who benefit are excluded, they will escape having to pay for it, and the cost will be higher for the remainder. If the provision of a good can be extended to additional persons at less than average cost, then it would be irrational to exclude them. In the language of contemporary public goods analysis, governance should be adapted to the externalities and economies of scale of the problems it confronts.

Hobbes (2001 [1651]: ch. XXI: 161) saw the problem clearly:

> For as amongst masterless men, there is perpetual war of every man against his neighbour; no inheritance to transmit to the son, nor to expect from the father; no propriety of goods or lands; no security; but a full and absolute liberty in every particular man: so in states and Commonwealths not dependent on one another, every Commonwealth, not every man, has an absolute liberty to do what it shall judge, that is to say, what that man or assembly that representeth it shall judge, most conducing to their benefit. But withal, they live in the condition of a perpetual war, and upon the confines of battle, with their frontiers armed, and cannons planted against their neighbours round about.[16]

The puzzle is not just hypothetical. The functional pressures that have led individuals to combine in states have also led states to merge into larger units. Many states have in fact done so voluntarily, most commonly in federal states.[17] Federalism promises to provide the best of both worlds: increasing scale in the provision of public goods while retaining self-rule for the constituent units. The functional benefits are compelling. Federal states internalize the effects of authoritative decision making over a larger population and they can exploit economies of scale in security, taxation, and market making. However, the number of states that have merged into federal polities is small in relation to the number of states that would stand to benefit from scale in the provision of public goods.

Federal institutions are designed with great care to guarantee the rights of the constituent units while exploiting the benefits of scale, yet such rules are

---

[16] Kant (2010 [1795]) grappled with the same puzzle for which he developed the "law of nations."

[17] On alternative forms of hierarchy in the international domain, see Lake 2009.

always open to interpretation, and interpretation opens the door to opportunism. When independent states contract a federal constitution, they are making an enduring commitment. They are making a commitment not merely to a set of rules, but to perpetual union. This requires that they expect to be able to agree on how to interpret the rules when those who have written them are no longer alive. On the occasions when they cannot agree, they must have the expectation that this will not outweigh their desire to live in the same political community. Hence, the decision to willingly sacrifice independence is made possible when the peoples in question have shared understandings, a "mutual compatibility of major values" (Deutsch 1957: 66).

Ostrom (1979: 77, 81) emphasizes that federalism can only be undertaken if the participants have

> a common understanding and basic agreement upon the terms and conditions for making collective decisions.... Federal societies depend first upon a shared community of understanding and agreement about: (1) basic moral precepts and standards of value and; (2) the terms and conditions that apply to governance of a community... The level of common agreement and understanding must include reference to commonly shared standards of value that can serve as generally accepted criteria of choice, and to mutually agreeable terms and conditions for the governance of the shared community of interests.

This line of argument appears to travel—we will explore how far in the chapters ahead. But first, it can be illustrated by two examples of thick governance that are at the book-ends of Western civilization: ancient Greek city states and the contemporary European Union (EU).

The Greek state, or *polis*, was the epitome of a self-governing community. Its constitution was more than "an arrangement of offices"; it was "a manner of life" (Barker 2010 [1918]: 6). Outside of the *polis*, according to Aristotle, man was akin to a wild animal; within it he was "political man" (Lipset 1960; Rawls 1971: 500–1).[18] The intense sociality of citizens in the *polis*, its moral imperative, and the fact that the population of each *polis* was rooted in common descent "fostered in each community an attitude of jealous exclusiveness towards its neighbors" (Boak 1921: 376). The history of conflict among Greek *polei* shows that self-rule (*autonomia*) was considered worth dying for.

Under what circumstances were city states willing to give up self-rule in overarching governance? Existential insecurity was a necessary condition, but this does not help us much because war, or the threat of war, was almost

---

[18] "Hence it is evident that the state is a creation of nature, and that man is by nature a political animal. And he who by nature and not by mere accident is without a state, is either a bad man or above humanity; he is like the Tribeless, lawless, heartless one, whom Homer denounces—the natural outcast is forthwith a lover of war; he may be compared to an isolated piece at draughts" (Aristotle, *Politics*, bk 1, part 2; see also Hansen 2006: 115).

always present as a result of Persian expansion, internecine war among *polei*, and the rise of Macedon. The most common response was to form an alliance, which placed the militaries of the contracting states under unified command in time of war, but otherwise left their freedom of action intact.[19] But several city states with overarching identities to a regional *ethnos* were willing to voluntarily sacrifice self-rule in permanent confederation. In her book on the subject, Morgan (2003: 4) asks "How, and under what circumstances did different kinds of community constitute and define themselves, and on what level were they salient to their members?" She finds that "tiered identities were more common than not" (6). "Far from being distinct and alternative forms of state, *polei* and *ethne* were thus tiers of identity with which communities could identify with varying enthusiasm and motivation at different times" (1).

The confederations reached deeply into the internal life of their members. The Boeotian and Achaean confederations set up a joint assembly, council, and magistrates that had complete control of military and foreign affairs with the right to legislate on federal issues, arbitrate disputes among its member states, impose taxes, issue coinage, and fine citizens (Beck and Funke 2015; Cary 1923). "In nearly every case the federal states arose on an ethnic basis, that is to say, they were associations of cities or rural states belonging to the same *ethnos*" (Boak 1921: 381–2).

The contemporary European Union illustrates both the potential and the obstacles for deep international governance. The European Union was established following two world wars in which the European states system and its vaunted balance of power had proved a disaster. Not one of the six founding states had avoided occupation by a foreign power in World War II. Ideas that were considered utopian before the war now seemed worth trying. The logic of integration was to gain the benefits of scale among densely interacting peoples who shared a long history of conflict and cooperation. The European Union, and its precursor, the European Coal and Steel Community, were highly incomplete contracts for an ever closer union based on an explicit recognition of common values.

The functional pressures for shared rule in Europe are powerful and sustained. The EU encompasses countries and their regions in a continental system of economic exchange, individual mobility, dispute resolution, fundamental research, and external representation. The economic size of the Union makes it one of the three largest domestic markets in the world, the world's largest exporter, and a great power in global economic, financial, and

---

[19] The Peloponnesian League and the Delian League were alliances that interfered heavily in the internal affairs of *polei* only after the Leagues came under the coercive hegemony of Sparta and Athens, respectively.

environmental governance with "equal bargaining power vis-a-vis the United States" (Drezner 2007: 121).

The assumption was that community would follow. Trust among Europeans has grown (Klingemann and Weldon 2013), and around 50 million Europeans have acquired a European identity that they attest is prior to their national identity (Kuhn 2015). However, powerful currents run in the opposite direction, framing national identity in opposition to European integration (Hooghe and Marks 2009b; Kriesi et al. 2008). The hard edges of European states have been softened in a system of multilevel governance, but a series of crises reveals both the functional pressures and the constraints in bringing communities under a single jurisdictional roof (Hooghe and Marks 2019).

The severity of the Eurozone crisis was an unintended consequence of economic and monetary integration, formalized in the Maastricht Treaty, itself the outcome of the single market in the 1980s. Monetary union in Europe was half-baked because it eliminated monetary flexibility at the national level but made no provision for European-wide fiscal insurance. There was immense pressure on governments to coordinate a response to the crisis as early as October 2008 when the European economy was in freefall. However, nationalists stoked domestic resistance to pooling risk.

Politicization in the shadow of exclusive national identity decisively narrowed options for reform.[20] The predominant response was to shield decisions from democratic pressures by resorting to ad hoc constructs bypassing treaty reform and avoiding referendums. This brought the Eurozone close to collapse. The eventual cocktail of European Central Bank (ECB) measures, bailouts, heightened macro-economic surveillance, and banking supervision was partial, delayed, and Pareto-inefficient. Politicized procrastination carried a steep price for the North as for the South (Börzel 2016; Genschel and Jachtenfuchs 2018; Grande and Kriesi 2016).

Whereas the Eurocrisis raised issues of identity indirectly by tapping unwillingness to redistribute across national borders, the migration surge touched the nerve of national identity directly by intermixing culturally dissimilar populations. In the fall of 2015, for the first time in Eurobarometer's history, immigration became the number one concern across Europe. Following on the heels of the Eurozone crisis, the migration spike intensified a long-simmering

---

[20] In a study of the North American Free Trade Agreement (NAFTA), the EU, and regional integration in Latin America, Hurrelmann and Schneider (2015: 254) conclude that "The overall effect of politicization has been constraining, not in the sense of halting the integration process but rather in the sense of limiting the options available to political elites when considering the next integration steps" (see also Bickerton, Hodson, and Puetter 2015: 26).

divide that has strengthened radical nationalist political parties and polarized electorates into socially distinctive groups.[21]

Nationalist challengers impelled governments to introduce restrictions. By early 2016, electoral pressure to shut the door appeared irresistible. The German government, which had initially welcomed more than one million refugees, adopted restrictions through an asylum law reform (Asylpaket II) and the EU-Turkey Statement of March 2016. Austria and Sweden also changed course.

The Brexit referendum in June 2016 reveals how functional pressures for shared rule can be thwarted by nationalism. For Prime Minister Cameron the decision to call a referendum on UK membership of the EU was a Mephistophelean pact: the referendum would take place only if he won the election, and he was convinced that victory in the election would be followed by victory in the referendum. He was wrong. The two sides of Brexit never connected. Remainers predicted economic dislocation while avoiding mention of European identity. Leavers emphasized national self-rule and control over immigration while sidestepping economics (Dennison and Geddes 2018; Hobolt 2016). Since then, polarization on the Remain/Leave divide has hardened (Hobolt, Leeper, and Tilley 2018). Nationalism can, and sometimes does, subvert multilevel governance.

Conclusion

The fundamental problem of governance, and the focus of this book, is that the externalities of many public goods stretch beyond any community. Dahl (1967: 960) makes the telling point that there is an inescapable trade-off between self-rule and the capacity to influence events beyond one's community. Small units sacrifice scale to achieve self-rule; large units sacrifice self-rule to achieve scale: "At the one extreme, then, people vote but they do not rule; at the other, they rule—but they have nothing to rule over."

The existence of states is both a resource and a constraint for governance beyond the state. It is a resource because states can act authoritatively for vast numbers of people within their territories. How else could one fashion cooperation among large, diverse, and distant populations? It is a constraint in

---

[21] We label this a transnational cleavage because it has as its focal point the defense of national political, social, and economic ways of life against external actors who penetrate the state by migrating, exchanging goods, or exerting rule (Hooghe and Marks 2018; Marks et al. 2018). The divide has spawned a multiplicity of terms, including cosmopolitanism vs. parochialism, multiculturalism vs. nationalism, universalistic vs. traditionalist-communitarian, integration vs. demarcation, fluid vs. fixed (De Vries 2018; de Wilde et al. 2019; Hetherington and Weiler 2018; Hutter and Kriesi 2018).

that states can be settings for exclusive nationalism and the conviction that international governance is the rule of foreigners. Because feelings of community are much stronger within than among states, the dilemma for governance among states is to gain the benefits of scale while adjusting to the shallowness of transnational community. To what extent are states willing to commit themselves to an incomplete contract for general purpose governance? How prepared are they to delegate authority to independent non-state actors? Under what circumstances will they be willing to bind themselves to majority rule?

Willingness to obey depends on more than its functional benefits. Governance is an expression of community and reflects the desire of those sharing a history, institutions, and norms to rule themselves. People care deeply about who they are expected to obey, and this exerts a powerful effect on the character of international governance.

We theorize that the differences among international organizations in their institutional architecture, their competences, and their decision making result from the contrasting ways in which human beings confront the dilemma of international governance. Overarching jurisdictions are uniquely able to manage problems that stem from the interaction of peoples. Yet the feeling of "we-ness" that underpins effective governance is at best weak. Still, even weak community among peoples makes possible general purpose international organization.

We now need to set out the implications of this theory and assess them against the evidence. How does the tension between scale and community produce distinctive forms of governance (Chapter 4)? Why do some IOs expand their policy portfolios while others are fixed (Chapter 5)? How can one explain the course of delegation and pooling over an international organization's lifetime (Chapter 6)? And why do some states pool authority in a collective body that makes joint decisions on behalf of its members, while in others, states retain national sovereignty (Chapter 7)? However, before we can do any of this, we must generate information that allows us to compare the exercise of authority in international organizations. This is the topic of Chapter 3.

3

Measuring International Authority

Causal models are sensitively dependent on how one operationalizes concepts, yet theory, concept, and measurement are intertwined in ways that can be difficult to perceive. There is always the danger that theoretical priors shape not only empirical expectations but also the observations that are used to test them. This chapter lays out how we measure the authority of an international organization.

Authority is the central focus of this book. In what respects, and to what extent, does an international organization (IO) exert political authority—the power to make collective decisions based on a recognized obligation to obey? What powers do non-state actors have in international decision making? To what extent, when, and how do states sacrifice the national veto in collective decision making? This is the basic distinction between delegation and pooling.[1]

This chapter discusses how we conceptualize and operationalize pooling and delegation and takes a first peek at the distribution of authority across the seventy-six IOs that we survey from 1950 to 2010. We eschew technical discussion and refer readers interested in the nuts and bolts to the Appendix, which contains a list of IOs with full names and coverage, a technical discussion of dependent and independent variables, and descriptives.

Measurement can be conceived in a sequence of six steps from the abstract to the particular. These form a system in which a choice at one level affects decisions at other levels. Figure 3.1 shows this process for international authority. As indicated by the arrows, the sequence runs in both directions.[2]

---

[1] The Measurement of International Authority (MIA) dataset is in the public domain on the authors' websites at https://hooghe.web.unc.edu, http://www.mwpweb.eu/TobiasLenz/further_1.html, and https://garymarks.web.unc.edu. An update with estimates through 2020 will be released in 2021. This chapter builds on ch. 2 in Hooghe et al. (2017).

[2] Figure 3.1 extends the four levels in Adcock and Collier (2001) by interposing a step in which the concept is broken down into dimensions as a basis for specifying indicators, and by adding a final step in which the analyst confronts gray cases.

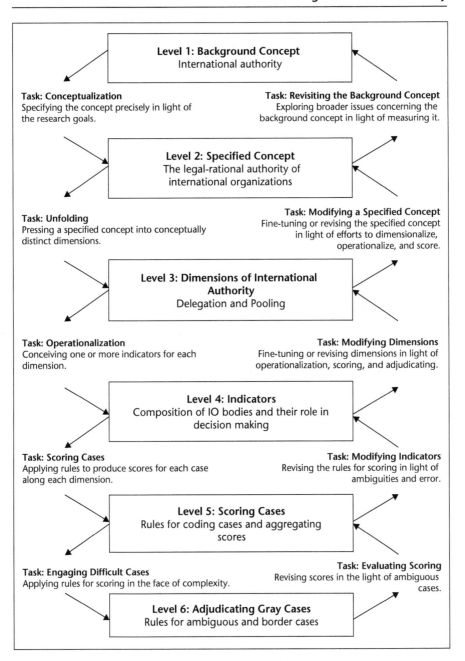

Figure 3.1 Measurement model
Note: adapted from Adcock and Collier (2001).

When one tackles the particularities of individual cases, one asks "Does the scoring make sense of the variation that we observe on the ground?" or more generally, "Do the indicators have similar connotations across diverse contexts?" and "Do the dimensions that aggregate the indicators capture the meaning of the overarching concept?" Each IO is, in certain respects, unique. We seek to evaluate them on a single set of indicators that can travel across diverse contexts while authentically grasping the overarching concept.

Defining Authority

Authority is relational: A has authority over B with respect to some set of actions C. This parallels Robert Dahl's (1957: 202–3; 1968) conceptualization of power as the ability of A to get B to do something that B would not otherwise do. A shorthand definition of authority is legitimate power. One speaks of authority if B regards A's command as legitimate and correspondingly has an obligation to obey. Authority implies power, but power does not imply authority. Whereas power is evidenced in its effects irrespective of their cause, authority exists only to the extent that B recognizes an obligation resting on the legitimacy of A's command. Such recognition may have diverse sources, including charisma, tradition, and religion (Weber 1958). We are concerned with the modern variant of authority—legal-rational authority based in a codified legal order.

Legal-rational authority is:

- institutionalized, i.e. codified in recognized rules;
- circumscribed, i.e. specifying who has authority over whom for what;
- impersonal, i.e. designating roles, not persons;
- territorial, i.e. exercised in territorially defined jurisdictions.

These characteristics distinguish legal authority from its traditional, charismatic, and religious variants. Weber (1968: 215–16) observes that "In the case of legal authority, obedience is owed to the legally established impersonal order. It extends to the persons exercising the authority of office under it by virtue of the formal legality of their commands and only within the scope of authority of the office." The exercise of legal authority over a large population involves a minimum level of voluntary compliance with codified rules that have a specific sphere of competence, and which are exercised through formal institutions, including a differentiated administration (Weber 1968: 212–17).

A focus on legal authority distinguishes the structure of governance from related but conceptually distinct phenomena such as the political resources of participants, their preferences over policy, reputational considerations, and the effects of IO decisions. These are precisely the phenomena that one might wish to analyze as causes or consequences of international authority, and it makes sense to set them apart.

Specifying the Concept

Unit of Analysis

The unit of analysis is the international governmental organization (IO), which is defined as a formal organization for collective decision making constituted by three or more states.[3] An IO is *formal* in that it is based on a written contract formally entered into by its member states. The contract can be scattered across several documents and may be subject to serial amendment. An IO is an *organization* in that it is structured by rules for a continuous purpose. Unlike an informal coalition or alliance, an IO has an institutional structure. Unlike an ad hoc agreement, an IO has an ongoing capacity for collective decision making. As a formal organization structured for a continuous purpose,[4] an IO has a permanent administrative capacity,

---

[3] This is consistent with the Correlates of War definition of a formal intergovernmental organization as an entity formed by an internationally recognized treaty among three or more states and which has a permanent secretariat or other significant institutions (Pevehouse, Nordstrom, and Warnke 2004).

[4] "Continuous purpose" implies that the IO has a track record of annually recorded activities, i.e. one or more annual executive or assembly meetings, secretariat output, and a budget. We detect two formal dissolutions: the East African Community (EAC), dissolved in 1976, and the Council for Mutual Economic Assistance (COMECON), disbanded in 1991. There are several challenges in assessing "continuous purpose." One is that states may let an IO exist even though it has ceased to function (Gray 2018). In this case, we need to delve into sources to verify whether there is a track record of activity. The Organization of Central American States (ODECA) illustrates the challenge. Founded in 1951 among states that once formed an overarching federation, it was off to a dynamic start but from the late 1960s it was hampered by the Cold War and civil strife (Nye 1967; Schmitter 1970b). There is little doubt that ODECA bureaucrats and, especially, the national ministers of economics, were intent on "maintaining some continuous political process within regional economic organs" (Schmitter 1970b: 46), but this became ever more difficult as the wars destabilized the region. However, the sources available to us suggest ongoing low-level activity in human resources, budgetary allocation, and common market coordination (Bulmer-Thomas 1998: 315, 316; Peralta 2016: 94–5). In the early 1980s, politicians and bureaucrats intensified cooperation efforts, and this prepared the ground for a renegotiated contract in 1991 for the same IO under a new name, the Central American Integration System (SICA) (Caldentey del Pozo 2014; Hooghe et al. 2017: 409–29). We code ODECA/SICA uninterruptedly but note retrenchment in authority and policy scope in the 1970s and 1980s. A second challenge is how to interpret changes in name, purpose, or institutions: Do they constitute a continuation of the same IO or a different IO? In most cases, continuity is the most sensible interpretation, as for example from ODECA to SICA, Caribbean Free Trade Association (CARIFTA) to Caribbean Community (CARICOM), or Preferential Trade Area for Eastern and Southern Africa (PTA-ESA) to Common Market for Eastern and Southern Africa (COMESA), but some cases are ambiguous. In those situations, we examine institutional continuity, membership, and how the founders conceive their mission. Perhaps the trickiest case in our dataset is the most intensely studied: the European Union. Should one conceive the European Coal and Steel Community (ECSC) and the European Economic Community (EEC) as the same IO or separate IOs? While the founders considered the ECSC and the EEC as expressions of a single European unity project and while the organizations had the same membership, they had separate institutions until 1967. Moreover, the ECSC had distinctive legal personality until 2002, when it was

"a hierarchically organized group of international civil servants with a given mandate, resources, identifiable boundaries, and a set of formal rules of procedure" (Biermann et al. 2009: 37). However, there is no a priori limit to its purpose, which may range from settling trade disputes, regulating tolls along a river, conserving whale stocks, to achieving an ever closer union.

This definition is conceptually specific and empirically inclusive. It puts under the same roof phenomena that are often treated separately. It encompasses global organizations, such as the United Nations (UN), the World Bank, and the World Health Organization (WHO), alongside regional IOs, such as the European Union, the Southern Common Market (Mercosur), and the Association of Southeast Asian Nations (ASEAN). It encompasses organizations that have wide-ranging policy portfolios alongside organizations responsible for a specific task. It excludes alliances that lack permanent organs for collective decision making (e.g. the Cairns group), regular summits without an independent permanent secretariat (e.g. G-20 or the Visegrad Four), temporary secretariats or commissions (e.g. the Intergovernmental Panel on Climate Change), and agencies or programs supervised by other IOs (e.g. the Office of the United Nations High Commissioner for Human Rights, which is a UN agency).

To select the IOs, we consulted the Correlates of War dataset and identified organizations that have a distinct physical location or website, a formal structure (i.e. a legislative body, executive, and bureaucracy), at least thirty permanent staff, a written constitution or convention, and a decision body that meets at least once a year. This produces seventy-six IOs (twenty-three IOs that existed in 1950 and fifty-three IOs set up since) that are not emanations from other IOs, and that fit all or all but one of these criteria. The dataset contains annual estimates for IOs from 1950 to 2010.

The sample is limited to IOs that have standing in international politics. The first reason is practical. The questions posed in this study require much denser information than prior datasets on IOs, and given time and financial constraints, it makes sense to estimate IOs that have some footprint in primary sources. Second, states are likely to pay more attention to IOs that have some minimal level of resources. Hence our decision to exclude IOs that have no website, address, or are poorly staffed.

Why Formal Rules?

This study is concerned with an IO's formal institutions, the persistent structure of articulated rules that transcend particular individuals and their

---

fully absorbed into the European Union. Given the significance of independent institutions, we come down on coding the ECSC and the EEC as separate IOs until the 1967 Merger Treaty, which unifies the institutions, and as a single entity thereafter.

intentions. These rules frame the IO's bodies, who sits on them, what they are empowered to do, how they make decisions, how binding those decisions are for the member states, and how disputes are handled. The rules that underpin an international organization are set out in writing when states create an organization, but they are often revised or refined in protocols, conventions, declarations, special statutes, rules of procedure, and annual reports.

We focus on formal rules for several reasons. First, an examination of the formal rules of an organization is essential if one wishes to measure its legal authority. Whereas the power of actors in getting others to bend to their will depends on charisma, expertise, and resources, legal authority is specified, impersonal, and institutionalized. Second, because they are written, the formal rules of an organization can be reliably researched. Most importantly, formal rules are firm guides to human behavior in that they can compel even in the face of controversy. Written rules record prescriptions in a public and intersubjective way in order to constrain subsequent interpretation. This is why people write down the rules they negotiate. Hence, formal rules of international organizations are rarely taken lightly. How IO bodies are constituted, their powers, their voting rules are topics of intense concern to national governments, and they negotiate accordingly. When a government signs a treaty of accession to an international organization it establishes an expectation that it will comply with the legal commitments in the treaty. Such commitments are in the public domain, and they can be difficult to escape and costly to change (Johnson 2013).

Informal rules, on the other hand, express understandings shared by the relevant actors. Because they are unwritten, informal rules exist only as long as there is substantial agreement about what they mean and when they apply. This is unproblematic for many informal rules, e.g. rules of the road, which are in everyone's interest to keep (North 1990: 41; Sugden 1986: 54). However, when consensus about the meaning of an informal rule unravels, so can the informal rule. Those who are party to it may have different recollections of its purpose or they may bend those recollections to their interests. Whereas a written rule exists in the face of contending interpretations, an informal rule exists only when the participants agree.

The formal rule casts a long shadow even in the presence of an informal rule. It may be costly for states in a minority to appeal to an informal rule for consensus. They must hope that the value of the informal rule to the winning coalition is greater than the value of making the decision by majority. Following the Single European Act, there was an informal rule for consensus when a member state government was under intense domestic pressure. However, for the informal rule to kick in, a member state had to plead extenuating circumstances. The UK government under Prime Minister Cameron repeatedly sought to block EU legislation on this ground—the domestic pressure was real enough—but the response on the part of other member states was typically unyielding. Between 10 and 20 percent of EU legislation subject to qualified majority has been opposed in formal votes by losing minorities (Novak 2013: 1092; see also Hagemann, Hobolt, and Wratil 2017; Hayes-Renshaw, van Aken, and Wallace 2006; Heisenberg 2005; Kleine 2013; Mattila 2009; Thomson 2011).

If one expects an analysis of the formal rules to point-predict IO decision making, one is clearly asking too much. However, to assess the authority of an IO the natural place to start is its formal rules—how its bodies are constituted, how they interact, and how they make decisions. The written word has for millennia provided the means to preserve memory, and today representatives of states choose words with care when they establish and reform an IO. This is perfectly consistent with the claim that informal rules can be important. No set of formal rules can interpret itself. However, there is no substitute for written rules in contracting relations of authority in the international domain.[5]

Dimensions of International Authority

Our first step in disaggregating IO authority is to break it into two parts, delegation and pooling. This distinction provides the conceptual frame for our measurement.

Delegation is a conditional grant of authority by member states to an independent body, such as a general secretariat that can set the agenda for decision making, an executive that takes day-to-day decisions, or a court that can impose a sanction on a non-compliant state. Delegation comes from the noun "legate," the authorized representative of the Pope who handled "Matters which the governor and ruler of the Roman Church cannot manage to deal with by his own presence" (Gregory 1077: 56; quoted in Rennie 2013: 3). The concept is taken up in the principal-agent literature, which makes the conditions under which principals delegate its chief puzzle. Delegation is designed to overcome issue cycling, sustain credible commitments, provide information that states might not otherwise share and, in general, reduce the transaction costs of decision making (Hawkins et al. 2006b; Koremenos 2008; Lake 2007: 231; Pollack 2003; Tallberg 2002). The delegate—in this case, the non-state actor—gains some influence over decision making; the principals—the member states—gain a capacity for governance that does not depend on their active presence.

---

[5] And, one might add, within states (Hooghe and Marks 2016).

A key virtue of the concept is that it provides a way to compare "completely dissimilar acts of delegation" (Brown 2010: 144). It highlights an underlying functional coherence among institutions—IO secretariat, executive, assembly, and court—that otherwise play contrasting roles. In each case, member states may grant authority to a non-state body to make decisions or take actions on their behalf (Bradley and Kelley 2008: 3).

However, international bodies are unlike most other delegated actors in one important respect: the member states are themselves part of the decision-making process. The divide between voters and members of parliament or between Congressional representatives and bureaucrats in federal agencies does not exist in an international organization. The principals do not stand apart from an IO; they operate within it. They may monopolize the IO's assembly, they may dominate the IO's executive, and they may play a pivotal role at every stage of decision making.

This has a fundamental implication for international authority. It requires that one considers decision making *among* states as well as delegation to independent IO bodies. An authoritative body may be composed of the principals themselves. It is perfectly possible to conceive an authoritative international organization in which non-state actors play no role at all if the principals collectively make decisions that are binding on individual states. This mode of authority is called *pooling*, and it is at least as consequential as delegation.

Delegation and pooling are distinct phenomena (Hooghe and Marks 2015; Kahler and Lake 2009; Lake and McCubbins 2006; Lenz et al. 2014). Delegation describes the autonomous capacity of international actors to govern. Pooling describes collective governance by states themselves. The strategic problem in delegation is the trade-off between the benefit of international governance and the cost of shirking when an international agent pursues its own agenda. The strategic problem in pooling is the trade-off between the benefit of eliding the national veto and the cost imposed on a government when it is on the losing end of a decision.

To what extent do non-state actors exercise delegated authority in an IO? To what extent do member states pool authority? To make headway one must model decision making in an international organization.

Developing Indicators

Delegation and pooling describe which actors make decisions, the rules under which they make decisions, and the kinds of decisions they make. This section explains how we disaggregate IO decision making to estimate delegation and pooling.[6] Figure 3.2 disaggregates IO decision making by IO body, decision stage, and decision area:

- *IO bodies*: assemblies, executives, secretariats, consultative bodies, and dispute settlement mechanisms;
- *Decision stages*: agenda setting, final decision making, opt-out, ratification, and dispute settlement;
- *Decision areas*: accession of new member states, member state suspension, constitutional reform, budgetary allocation, financial compliance, and up to five streams of policy making.

What role does each IO body, having a particular mode of state or non-state composition, appointment, and representation, play at each stage of decision making in each decision area? This produces a matrix where the unit of observation is the *IO body at a decision stage in a decision area in a year*.

At the left, the member states and their representatives compose the assembly, executive, and other IO bodies. The dashed arrows represent the simplest set-up. Most IOs have more than one assembly, executive, or general secretariat. In many IOs, the assembly has an independent role in the composition of

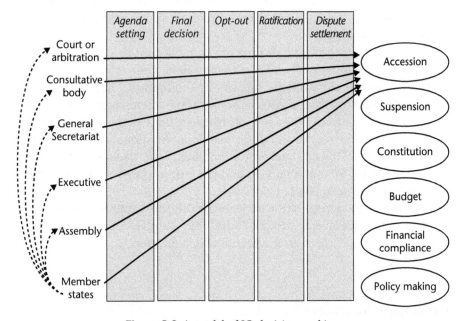

Figure 3.2 A model of IO decision making

---

[6] Hooghe et al. 2017 (ch. 3: 107–17) set out the algorithm for delegation and pooling.

the executive and general secretariat, and the dashed arrow connections among the bodies can be diverse. Indicators for each IO body assess its composition, member state representation, appointment, and removal procedures.

The solid arrows in the figure traverse stages of decision making in a single area, member accession. The full model treats all six decision areas. For agenda setting and the final decision, we code the relevant voting rule for each IO body at each stage in each decision area. The subsequent decision stage taps the depth of member state obligation, i.e. how binding a decision is in each area. To use a domestic analogy, our focus is on the rules specifying the speed limit rather than on the incidence of speeding. Bindingness is estimated on a scale of three institutional alternatives. A decision is non-binding if there is a voluntary provision or if objections by one or several countries can postpone or annul a decision. A decision is partially binding if there is a procedure for an individual member state to opt out or postpone a decision that does not affect its binding character for other member states. Finally, a decision is coded as binding if there is a legal provision to this effect or if there is no provision for a member state to opt out or postpone implementation.

Beyond this, there is the possibility that a collective decision is subject to ratification before it becomes binding. We distinguish four possibilities: the decision comes into force for all states if ratified by all; the decision comes into force only for those member states that ratify; the decision comes into force for all states after ratification by a subset of states; the decision comes into force without ratification.

Third-party legal dispute settlement—the authority of an IO to take on legal disputes concerning the constitution, principles, or policies of an international organization—is assessed separately (Alter and Hooghe 2016; Merrills 2011: 1; Romano, Alter, and Shany 2014). Legal dispute settlement is concerned with arbitration and adjudication, and not diplomatic or political forms of dispute settlement, such as negotiation, mediation, or conciliation. Labor disputes within an IO or disputes that involve only private actors are excluded.

Third-party dispute settlement is tapped by seven indicators that assess the authority of an IO's legal dispute settlement mechanism. This refines McCall Smith's (2000) coding scheme and extends it to task-specific alongside general purpose IOs. The first four indicators evaluate the extent of state control and the final three indicators evaluate the supranational character of dispute settlement.

- *Coverage*. How inclusive is international dispute settlement? Can member states opt out of the dispute settlement system or is it obligatory for all member states?

- *Third-party review.* How compulsory is international dispute settlement? Is there recourse to third-party judicial review? Can a member state initiate litigation only with the consent of a political IO body? Or is there an automatic right for third-party review of a dispute over the objections of the litigated party?
- *Tribunal.* How institutionalized is international dispute settlement? Are ad hoc panels selected to hear particular cases or is there a standing tribunal that can build precedence?
- *Binding.* How binding is international dispute settlement? Is dispute resolution merely advisory? Is dispute settlement binding only on condition that a state consents ex ante to bindingness; can a state register a derogation or exception; does a court decision require post hoc approval by a political body? Or are rulings unconditionally binding?
- *Access.* How accessible is international dispute settlement? Is litigation closed to non-state actors or can the general secretariat litigate? And what about other non-state actors?
- *Remedy.* How enforceable is international dispute settlement? Is no remedy available? Are states authorized to take retaliatory sanctions? Can a remedy be imposed by direct effect that binds domestic courts to act?
- *Preliminary ruling.* How domestically integrated is international dispute settlement? Is preliminary ruling an option for domestic courts? Is there a compulsory system in which domestic courts must refer cases of potential conflict between national and international law to the court or must abide by international rulings?

Now we have assembled the Lego blocks needed to construct the two dimensions. Delegation depends on the extent to which IO bodies—assemblies, executives, general secretariats, consultative bodies, or courts—are institutionally independent of state control and the role of these bodies in IO decision making. Independence from state control can arise in several ways, most commonly because those who sit in an IO body are not selected by or responsible to member state governments. The model includes several indicators relating to the role of an IO body in agenda setting and the final decision, which are aggregated across decision areas.

Pooling refers to the joint exercise of authority by member states in a collective body to which they have ceded the national veto. These are the assemblies and executives composed of member state representatives who are directly responsible to the member states that select them. Pooling depends on the extent to which member states collectivize decision making in one or more IO bodies, the role of such bodies in agenda setting and the final decision, the decision rule in these bodies, and the extent to which the decisions made by these bodies are binding on member states.

These components are summed up into scales that range from 0 to 1, where 0 stands for pure intergovernmentalism and 1 for pure supranationalism. Throughout the book, we use summated rating scores for delegation and pooling. Summated scores correlate very highly with factor scores derived from principal components analysis (see Appendix). Both types of aggregation generate estimates with high internal consistency. We go with summated scores because the results can be interpreted more directly.

Scoring and Adjudicating Cases

Scoring cases consists of obtaining and processing information in order to place numerical values on objects (Bollen and Paxton 2000). One perennial challenge is that information is unevenly available. A necessary first step is to compile IO foundational documents, IO manuals, official webpages, fact sheets, meeting minutes, committee reports, rules of procedure, and annual reports alongside secondary sources, news reports (e.g. on accession or suspension), and information from the Yearbook of International Organizations. The Union of International Associations library in Brussels and the Peace Palacy Library at the International Court of Justice in The Hague are useful for less prominent organizations, as is inquiring directly from the relevant IO. Over the past decade, many IOs have developed more informative websites that provide open access to organizational, policy, and budgetary documents and sometimes to searchable historical archives. Increased IO transparency has made our task a lot more manageable!

Our strategy in using this information can be described as interpretation through dialogue. Interpretation is the act of explaining meaning across contexts or persons. As one moves down the steps of measurement in Figure 3.1, the concept becomes less abstract, but even apparently simple concepts, such as majority voting rule, are often not directly observable. "The bridge we build through acts of measurement between concepts and observations may be longer or shorter, more or less solid. Yet a bridge it remains" (Schedler 2012: 22). Dialogue is sustained, open-ended discussion among coders. We choose to pool information and interpretation rather than to interpret information separately. Our primary concern is to produce valid judgments—even if this means foregoing intercoder reliability.

There will always be ambiguities in applying rules to particular cases. There will also always be gray cases that lie between the intervals. Our approach is to

A Theory of International Organization

document the basis of judgment and, where necessary, devise additional rules for adjudicating such cases.[7]

A Bird's-Eye View

The Measure of International Authority (MIA) reveals a marked, though uneven, increase in the authority of international organizations.

Figure 3.3 displays the mean delegation and pooling scores for the fifty-one IOs that are in the sample continuously from 1975 to 2010.[8] International governance entered a dynamic phase after the end of the Cold War (Hooghe, Lenz, and Marks 2018; Ikenberry 2018; Zürn 2018). Delegation increased more than pooling, but both saw a marked increase from 1992. The mean

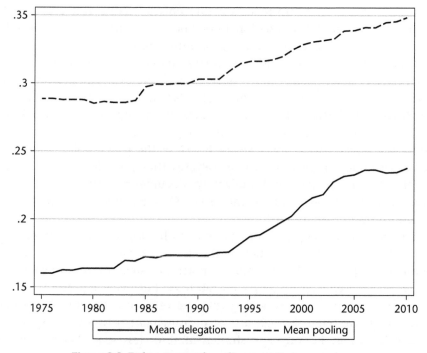

Figure 3.3 Delegation and pooling over time
Note: N = 51 IOs that were in existence between 1975 and 2010.

---

[7] In order to make these judgments transparent we explain coding decisions in extended profiles of individual IOs. Forty-six profiles are published in Hooghe et al. (2017), and the remainder are available from the authors upon request.

[8] This allows us to exclude the effects of change in the sample over time.

delegation score creeps up from 0.16 in 1975 to 0.17 in 1992 and then rises to 0.24 by 2010. This is equivalent to replacing ad hoc arbitration for state parties with a standing tribunal that can hear cases filed by private parties and that can authorize retaliatory sanctions, or to an independent secretariat acquiring sole agenda-setting power in at least two additional decision areas.

The mean pooling score increases from 0.29 in 1975 to 0.30 in 1992 and then climbs steadily to 0.35 in 2010. An increase of 0.06 points is equivalent to relaxing the decision rule from consensus to supermajoritarian voting or from supermajoritarian voting to simple majority in two decision areas. It is also equivalent to replacing policy instruments that are conditionally binding and require ratification by each member with directly binding instruments (e.g. by replacing conventions with acts, directives, or regulations).

Table 3.1 shows that this trend is not uniform. Nineteen of the fifty-one IOs in our dataset from 1975 to 2010 saw an increase in both pooling and delegation. A further seven IOs saw an increase in pooling and stasis on delegation, or an increase in delegation and stasis on pooling. Sixteen IOs have seen no change. Four IOs have seen an increase in one form of authority and a decline in the other, and just five have seen a rollback in pooling and stasis on delegation or a rollback on delegation and stasis on pooling. No IO has witnessed a decline in both delegation and pooling. A chief objective of this book is to understand why IOs evolve in such contrasting ways.

One reason for the general upward trend is that governments, particularly in the West, became more willing to impose international rules on suspension and financial compliance. Many IOs gave their secretariats more autonomy in initiating proceedings against non-compliant states, set up stronger dispute settlement mechanisms, and dropped the national veto for penalizing non-compliant member states.[9]

Table 3.1. Change in delegation and pooling compared

Change in delegation	Change in pooling Decline	Status quo	Small increase	Large increase	Overall
Decline	0	1	0	1	2
Status quo	4	16	2	1	23
Small increase	2	3	1	2	8
Large increase	1	1	1	15	18
Overall	7	21	4	19	51

Note: 51 IOs that were in existence 1975 to 2010. *Decline* is a negative change greater than 0.01 on a 0 to 1 scale for delegation (pooling). *Status quo* is a change equal to or less than +/− 0.01 for delegation (pooling). A *small increase* is smaller than the average increase for delegation (pooling). A *large increase* is greater than or equal to the average increase for delegation (pooling). The average increase in delegation is 0.08, and in pooling it is 0.06 for 51 IOs between 1975 and 2010.

[9] Hooghe et al. (2017: ch. 3) disaggregates these trends by decision area.

A Theory of International Organization

Figures 3.4 and 3.5 summarize variation in delegation and pooling for seventy-six IOs. The diamonds in the boxplots represent the median level of delegation (pooling) for an IO over the period from 1950 to 2010, or the years that an IO existed if less. The boxes indicate the interquartile range; the whiskers are the 95 percentiles, and the solid circles are outlying values. The panels order IOs according to the extent of change in delegation (pooling) and then by the absolute level of delegation (pooling). Median delegation is zero for the Central Commission for the Navigation of the Rhine (CCNR) in the left panel of Figure 3.4 and the Southern African Customs Union (SACU) in the right panel. At the other extreme, delegation has a median value of 0.50 or more for the renewed East African Community (EAC2), the European Economic Area (EEA), and the European Union (EU). The range for pooling runs from 0.01 for ASEAN to over 0.60 for the International Civil Aviation Organization (ICAO), the UN Educational, Scientific and Cultural Organization (UNESCO), and the International Atomic Energy Agency (IAEA).

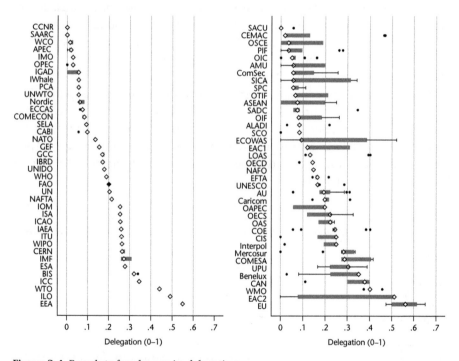

Figure 3.4 Boxplots for change in delegation

Note: N = 76 IOs over 1950–2010. The boxplots summarize the median (diamonds), interquartile range, and 95 percentile whiskers for the values that each IO takes across its years of existence in the dataset. The dark circles mark outside values beyond the range of the whiskers. The left panel contains the 38 IOs with the lowest absolute change in delegation, and the right panel the 38 IOS with the highest absolute change in delegation; each panel is ranked from the lowest to highest median value of delegation.

Measuring International Authority

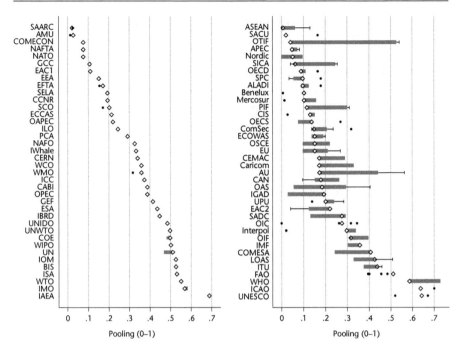

Figure 3.5 Boxplots for change in pooling

Note: N = 76 IOs over 1950–2010. The boxplots summarize the median (diamonds), interquartile range, and 95 percentile whiskers for the values that each IO takes across its years of existence in the dataset. The dark circles mark outside values beyond the range of the whiskers. The left panel contains the 38 IOs with the lowest absolute change in pooling, and the right panel the 38 IOS with the highest absolute change in pooling; each panel is ranked from the lowest to highest median value of pooling.

Comparing medians with boxplots reveals that the *level* of authority does not tell much about *change* in authority. One can get a sense of this by contrasting the two panels in Figure 3.4 with the two panels in Figure 3.5. Statistically, there is a weak association between an IO's median level of delegation or pooling and the extent of change. For delegation, the association is less than 0.02.

For pooling there is a negative association of −0.33 between the median level and extent of change. IOs with higher median values tend to shift less than those with lower median values, which results in a slight reduction in the standard deviation of pooling over time. Figure 3.5 shows that this is primarily driven by high-pooling IOs, where change is subdued. Of the fifteen IOs with a median pooling score of 0.45 or higher, eleven are static (left panel), and four are dynamic (right panel) and in just two of these has pooling increased. There appears to be a ceiling effect for pooling. The organizations that have changed the most are those with low initial values, including the uniquely dynamic Intergovernmental Organization for International Carriage by Rail

41

(OTIF)—now "intergovernmental" in name only—which entered the dataset in 1950 with a score of 0.04 and in 2010 scores 0.54.

The figures suggest also that the general trend is upward. Forty-seven of the fifty-three IOs that move on delegation have experienced an upward shift, and thirty-seven of the forty-nine IOs that move on pooling increase their score. For pooling and delegation, the average decrease is five to six times smaller than the average increase (−0.04 against +0.15 and −0.03 against +0.16 respectively).

One might expect delegation and pooling to offset each other on the rationale that states that concede IO delegation may seek to claw back control by tightening pooling, or vice versa. This does not appear to happen. Instead, when states increase IO authority, they tend to increase both delegation and

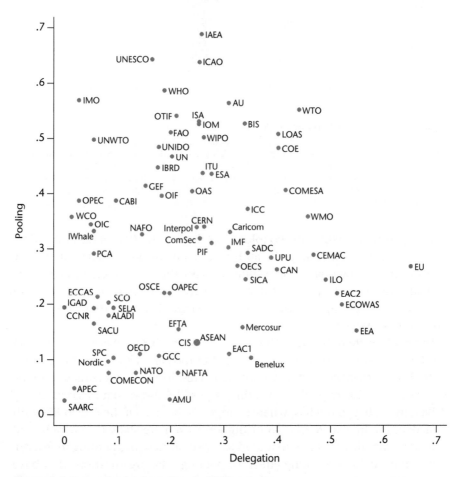

Figure 3.6 Delegation and pooling in 2010

Note: N = 76 IOs in their final year, which is 2010 except for EAC1 (1976) and COMECON (1991).

pooling (r = 0.43 for directional change). We shall find that common factors explain change in both delegation and pooling.

While directional change in delegation and in pooling is related, the association between levels of delegation and pooling is weak (r = 0.12). Figure 3.6, which maps the level of delegation and pooling for the seventy-six IOs in their final year in the dataset, reveals this quite clearly. Pooling and delegation provide distinctive design strategies for authority in international organizations. Very few IOs combine high levels of delegation and high levels of pooling. The upper-right quadrant is thinly populated, but the other quadrants are populated in about equal numbers suggesting that delegation and pooling are responses to different causal logics.

Conclusion

This chapter introduces the *Measure of International Authority* (MIA) covering seventy-six IOs from 1950 (or the year of founding) to 2010 (or the year of dissolution).

We disaggregate the concept of IO authority into two dimensions. States can *delegate* authority to non-state bodies that set the agenda, monitor compliance, oversee implementation, and more rarely, make the final decision. States can *pool* authority among themselves by making collective decisions that outflank the national veto. The distinction between delegation and pooling lies at the core of our effort to estimate international authority.

Delegation and pooling are built from observable components—Lego blocks—that can serve as a flexible toolkit for testing theory. For international authority, the components summarize the composition and role of individual IO bodies at each stage in policy making, constitutional reform, the budget, financial non-compliance, membership accession, and suspension. Uncovering the causal logics of delegation and pooling is the purpose of this book, beginning in Chapter 4 with a theory of an IO's basic set-up.

4

The Basic Set-Up

How International Organizations Vary

The purpose of this chapter is to explain the basic set-up of an international organization—its membership, policy scope, and contractual basis. Why are some IOs highly selective in their membership while others span the globe? Why are some IOs narrowly targeted at specific problems, while others have policy portfolios almost as broad as that of a national state? All IOs are based on contracts among their member states, but while some are highly specified, others are almost as incomplete as marriage contracts. Why, in short, are some IOs limited arrangements of mutual convenience while others are journeys to an uncharted destination? How do these basic features of IO design interconnect? Can one identify an underlying logic to IO design?[1]

To answer these questions it makes sense to consider the entire population of IOs rather than regional or global subsamples. We wish to explain the trade-offs that shape an IO's institutional structure across the full range of possibilities.

All IOs face the tension between scale and community. On the one hand, an IO is a means to facilitate cooperation among states. From this angle, an IO is a

---

[1] Prior research theorizes delegation (Hawkins et al. 2006b), rational design (Koremenos, Lipson, and Snidal 2001), legalization (Goldstein et al. 2000), and trade agreements (Dür, Baccini, and Elsig 2014). There is also an extensive literature on (a) voting, accession, expulsion, and flexibility clauses in IOs (Blake and Lockwood Payton 2015; Davis and Wilf 2017; Grigorescu 2015; Koremenos 2016; Koremenos and Lerner 2017; Kucik and Reinhardt 2008; Mansfield and Milner 2012; Rosendorff and Milner 2001; Pelc 2016; Rosendorff 2005; Vabulas 2017); (b) IO bodies, including dispute settlement mechanisms, courts, parliaments, secretariats, consultative bodies, and emanations (Allee and Elsig 2016; Alter 2014; Arnold and Rittberger 2013; Barnett and Finnemore 2004; Biermann and Siebenhüner 2009; Cockerham 2007; Duina and Lenz 2016; Elsig and Eckhardt 2015; Haftel 2013; Jo and Namgung 2012; Johns 2015; Johnson 2014; Lenz, Burilkov, and Viola 2019; McCall Smith 2000; Manulak 2017; Mitchell and Powell 2011; Rocabert et al. 2018; Tallberg et al. 2013; Voeten 2007); and (c) IO policies, including trade, economic liberalization, security, social policy, environmental protection, and human rights (Barnett and Coleman 2005; Bernauer 1995; Davis 2012; Hafner-Burton 2005; Haftel 2011; Hoffman 2013; Mansfield 1998; Simmons 2009).

functional adaptation to the provision of public goods at an international scale. However, an IO is, at the same time, a form of collective rule. Collective rule depends on its sociality as well as its functionality. Do the participants have some normative commonality that underpins the legitimacy of an IO, or do they perceive collective rule as rule by foreigners?

In this chapter we describe and explain the basic choices that characterize an international organization. General purpose IOs build on transnational community to contract cooperation as an open-ended venture among peoples. Task-specific IOs have a clear-cut focus so that states, no matter how diverse, can come together to problem-solve in a targeted way. We then test our theory with an original data set covering seventy-six IOs from 1950 to 2010.

The Basic Set-Up

Governance—binding rule making in the public sphere—raises three fundamental questions which decision makers must engage with when constructing an IO. First, how is governance contracted? Second, who is governed? And third, what is governed? The response to these questions can be described as the *basic set-up* of an international organization.

- *How* is governance contracted? What is the nature of the contract underpinning the IO? Is the purpose of the IO contractually open-ended or is it precisely specified?
- *Who* is governed? Who does the IO encompass? Is the membership of the IO unrestricted or is it limited?
- *What* is governed? How diverse are the policy competences of the IO? Does the IO have a broad-ranging policy portfolio or is it task-specific?

These questions are fundamental in the sense that they are logically prior to other questions that one may wish to ask, including how decisions are made or what decisions are made. The *basic set-up* is resolved in decisions that cannot be avoided in designing a jurisdiction, whereas the policy outputs of an IO are negotiated along the way. As we move forward in subsequent chapters we will find that the basic set-up of an IO is institutionally sticky and highly consequential for other features that we care about, including the authority that an IO exercises vis à vis its member states.

IOs vary widely on each of the questions set out above. Some IOs, like Mercosur or the Central Commission for the Navigation of the Rhine (CCNR), encompass just a few member states; others, including the World Health Organization (WHO) or the International Monetary Fund (IMF), are worldwide. Some IOs focus on a single policy, such as regulating whale hunting (the International Whaling Commission: IWhale) or research in high-energy particles (the European Organization for Nuclear Research: CERN); whereas others, such as the United Nations or the European Union, have policy portfolios that are almost as diverse as that of their member states. Some IOs, such as NAFTA and the World Customs Organization, have contracts that specify their purpose in considerable detail; whereas others, such as the Andean Community and the European Union, set out open-ended goals for cooperation among peoples.

It is worth noting at the outset that this variation cannot be reduced to the conventional regional/global distinction. Some regional IOs are general purpose, but others are task-specific. To say that an IO is regional does not tell one about the breadth of an IO's policy portfolio, who the IO governs, or how it is contracted. Most regional IOs, such as the Southern African Development Community, the European Union, and the Andean Community, are contractually open-ended, but there are many exceptions, including NAFTA and the European Space Agency, that have contracts specifying the goals of the organization with considerable precision. Many regional IOs have a broad policy portfolio, but several, including the Southern African Customs Union and the Commission for the Navigation of the Rhine, target specific problems. Beyond this, the regional/global distinction is theoretically inert, serving merely to partition the study of international organization. Our intent is to provide an explanation that puts the conventional classification in its place. Is it possible that a distinction that is regarded as obvious and unproblematic is actually puzzling and theoretically interesting?[2]

Theorizing Variation in the Basic Set-Up

The premise of our theory is that the basic set-up of an IO is a response to the tension between scale and community. This section explains how.

Scale and Community

Our point of departure is the idea—shared with functional theories of international cooperation—that the purpose of an IO is to facilitate the provision

---

[2] Lakatos describes a progressive theory as "having some excess empirical content over its predecessor, that is, if it predicts some novel, hitherto unexpected fact" (Lakatos 1970: 118). "Typically, when questions are more sharply formulated, it is learned that even elementary phenomena had escaped notice, and that intuitive accounts that seemed simple and persuasive are entirely inadequate" (Chomsky 2015: 4).

of public goods.[3] Governance is scale efficient if it is guided by the costs and benefits of providing a particular bundle of public goods at a particular population scale. If the externalities of human interaction are transnational, then the jurisdiction that reduces the transaction costs of internalizing those externalities should also be transnational (Deutsch 1966 [1953]; Hooghe and Marks 2009a; Keohane 1982). There may also be economies of scale. The greater the number of persons who pay for a public good such as disease prevention or weather prediction, the cheaper it is for any one person. In order to internalize externalities and exploit economies of scale, the benefits of international governance encompass the entire range of transnational public goods, including those related to economic exchange, common pool resources, cross-border communication, and the environment.

However, international governance depends also on the willingness of the parties to share rule (Hooghe and Marks 2009a, 2009b). Do the participants conceive shared rule as rule by foreigners with whom they have little normative commonality? This is the constraint of community (Hooghe and Marks 2016; Lenz et al. 2015; Marks 2012). Community beyond the national state is thin by comparison to that within states. Still, national states have never been able to homogenize their populations into normatively insulated peoples. Most states encompass normatively diverse peoples and norms flow across the borders that separate a state from its neighbors. Hence, normative affinities both divide states and extend beyond them. Where transnational community exists it may ground general purpose governance.

The tension between scale and community produces a strategic terrain for IO design. This gives rise to distinct responses—either root international governance in transnational community or carve out a cooperation problem that can be handled by a diverse membership. These responses take the form of logically coherent alternatives, and we conceptualize them as ideal types. Both reflect human ingenuity in providing governance at a scale beyond the national state.

Types of Governance

We conceptualize two contrasting types of governance, one that builds on transnational community and one that finesses community by searching for Pareto-optimal solutions to problems on a narrow policy front (Hooghe and Marks 2003). General purpose and task-specific IOs relate to their constituencies differently. This is expressed in their contractual specificity, the scale of their membership, and the breadth of their policy portfolios (Table 4.1).

---

[3] Including collective goods.

Table 4.1. General purpose and task-specific governance

	General purpose (Type I)	Task-specific (Type II)
How is governance contracted?	The IO has a contract that specifies its purpose incompletely.	The IO has a contract that specifies its purpose relatively completely.
Who is governed?	The IO encompasses normatively related peoples.	The IO encompasses those affected by a problem.
What is governed?	The IO has a diverse policy portfolio.	The IO has a narrow policy portfolio.

General purpose IOs handle the problems that confront a given set of peoples as they interact across national borders. Such IOs are formed by states whose peoples have some mutuality of expectations grounded in a shared sense of purpose. A general purpose IO bundles the provision of public goods for a transnational community possessing what Elinor Ostrom (2005: 106–7) describes as "shared mental maps"—a bed of common understandings that facilitate convergent interpretation of behavior. That eases open-ended cooperation based on highly incomplete contracts, which require not only that others believe one's promises but that they also understand one's promises (Gibbons and Henderson 2012: 1351).

General purpose (or Type I) governance is oriented to peoples who share a "common ethos" (Schimmelfennig 2002: 417) or a "sense of common identification" (Ellis 2009: 8–9; Jackson 2000). This may be as liberal democratic Europeans, Central Latin Americans, Arab Gulf people, Pacific Islanders, or Africans in anti-imperial struggle. It may be rooted in a shared federal past or a history of subjugation. In each case, there is the possibility that overarching norms rather than a specific transborder problem can provide a basis for governance.

Because the problems that arise as peoples interact are difficult to predict, the contract that underpins a general purpose IO is attuned to flexibility. Solving one problem may generate others (Haas 1958, 1980; Schmitter 1970a). Hence, the contract underpinning a general purpose IO signals an ambition to provide public goods to an evolving political community rather than to groups that happen to share a problem. For example, the European Union's Article 352 effectively grants the EU subsidiary powers and explicitly authorizes the Union to take up a policy problem unforeseen in the Treaty.[4]

---

[4] The clause was first included in the Treaty of Rome and has been amended several times. Article 352 of the Lisbon constitutional treaty is the most recent version, and begins as follows:

"If action by the Union should prove necessary, within the framework of the policies defined in the Treaties, to attain one of the objectives set out in the Treaties, and the Treaties have not provided the necessary powers, the Council, acting unanimously on a proposal from the Commission and after obtaining the consent of the European Parliament, shall adopt the appropriate measures."

As an organization oriented to a community, a general purpose IO is conceived as a commitment among peoples as well as states. Its contract invokes an aspiration as well as a bargain—the "formation of a subregional community" (Andean Community), "creation of a homogenous society" (Economic Community of West African States: ECOWAS), "comprehensive integration" (Arab Maghreb Union: AMU), "an ever closer union" (European Union).

Task-specific governance, by contrast, minimizes uncertainty that might arise from contending interpretations. The issue domain of a task-specific IO is contractually specified in advance. The agreement details a particular cooperation problem, such as lowering barriers to trade or coordinating the use of a common pool resource. While it is true that no contract can specify "the full array of responsibilities and obligations of the contracting parties, as well as anticipate every possible future contingency" (Cooley and Spruyt 2009: 8), the contract for a task-specific IO is considerably more complete than the contract for a general purpose IO.

Whereas general purpose governance is comprehensive in its policy portfolio, but selective in its membership, task-specific governance is comprehensive in its membership, but limited in its policy portfolio. Task-specific governance is suited to problems that are amenable to Pareto optimal solutions, and to problems that have been decomposed into discrete policies that are connected to others only in the medium term, but not in the short term (Simon 1981). These features of task-specific governance have the considerable effect of reducing dependence on shared norms.

A task-specific IO encompasses all those affected by a problem. Hence, it is prevalent in dealing with problems that have global externalities and a correspondingly weak community basis. However, some task-specific IOs handle local problems that are decomposable. For example, the CCNR regulates social rights and environmental externalities related to shipping on the Rhine; the Organization of Petroleum-Exporting Countries (OPEC) coordinates production and price-setting among oil-exporting economies; and OTIF sets standards for railways in Europe and contiguous countries in Central Asia and the Middle East. The size or geographical span of membership is secondary; what distinguishes these IOs is that they target a specific problem.

General purpose IOs and task-specific IOs are distinct responses to the basic dilemma of international governance: how to achieve scale in the provision of public goods in the absence of national community. The answer from general purpose governance is to build cooperation on existing community even if this is thin compared to that within states. The answer on the part of task-specific governance is to focus on a discrete problem. We conceptualize general purpose and task-specific governance as ideal types because they appear to be different in kind. General purpose IOs combine a small membership with an open-ended contract and broader policy portfolio. Task-specific IOs combine a clearly specified contract with a narrow policy portfolio for an undefined membership. Hence, the basic set-up of an IO appears to be the result of a choice between stark alternatives, each of which is internally coherent. We next hypothesize some key implications for an IO's basic set-up.

Key Expectations

We are hypothesizing a system of mutual constraint arising from *deliberatively produced regularities*. Deliberatively produced regularities occur when individuals anticipate the consequences of their choices (Pearl 2009: 108; Snidal 1994: 450, 455–8).[5] We are dealing with forward-looking human agents who have expectations about the likely effects of their institutional designs, and then build this into their choices. Hence, it makes little sense to say that the contract *causes* the policy portfolio or that the scale of membership *causes* the contract in a "before and after" sense. Our argument is that member states anticipate the constraints of scale and community when they design an international organization, and so one can say that scale and community are mutually constraining. This is no different from how you might react to a weather forecast of rain. If you decide to arm yourself with an umbrella, in what sense does the forecast *cause* your behavior? You could of course decide to ignore the forecast and get soaked even if you are convinced it will indeed rain. Likewise, member states can simply ignore the logics of scale and community. However, if they choose not to, the international organizations they create will have features that one can predict. Hence, general purpose and task-specific governance can be conceived as equilibrium institutions that constrain how forward-looking states manage the tension between scale and community.

A theory that engages the sociality of governance alongside its functional benefits has several empirical implications. We begin by considering the trade-off between scale and community and then draw out its effects for the *basic set-up*.

- H_1: *There is a convex association between the scale of an IO's membership and the extent to which it encompasses a community of peoples.*

We theorize that the trade-off between scale and community is non-linear. An additional member state in an IO will reduce the normative coherence of the IO as a whole. However, the marginal effect of an additional member state

---

[5] The concept of deliberatively produced regularities is consistent with Pearl's conception of the "marriage of the counterfactual and probabilistic approaches to causation" (Pearce and Lawlor 2016: 1895). "A variable X is a cause of a variable Y if Y in any way relies on X for its value...X is a cause of Y if Y listens to X and decides its value in response to what it hears" (Pearl, Glymour, and Jewell 2016: 5–6).

The Basic Set-Up

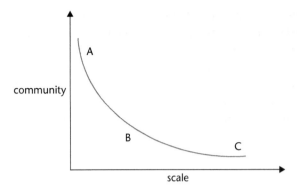

Figure 4.1 The community versus scale trade-off

will diminish with the number of member states in an IO. This is represented in Figure 4.1 by a convex curve plotting the number of member states in an IO against the proportion of the IO population that regard themselves as part of an overarching community.

The intuition here is that the decision to set up or enlarge an IO involves contrasting considerations at different levels of membership. The normative coherence of an IO with just a handful of members is sensitive to just a single additional member state. For example, the Nordic Council, which is composed of Denmark, Finland, Iceland, Norway, and Sweden, would become a lot more diverse if it extended to the Netherlands or Estonia. Even a single additional member can change the dynamics of a general purpose IO. The enlargement of the European Union to the United Kingdom transformed the organization as a whole by encompassing a country in which around half of the population felt little community with Europe and regarded EU legislation as rule by foreigners. Each IO will have unique discontinuities in its scale/community trade-off. The conjecture is that, in general, the sensitivity of community to an increase in the membership of an international organization is greater for a small, normatively cohesive IO than it is for a large, already diverse, IO.

- H_2: *The distribution of IOs with respect to the scale of their membership is bimodal.*

The convex trade-off between scale and community has a strong implication for the basic set-up of an IO and for the overall pattern of international organization. An IO is faced with a stark choice—either sustain community by limiting the scale of membership, or go for scale irrespective of community. The choice is discrete rather than continuous. In Figure 4.1, moving from *A* to *B* leads to a large loss of community, but not much increase in the number of member states. Conversely, moving from *C* to *B* leads to a large decrease in the number of member states, but not much increase of community. Of course,

51

the curve *ABC* will vary across IOs depending on the distribution of political, religious, and cultural norms among the peoples in its neighborhood. However, if the convexity hypothesis is valid as a general description of the trade-off, the effect will be to bifurcate the basic set-up of international organization towards the extremes. This would mean that IOs would cluster at *A* or at *C* in Figure 4.1. The overall distribution of IOs with respect to the scale of their membership would then be bimodal.

- H_3: *A general purpose IO has considerably less membership growth than a task-specific IO.*

The convexity hypothesis underpins the idea that general purpose and task-specific IOs have contrasting logics of membership growth. General purpose IOs are located at *A* in Figure 4.1, while *C* is populated by task-specific IOs. IOs sited at these points will have distinctive strategies of membership accession producing divergent trajectories of membership growth. A task-specific IO will seek to encompass all those affected by a particular policy problem, no matter who they are or where they live. Local problems will produce a small-*N* IO, global problems a large-*N* IO. The externalities of the policy problem, rather than the character of the participants, determine the scale of membership. Where the problem is global, a task-specific IO will expand as the number of states in the system increases. A general purpose IO, by contrast, is more discerning because it cares about the normative coherence of its membership. It is one thing to admit a new member when the purpose is clearly specified, and quite another when it is contractually open. Membership in a general purpose IO involves a commitment to join a community of peoples, and an applicant for membership can expect to be carefully vetted. Whereas the membership of a task-specific IO can increase quickly, the membership of a general purpose IO will increase slowly, if at all.

- H_4: *A general purpose IO has a dynamic policy portfolio; a task-specific IO has a stable policy portfolio.*

A general purpose IO is contracted incompletely in the expectation that it will adjust its competences to problems that arise for a community of peoples. It is oriented to peoples sharing a way of life, and this requires flexibility in responding to changing circumstances. Hence, a general purpose IO is involved in making decisions about its policy competences. It is a forum for negotiation about its mission as well as an instrument to make policy. And given the dense connections among policies, the portfolio of a general purpose IO will tend to grow over time. By contrast, the purpose of a task-specific IO is contracted more completely around the challenge of problem solving on a given front. Task-specific governance is grounded on the belief that no matter how diverse their religious beliefs or cultural practices, human beings can cooperate to solve a pressing problem. Complex problem solving involves continuous learning and adaptation, which in a task-specific IO will be focused around a given problem. Only if the problem confronting a task-specific IO were to creep into new areas, would one expect a task-specific IO to broaden its policy portfolio.

Key Variables

We assess the validity of these expectations for seventy-six international organizations on an annual basis from 1950 to 2010.[6]

How governance is contracted refers to the contractual incompleteness of an IO's purpose. *Contract* is a dichotomous variable for the extent to which the purpose of an IO's contract is incomplete, which we code annually using a lexicon of words to assess an IO's foundational documents. We describe an IO with a highly incomplete contract as general purpose, and an IO with a relatively complete contract as task-specific.

Who is governed refers to the number of member states in the IO. *Membership* is a discrete annual measure for the number of states that are formal members of an IO. Unless otherwise stated, we use the logarithm (log10).

What is governed refers to the breadth of an IO's policy portfolio. *Policy scope* is a discrete variable for the range of policies for which an IO is responsible from a list of twenty-five policies assessed annually using eight legal, financial, and organizational indicators.

Community refers to normative commonality among the members of an IO. This variable is a principal components factor for indicators of the extent to which the members of an IO share an overarching religion, culture, geographical location, type of political regime, and legal tradition. These are indicators of deeply rooted norms expressed in distinctive ways of life.[7]

Results

We are now equipped to examine the four hypotheses concerning the basic set-up of IOs. Our prior is that the basic set-up of an IO is a trade-off between

---

[6] The Appendix provides details on all variables in this chapter.
[7] In the absence of comparative surveys, these indicators have the additional virtue of providing annual observations for all countries. Using any four rather than five indicators makes little difference. *Community* has an alpha of 0.94.

A Theory of International Organization

community and scale. The linear association between community and the number of member states for seventy-six IOs in their last year in the dataset is −0.85. We expect the relationship to be convex because the decline in community will be greater for a given increase in membership in an IO with few members than in one with many members (H_1). This is exactly what we find when we plot a factor for five indicators of community against the absolute number of member states in an IO in Figure 4.2. The fit is impressively strong.[8]

No IO is as much as two standard deviations from its expected value under the convexity hypothesis. The two IOs that are furthest from the predicted value of community are the Intergovernmental Authority on Development (IGAD) (sd = 1.25) and the Common Market for Eastern and Southern Africa (COMESA) (sd = 1.12). These IOs are more diverse than expected given the size of their membership. IGAD came into being in 1986 after pressure by international donors and the United Nations Environment Programme for an intergovernmental organization that could coordinate drought and famine relief (El-Affendi 2009: 5–6). Its seven member states are all located in Eastern

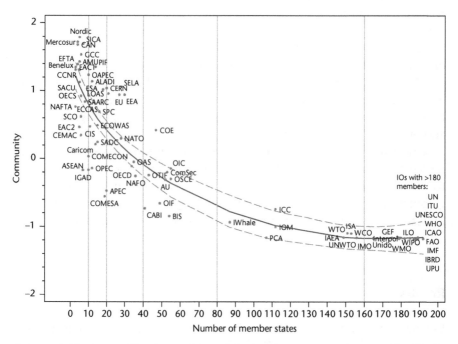

Figure 4.2 The trade-off between scale and community

Note: N = 76 international organizations in their last year in the dataset. Community is standardized, and ranges from −1.1 to 1.8. The fit line is a fractional polynomial function.

---

[8] A fractional polynomial that regresses members on community in the final year of the dataset has an R^2 of 0.81.

Africa, but are diverse in religion (Orthodox, Christian, Sunni), political regime (ranging from −7 to +8 on the Polity scale), and legal tradition (common law, civil law, Islamic law, mixed law). Set up in 1966, COMESA was a product of efforts by the United Nations Economic Commission for Africa and the Organization of African Unity (OAU) to ensure the continuation of trade in post-colonial Eastern and Southern Africa (Mwale 2001: 39). With nineteen members, COMESA is a conglomerate of former British and French colonies with diverse legal traditions, political regimes, and cultures.

One implication of the theory is that IOs will cluster at high and low values and away from the middle range. This is broadly confirmed in Figure 4.2. Three things are worth paying attention to. The first is that many IOs are, as expected, located at the high member, low community end of the curve (at C in Figure 4.1). The second is that almost all remaining IOs are densely packed at the low member, high community end of the curve (A in Figure 4.1), though it is notable that the distribution extends to the range of forty to fifty-five member states. Four IOs in this range deal with specific problems that have limited geographical externalities.[9] The remaining IOs in this group reveal how the scale/community trade-off can be tempered by non-spatial forms of community. The Organization of Islamic Cooperation has sixty-seven member states in four continents sharing a religious vocation. La Francophonie and the Commonwealth encompass geographically diverse countries that have been shaped by the experience of the French or British empires. The African Union, with fifty-five member states, is rooted in shared resistance to colonial rule and racial exclusion. In each case, an unusual source of normative affinity is robust to an increase in membership of the organization, up to a point.

A third thing to notice is the nearly empty space in the middle of the curve in Figure 4.2 corresponding to B in Figure 4.1. Strikingly, more than half of the entire range in Figure 4.2 is very sparsely populated.[10] The key expectation is that the overall distribution of IO membership is bimodal (H_2). Figure 4.3 confirms this by estimating a kernel density function which smoothens the sample distribution of IOs with respect to their membership.[11] The probability distribution is bimodal, and comfortably meets the Hartigan dip test (Table 4.2).

---

[9] These are the Bank for International Settlements (BIS), the Organization for Security and Cooperation in Europe (OSCE), the Centre for Agriculture and Bioscience International (CABI), and the Intergovernmental Organization for International Carriage by Rail (OTIF).

[10] The entire range for the number of member states in IOs is from three (NAFTA and Benelux) to 192 (the United Nations). Precisely 49.7 percent of the range—the middle part—is home to just 5.3 percent of the cases.

[11] Kernel density estimation is a non-parametric method in which the data are treated as a randomized sample and the distribution is smoothened. We have no prior about the smoothing bandwidth, and so use Stata's default, the Epanechnikov estimator.

A Theory of International Organization

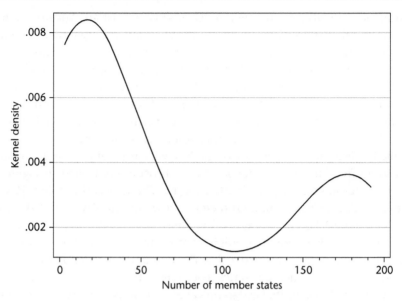

Figure 4.3 Bimodal distribution of international organizations
Note: N = 76 IOs in latest year in dataset. Kernel density function (gaussian, n = 450).

Table 4.2. Predictions and findings

	Prediction	Finding
H_1	As the number of IO members increases, community diminishes non-linearly.	The trade-off between scale and community is convex (see Figure 4.2).
H_2	The distribution of IO membership is bimodal.	The Hartigan diptest for bimodality = 0.087 ($p < 0.000$).[a]
H_3	A task-specific IO has greater membership growth than a general purpose IO.	Mean annual membership increase for task-specific IOs = 1.304. Mean annual membership increase for general purpose IOs = 0.310. Paired t-test = 13.650 ($p < 0.000$).[b]
H_4	The policy portfolio of a general purpose IO is more dynamic than that of a task-specific IO.	Mean annual increase in policy scope for task-specific IOs = 0.022. Mean annual increase in policy scope for general purpose IOs = 0.185. Paired t-test = −5.715 ($p < 0.000$).[b]

Note: Analyses for H_1 and H_2 use data for 76 IOs in their last year in the dataset; analyses for H_3 and H_4 use the full time series. See the Appendix for operationalization.
[a] The Hartigan dip test estimates whether a distribution is bimodal or unimodal. It is the maximum difference between the empirical distribution and the reference unimodal distribution that minimizes the maximum difference. The dip measures how much a sample departs from unimodality, whereby lower values indicate significantly different departures from zero (Hartigan and Hartigan 1985).
[b] Two-tailed significance paired t-test with unequal variances.

Just four IOs have more than 55 member states and fewer than 149 in 2010: IWhale (87 member states), the Permanent Court of Arbitration (107), the International Criminal Court (112), and the International Organization for Migration (112). Each of these IOs has a particular reason for being in the convex region of the scale/community trade-off. IWhale and the International Criminal Court (ICC) have global intent, but they have been stymied by the refusal of states to join. Both are contested organizations: IWhale because it pits states supporting whale hunting against those opposing it, and the ICC because several countries resist its efforts to bring human rights abuses to trial (Berger-Eforo 1996; Kelley 2007; Mills and Bloomfield 2018; Simmons and Danner 2010). The Permanent Court of Arbitration (PCA) is the oldest worldwide international court, but it has had to contend with alternative venues for international dispute settlement, including the International Court of Justice and private arbitration channels. The International Organization for Migration (IOM) is in transition. It began as an IO concerned with refugees in post-war Europe, and it went global only in the 1980s. Its membership has been on the rise, and by 2019 it stood at 172.

The findings suggest that the population-wide distribution of member states in IOs has a micro logic rooted in the trade-off between scale and community for an individual IO. General purpose governance in the international domain requires that an IO limit the scale of its membership. Beyond the national state, it is certainly possible to find peoples who, despite living in separate states, have normative affinities arising from a history of interaction that can sustain general purpose governance.[12] However, the orbit of such peoples is usually limited by geographical proximity, or more unusually by the reach of empire or religion. A general purpose IO encompassing normatively related states may face a sharp trade-off when it enlarges its membership. The alternative mode of governance—task-specific governance—relaxes this constraint by contracting around a specific problem that can be handled by the affected group no matter how diverse. Whereas a general purpose IO is constrained to a select membership, a task-specific IO adjusts the scale of its membership to the collective goods it provides. Hence, a task-specific IO is attuned to handle global problems. This contrast is reflected in the scale of IO membership. The median general purpose IO in our dataset has ten member states; the median task-specific IO has 110 member states.

---

[12] General purpose IOs have an average value of 0.59 against 0.26 for task-specific IOs on *Community*, rescaled from zero to one. The coefficient of variation for task-specific IOs is 1.23 compared to 0.45 for general purpose IOs, which is consistent with the notion that task-specific governance exists under conditions of weak or strong community but general purpose governance requires strong community. A difference of means t-test shows these averages to be significantly different ($t = -4.95; p = 0.000$).

We theorize that these contrasting modes of governance have dynamic effects. One expectation is that a task-specific IO will have considerably greater membership growth than a general purpose IO (H_3). Table 4.2 reports that the average annual rate of membership growth in a task-specific IO is more than four times greater than that for a general purpose IO (1.3 versus 0.31). This easily meets a paired t-test for difference of means. The median membership of a task-specific IO has increased from thirty-four to ninety-seven over the sixty-year period we consider, while the median membership of a general purpose IO inched up from seven to ten.

In line with this, task-specific IOs generally impose less restrictive conditions of entry than general purpose IOs. Many task-specific IOs allow entry if a state meets a written condition, most commonly, membership of the United Nations (Bezuijen 2015). When a task-specific IO imposes a more substantive requirement for prospective members, it is usually to protect the organization's core function, e.g. the Organization for Economic Co-Operation and Development (OECD) is expressly committed to "liberal values whether those are achieved by liberal political institutions, economic policies, or commitment to the western alliance" (Davis 2016: 52). Enlargement in a general purpose IO has to pass a higher hurdle on both the side of the applicant and that of the existing members for it involves joining an incompletely contracted community of peoples. Enlargement usually involves intrusive screening and prolonged negotiation. In almost all cases it concludes in a formal vote that must meet the threshold of unanimity.[13]

Our final expectation is that the type of governance affects an IO's policy development (H_4). Contracts are commitments that can be anticipated to constrain future behavior. This motivates clear expectations about the breadth of the policy portfolio many years, or even decades, down the road. A general purpose IO is based on a highly incomplete contract that builds in flexibility. Because it caters to the problems faced by communities, a general purpose IO will sponge additional competences over time as it grapples with unanticipated problems. By contrast, a task-specific IO is designed to reduce the uncertainties of cooperation, and it will expand its competences only if its problem spills over into other policy areas. On average, general purpose IOs take on 6.2 additional policies from the year of their founding to 2010. A task-specific IO, by contrast, tends to have a relatively static policy portfolio, picking up just one policy over the period as a whole. The difference, as reported in Table 4.2, is highly significant.

---

[13] Twenty eight of thirty-two general purpose IOs require unanimity for enlargement in 2010 or their final year in the dataset. The exceptions are the League of Arab States, the Organization of American States, the African Union, and the Council of Europe. Thirty-one of forty-four task-specific IOs require only a majority vote for enlargement. For seventy-six IOs, the Pearson Chi2(1) is 31.69 ($p < 0.000$).

Conclusion

This chapter takes a fresh look at the field of international organization. It asks some fundamental questions about institutionalized cooperation among states. How is cooperation contracted? Who is encompassed? What is decided?

One needs to probe the sociality of international governance to answer these questions. Governance depends on a willingness to be governed as well as on its functional benefits. People care deeply about who exercises authority over them and this, we argue, powerfully constrains governance among states. To what extent do those contracting governance share understandings that can underpin diffuse reciprocity?

The hard core of the theory is that governance confronts a tension between scale and community, between the functional benefits of governance at diverse scale and the desire on the part of those who are governed to rule themselves. General purpose IOs structure cooperation around community. They discover, as well as implement, cooperation. Membership of a general purpose IO involves commitments that can affect national sovereignty on a broad front. States therefore pay close attention to who is part of the club. Hence, the membership of a general purpose IO is bounded. Enlargement is a serious matter usually requiring consensus among existing members.

A task-specific IO, in contrast, structures cooperation around a problem and this fixes the scale of membership. By clearly specifying its purpose, a task-specific IO reduces uncertainty, and so opens the door to cooperation in the absence of shared norms. Whereas the membership of a general purpose IO tends to be stable, that of a task-specific IO is flexible. Whereas the policy portfolio of a general purpose IO is flexible, that of a task-specific IO tends to be stable.

This approach to international governance explains phenomena that are often taken for granted, and goes far beyond the regional/global classification of IOs. Why is the membership of IOs not distributed normally around a mean value, but instead clumps towards the ends of a continuum? Why do IOs follow contrasting paths of membership growth? Why do their policy portfolios develop in differing ways?

Our theory is that the tension between scale and community is expressed in the basic set-up of an IO—its contract, membership, and policy portfolio. In the remainder of the book we probe how scale and community also shape an IO's authority.

5

Why Do Some IOs Expand their Policy Portfolio?

Why do some IOs expand their policy portfolios while others are fixed? We make two claims. The proximate claim is that the policy trajectory of an IO is sensitive to the incompleteness of its contract. This raises the question why some IOs have a highly incomplete contract and others do not. Our prior claim is that the willingness of states to engage in incomplete contracting depends on shared norms which can allay fears of exploitation arising from open-ended commitment.

Incomplete Contracting and Policy Scope

All international organizations are based on contracts in the form of treaties, conventions, protocols, and rules of procedure that set out what the organization is intended to do and how it makes decisions. All such contracts are incomplete because it is never possible to anticipate every eventuality. Yet the degree of incompleteness varies greatly. Some IO contracts specify the purpose of the organization with careful precision, as does NAFTA, a meticulously drafted agreement covering almost every conceivable contingency in the trade of certain goods.[1] By contrast, some IO contracts set out the goals of the organization with studied imprecision, as in the Rome Treaty of the European Union which begins by calling for "an ever closer union" and goes on to make a series of broad declarations for "common action," "improving the living and working conditions of their peoples," "concerted action," and "solidarity," while leaving the content of these objectives to subsequent negotiation.

---

[1] The same applies to its successor, the United States–Mexico–Canada Agreement (USMCA).

The decision to write a relatively complete or incomplete contract involves a trade-off between ambiguity and flexibility. A relatively complete contract seeks to minimize ambiguity in a relationship, but it does so by limiting flexibility as new circumstances arise. The participants to a complete contract bind themselves to a precisely articulated set of objectives and thereby reduce ambiguity ex ante. It is true that contracts for ongoing cooperation can never fully eliminate ambiguity for there is always going to be some room for contending interpretation as the world changes.[2] However, the parties to an IO can try to fix the contract around a clearly specified task. In the words of two economists who have pioneered contract theory, a relatively complete contract "pins down future outcomes very precisely, and...therefore leaves little room for disagreement and aggrievement. The drawback of such a contract is that it does not allow the parties to adjust the outcome to the state of the world" (Hart and Moore 2008: 2).

A highly incomplete contract reverses the trade-off, gaining flexibility at the cost of ambiguity. A contract that sets out the purpose of an IO in non-specific terms can easily be adjusted to changing circumstances.[3] This is particularly useful in an unpredictable environment which does not "disclose the alternatives available or the consequences of those alternatives" (Thompson 2003: 9). The cost is that flexibility raises the fear of exploitation arising from divergent interpretation about what was agreed in the contract.

Under what circumstances are the member states of an IO willing to tolerate ambiguity to gain flexibility? When will states enter into something that looks more like a marriage than a rental agreement? To answer this question one must inquire into the willingness of the participants to continuously negotiate their way through the dense thicket of general purpose governance. In the model in Figure 5.1, community, which underpins diffuse reciprocity, trust, and a reputation for keeping one's word, shapes the contractual basis of an IO.

Community lies behind contractual incompleteness because it diminishes the potential for contending interpretations of behavior in relation to the

---

[2] Even NAFTA is not as complete as it may have looked when it came into force. The treaty binds states, but not subnational units within them, and says nothing about how a state should enforce the treaty when one of its provinces is noncompliant. Article 105 states that all parties "shall ensure that all necessary measures are taken in order to give effect to the provisions of this Agreement, including their observance...by state and provincial governments." But, as Herman (2010: 3) points out, "that is an obligation placed on the federal levels of government, not on the sub-federal units." This has provoked a series of trade remedy cases brought by US investors against Canada. Multilevel governance can blindside even the most complete treaty if it assumes that states are unitary actors.

[3] Jupille, Snidal, and Mattli (2013) distinguish between "change" and "use" as institutional responses to a new cooperation problem. "Change" involves high transaction costs because it requires a "significant modification of an existing institution," i.e. rewriting an IO's contract. "Use" is "a relatively unproblematic activation of a single existing institution" and "usually the least costly solution if the institution is agreeable" (Jupille, Snidal, and Mattli 2013: 39–41). The virtue of an incomplete contract is that it biases an IO's response to a new cooperation problem to "use."

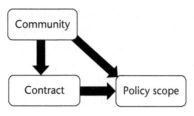

Figure 5.1 A model of policy scope

contract. Our reasoning, following Ostrom (2005: 106), is that the greater the scope for different perceptions of the same objective behavior, the greater the importance of "shared mental models" for identifying mutual gains and negotiating institutions for reaping them. In order for states to make a highly incomplete contract they must expect not merely to be able to enforce the letter of the contract, but to share priors about its interpretation.[4]

Shared norms affect the growth of an IO's policy portfolio. Diffuse reciprocity, trust, and a reputation for keeping one's word may help the parties discover the benefits of cooperation and so enlarge an IO's policy portfolio. Decision making in an IO can be conceived as an iterated process in which shared norms build confidence in the other participants.[5] In short, community allows cooperation "to unfold over time without placing either party at the mercy of the other" (Posner 2004: 1583; Knack 2001). Hence, an IO composed of those who share norms of appropriate behavior and who come to have mutually convergent expectations about the behavior of others is likely to be more dynamic than one in which participants do not share such norms.

Key Variables

We assess these expectations for seventy-six international organizations on an annual basis from 1950 to 2010. Not all IOs are in the dataset for the entire period. At the extremes, two IOs are observed for nine years and twenty-four IOs for sixty-one years. The median IO is observed for 44.5 years.

---

[4] Greif and Laitin (2004: 637–8) make the point that self-enforcing institutions are those in which "socially articulated and distributed rules provide individuals with the initial 'grain of truth' to develop subjective beliefs regarding others' behavior."

[5] Cooperation can be considered "a creative enterprise through which the parties not only weigh the benefits and burdens of commitment but explore, redefine, and sometimes discover their interests" (Chayes and Chayes 1993: 180). Checkel (2001: 568) suggests that "whether agents comply with regime norms through processes of persuasion and social learning" depends "on their cognitive priors and, more generally, their broader normative environment."

Why Do Some IOs Expand their Policy Portfolio?

This section introduces the key variables in our theory: policy scope, contract, and community. We then examine the conjecture that an IO's contract depends on its community and that community and contract explain the course of its policy scope.

Policy Scope

We measure the breadth of an IO's policy portfolio across twenty-five policies identified by Lindberg and Scheingold (1970) and updated by Schmitter (1996), Hooghe and Marks (2001), and Hooghe et al. (2017). Eight legal, financial, and organizational indicators assess whether a policy is part of an IO's portfolio for each year of the IO's existence (see Appendix). In most cases, a change in *Policy Scope* leaves a clear footprint in the budget or in the establishment or elimination of an institution (e.g. a commission, a crisis management mechanism, or a high-profile position).

The number of policies handled by an IO and the change in its policy portfolio vary widely. Figure 5.2 summarizes the sample variation in *Policy*

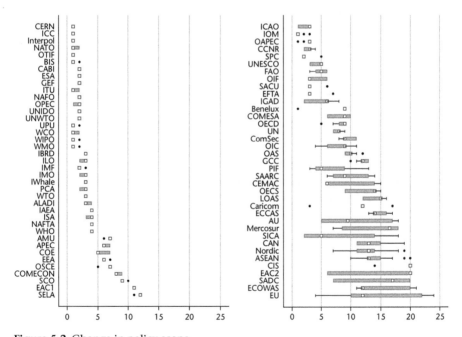

Figure 5.2 Change in policy scope

Note: 76 IOs over 1950–2010. The left panel arrays IOs whose policy scope shifted 1 or less between first and last year in the dataset; the right panel arrays IOs whose policy scope shifted 2 or more between first and last year in the dataset. Each panel orders IOs from the lowest to the highest scope in their final year of observation. The box plots display the median policy scope (squares), the interquartile range in policy scope (shaded rectangles), the 5 to 95 percentile (whiskers), and outlying observations (dots).

Scope in box plots. The squares in the box plots indicate the median number of policies for each IO. This ranges from one policy in twelve IOs to ten or more policies in sixteen IOs. Eleven IOs have extended their portfolios by at least ten policies. The European Union is an extreme case. It begins in 1952 with four policies (competition, energy, social policy, and trade) and acquires an additional twenty policies over nine subsequent reforms. Today it is the only IO covering all policies on a list of twenty-five.[6]

The re-founded East African Community has the fastest annual rate of change, from six policies at its formation in 1993 to twenty in 2010. ASEAN grew from ten policies in 1968 to twenty in 2010. This was put into practice by routine ministerial councils, and was mandated through intergovernmental declarations, concords, and agreements. In 2007, ASEAN consolidated its incremental expansion in a new charter, adding human rights and research.

Contract

Contract assesses whether an IO's foundational contract formulates its objectives in specific or open-ended terms. We code a contract as complete (value = 1) if its purpose is to achieve a fixed objective under clearly specified conditions. For example, the objectives of the Bank for International Settlements (BIS) are precisely formulated as fifteen operating tasks facilitating central bank cooperation and its role as trustee for intergovernmental financial operations (Article 21). Moreover, these objectives are delimited by explicit prohibitions (Article 24).

A contract is incomplete (value = 2) if its purpose is to achieve broad-ranging cooperation that is only vaguely specified, for example, as a "community of peoples," "political federation," or in terms of "unity" or a "common identity." The best known example is the European Union, which involves a diffuse and open-ended commitment to an "ever closer union among the peoples of Europe."[7] The Caribbean Community's 1974 Treaty is an example of an incomplete contract calling for economic cooperation as a step to "fulfil the hopes and aspirations of their peoples for full employment and improved standards of work and living" (Article 4). While the treaty focuses on economic cooperation, it commits member states to "take all appropriate measures" for "the achievement of a greater measure of economic independence and effectiveness of its Member States" (Articles 4 and 5).

---

[6] The EU accreted the twenty-fifth policy (financial stabilization) in 2012. The Fiscal Stability Treaty was designed to force member states to balance their budgets over the business cycle, and its provisions are binding on Eurozone members (Börzel and Risse 2018; Copelovitch, Frieden, and Walter 2016).

[7] In the absence of an existing measure, we developed the coding scheme ourselves and tested its reliability with independent coders who produced convergent scores (see the Appendix).

Table 5.1. IOs by contract

	First year	Last year
Complete	47	44
Incomplete	29	32

Note: N = 76 IOs over 1950–2010 (or last year in dataset).

Table 5.1 shows the distribution of IOs by type of contract in their first and last year in the time series. While an organization can change its contract over time, this is rare.[8]

We are interested in how the policy portfolio develops over time as a function of its contractual basis. We need, therefore, to add a time dimension to the contract measure beyond the limited over-time variation that this variable exhibits. The baseline specification of *Contract dynamic* is the raw measure of *Contract*, ranging from 1 to 2, multiplied by the age of the international organization (1 for the first year, 2 for the second year, 3 for the third, and so on). The resulting measure uses the full variation in our data, capturing the depth and breadth of interaction that arises over time in relation to contractual incompleteness.

Community

Community is operationalized as the extent of normative commonality among the populations of an IO's member states. Surveys of trust and shared identity are not available for the countries and time period covered here. As a next-best solution, we use indicators for the extent to which an international organization encompasses populations that have a similar culture, religion, geographical location, and political/legal institutions (see the Appendix). These variables indicate the extent to which the populations share enduring norms across socio-political fields.

The bivariate associations among these variables are strong, ranging from 0.58 to 0.86.[9] Table 5.2 presents the results of a principal component factor analysis in which a latent variable, *Community*, accounts for 79 percent of the variance in the indicators. The coherence of the indicators is such that the results of the analyses below do not depend on the particular combination that we use.

We would like to know how an IO's policy portfolio changes over time in relation to change in community, and so we add a time dimension to

---

[8] Three IOs—Benelux, CARICOM, and IGAD—shift from complete to incomplete contracts. Results hold if we use the original or revised contracts.
[9] The Cronbach's alpha is 0.93.

Table 5.2. Principal components analysis for *Community*

Culture (Rae index)	0.48
Religion (Rae index)	0.44
Political regime (standard deviation)	0.40
Legal tradition (Rae index)	0.45
Geographical location (Rae index)	0.44
Eigenvalue	3.97
Proportion explained	79.5

Note: 3,279 IO-years. For a description of the components, see Appendix.

Community to calculate *Community dynamic*. The variable is useful for testing the expectation that a high degree of community facilitates policy expansion over time.[10]

Controls

We control for several variables that could affect policy scope:

- *Democracy* on the hypothesis that an IO with democratic member states will be more willing than one with autocratic states to expand international cooperation (Mansfield, Milner, and Pevehouse 2008; Simmons 2009).

- The *number of IO member states* because a larger membership may lead states to broaden the IO's policy portfolio to increase issue linkage and facilitate negotiation (Hawkins et al. 2006b; Koremenos, Lipson, and Snidal 2001: 785–6).

- *Power asymmetry*, i.e. heterogeneity of power capabilities, because hegemonic states are hypothesized to be more willing to subsidize public goods (Kindleberger 1973; Martin 1992; Mattli 1999; Snidal 1994).

- *Affluence* on the hypothesis that wealthier populations transact more across national borders, generating demand for international regulation across a wider range of issues (Keohane 1984; Stone Sweet and Brunell 1998).

- *GDP dispersion* on the expectation that an IO with member states having heterogeneous levels of GDP may have an incentive to engage in broader cooperation which can increase issue linkage and facilitate negotiation (Carnegie 2014; Koremenos, Lipson, and Snidal 2001: 785–6; Martin 1995).

---

[10] We also consider an alternative community measure, *Historical ties*, which taps whether the member states of an IO share historically rooted political bonds. This produces slightly weaker but convergent results. An IO scores 1 on *Historical ties* if its members meet one or both of the following conditions: (a) at least two-thirds of the IO's founding members were once territories in the same colonial empire; and (b) at least two-thirds of the IO's founding members were once constituent units of the same political federation.

- A *year count* to pick up the effect of an omitted variable that might produce an incremental increase in IO authority over time.[11]

Evidence

Let us now turn to the evidence to assess the argument that (a) community facilitates incomplete contracting, and (b) incomplete contracting facilitates an expanding policy portfolio. We also evaluate an alternative explanation that conceives trade as a source for policy expansion.

Community and Contract

We expect a strong affinity between shared norms and incomplete contracting for international governance. This is borne out in Table 5.3, which reports a cross-sectional and a dynamic estimation for *Community dynamic* on *Contract dynamic*. The first and third models show that the bivariate association is strong. *Community dynamic* alone accounts for slightly more than one-quarter of the variance in *Contract dynamic* in the between-effects model, and more than 40 percent in the fixed effects model. These associations survive under controls (second and fourth model).[12]

Table 5.3. Community and contract, 1950–2010

	DV: Contract dynamic			
	Cross-sectional (1)	Cross-sectional (2)	Over time (3)	Over time (4)
Community dynamic	0.162***	0.212***	0.370***	0.124***
	(0.032)	(0.033)	(0.027)	(0.026)
Controls	NO	YES	NO	YES
R^2 between	0.262	0.442		
R^2 within			0.619	0.920

Note: N = 3,279 IO-years (76 IOs) for 1950–2010. Columns 1 and 2 report between-effects estimation; columns 3 and 4 report fixed effects estimation. Columns 1 and 3 are bivariate estimations; columns 2 and 4 control (not shown) for democracy, power asymmetry, affluence, GDP dispersion, and year count (see online Appendix).
*** $p < 0.01$, ** $p < 0.05$, * $p < 0.1$.

---

[11] We also run all models with a fractional polynomial which provides a more flexible parameterization for time. This produces essentially the same results (see online Appendix).

[12] A Hausman test indicates that a random effects model is inappropriate. Hence, we report between-effects and fixed effects models separately. The online Appendix confirms that the results are robust (a) for an alternative specification for community, *Historical ties*; (b) for each of the five components of the *Community* factor; and (c) in logistic regression using *Contract* and *Community* rather than their dynamic siblings, *Contract dynamic* and *Community dynamic*.

A Theory of International Organization

The relationship is pictured in Figure 5.3 which takes a cross-section for 2010. For simplicity, *Community* is rescaled from zero to one. The distribution of IOs in the two panels is skewed in opposite directions because the member states in an IO with a complete contract tend to be normatively diverse and the member states in an IO with an incomplete contract tend to have greater normative commonality. Scores for *Community* are, on average, about twice as high in IOs with incomplete contracts (0.63 vs. 0.32; $p < .001$).

The expectation here is that an IO with heterogeneous membership is unlikely to have an incomplete contract. Only five IOs with relatively weak community (< 0.35 on a 0–1 scale) have incomplete contracts: in descending order of community, the Organization of American States (OAS), the Commonwealth of Nations, the African Union (AU), la Francophonie (OIF), and the United Nations. These are revealing cases, and later in this chapter we will

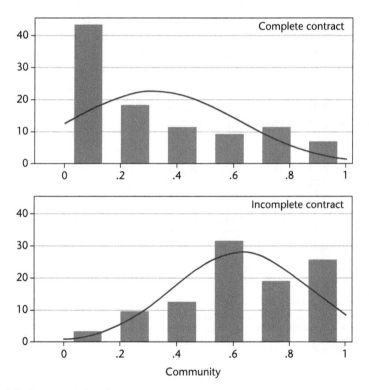

Figure 5.3 Community and contract

Note: 76 IOs in their last year in the dataset. *Community* is estimated at the foundation of an IO or in 1950. Higher values indicate that the founding members of an IO are more similar in religion, culture, political regime, legal regime, and geography. The top panel represents IOs with a complete contract, such as NAFTA, NATO, or the WTO. The bottom panel represents IOs with an incomplete contract such as the European Union, the Commonwealth of Nations, or ECOWAS. The lines are normal distribution functions for continuous data.

examine whether and how an IO can square the circle of contractual incompleteness and normative heterogeneity.

Our theory predicts that the normative coherence of the peoples encompassed in an IO facilitates incomplete contracting and the subsequent expansion of an IO's policy portfolio. Because we are interested in change over time our basic modeling choice is fixed effects. Pooling time series compounds inferential threats such as longitudinal heteroskedasticity and correlation of standard errors, and this complicates the choice of an optimal estimator (Beck and Katz 2011). Moreover, the panel is unbalanced because IOs vary in their year of founding. Hence, our exploration of how community and contract influence policy scope looks for consistency across a variety of model specifications.

Table 5.4 begins on the left with models predicting *Policy scope* with *Community dynamic* and with *Contract dynamic*, respectively, under controls for democracy, power asymmetry, the number of IO members, affluence, and GDP dispersion (models 1 and 2). These and subsequent models use one-year lags for predictors and include a year count to address pressures of time in an unbalanced panel. Model 3 includes both *Community dynamic* and *Contract dynamic*, and strongly confirms the hypothesis that the course of an IO's policy portfolio is affected both by the contract that underlies an IO and the normative diversity of its members. Finally, model 4 adds a lagged dependent variable to address autocorrelation and substantive time effects.[13] The lagged model also controls for possible endogenous development of policy scope (Wooldridge 2002).

Table 5.4. Explaining policy scope with the community-contract model

	DV = change in policy scope			
	(1)	(2)	(3)	(4)
Community dynamic$_{t-1}$	0.030***		0.015**	0.002**
	(0.007)		(0.006)	(0.001)
Contract dynamic$_{t-1}$		0.140***	0.110***	0.008**
		(0.031)	(0.031)	(0.003)
Policy scope $_{t-1}$				0.918***
				(0.012)
Controls	YES	YES	YES	YES
R^2 within	0.383	0.452	0.477	0.920
AIC	12,256	11,873	11,726	5,710

Note: N = 3,203 IO-years (76 IOs) for 1950–2010. Fixed effects estimation with standard errors clustered by IO. Controls (not shown) for democracy, membership size, power asymmetry, affluence, GDP dispersion, and year count.
*** $p < 0.01$, ** $p < 0.05$, * $p < 0.1$.

---

[13] Fixed effects estimation with standard errors clustered by IO controls for autocorrelation (Stock and Watson 2008). Results are similar for Poisson regression (online Appendix).

Community dynamic and *Contract dynamic* have a positive and significant impact on change in *Policy scope* across all specifications.[14] Furthermore, when both are present, each affects *Policy scope* independently (models 3 and 4). It is worth noting that *Contract* soaks up some of *Community*'s power which is consistent with the idea that the effect of community is mediated through an IO's contract. Community contributes to the discovery of cooperation over time (Marks, Lenz, Ceka, and Burgoon 2014; Ostrom 1990).[15] All but one control fail to reach significance. The exception is democracy which is positively and significantly related to policy expansion in three of the four models.

Notably, we find no robust effect for heterogeneity of preferences. Our analysis includes controls for power asymmetry; economic disparity measured by GDP dispersion; and foreign policy divergence measured by *Ideal points*, which relies on voting patterns in the UN. The field of international relations has long debated whether heterogeneity of preferences helps or hurts international cooperation (see e.g. the contributions in Keohane and Ostrom 1995), though recent research suggests that international organizations may be more valuable when they encourage cooperation among dissimilar states (e.g. Carnegie 2014). Our analyses find no systematic effect for power asymmetry, economic disparity, or foreign policy divergence for an IO's contract or policy scope.

Trade

A firmly grounded expectation in the literature is that international organization responds to interdependence, and in particular, to trade (Kahler 1995; Keohane 1982; Keohane and Nye 1993; Mattli 1999; Stone Sweet and Brunell 1998). Does trade affect the breadth of an IO's policy portfolio?

We test two lines of argument. The first is that an IO handling trade is likely to experience pressures for policy expansion because trade is difficult to insulate from other issues such as the environment, health, labor rights, or immigration (Haftel 2013; Kahler 1995; Milewicz et al. 2018). We find that, indeed, an IO with responsibility for reducing barriers to cross-border trade

---

[14] A two-stage model in which the first model regresses *Community* on *Contract* produces similar results (online Appendix).

[15] Benelux illustrates the potential dynamism of cooperation. Benelux began as a paired-down customs union in the final months of World War II when the Belgian, Luxembourg, and Dutch governments-in-exile signed the London Customs Convention (van Roon 1994: 11–37; Grosbois 1994: 39–69). Initially, as the Dutch ambassador in Brussels, Baron Harinxma Thoe Slooten, wrote to his minister of foreign affairs, there was concern about a weak *"compatibilité d'humeurs"* (Boekestijn 1994: 101, and n. 5). In subsequent years, governments, civil servants, and interest groups discovered that their differences paled against what tied their societies together (Kersten 1994; Spierenburg 1994; Weisglas 1994). This paved the way for the 1958 Treaty which, unlike the 1944 Treaty, was a highly incomplete contract (Benelux Treaty, Art. 1; Boekestijn 1994: 112; Mikesell 1958).

Table 5.5. Community, contract, and trade policy

	DV = Change in policy scope	
	(1)	(2)
Trade dynamic$_{t-1}$	0.106***	0.050**
	(0.026)	(0.020)
Community dynamic$_{t-1}$		0.011*
		(0.006)
Contract dynamic$_{t-1}$		0.093***
		(0.028)
Controls	YES	YES
R² within	0.392	0.500
AIC	12,208	11,586

Note: N = 3,203 IO-years (76 IOs) for 1950–2010. Fixed effects estimation with standard errors clustered by IO. Controls (not shown) for democracy, power asymmetry, membership, affluence, GDP dispersion, and year count.
*** p < 0.01, ** p < 0.05, * p < 0.1.

tends to have a more dynamic policy portfolio than an IO that does not have trade competence, but this does not suppress the effects of community and contract.

Trade takes on a value of 1 from the year when trade becomes an IO competence and zero otherwise, and *Trade dynamic* adds a time dimension. This variable is statistically significant in a fixed effects regression under full controls, with or without *Contract* and *Community* (Table 5.5). Adding trade improves the AIC statistic compared to a model without *Trade dynamic* (model 3 in Table 5.4).[16] The estimated substantive effect of *Trade* on *Policy scope* is modest, while that of *Contract* is around three times as large (based on model 2 in Table 5.5). A positive shift of one standard deviation in *Trade dynamic* increases the policy breadth of an IO by 0.80 whereas an IO moving one standard deviation on *Contract* produces an expected increase of 2.3 policies.

A second argument links trade interdependence to IO design. To examine the effect of trade interdependence on an IO's policy portfolio, we use three specifications: intra-IO trade, trade intensity, and trade introversion.[17] Each specification measures internal trade among IO members in comparison to trade between IO members and third parties (see Appendix).[18] To assess trade

---

[16] *Trade dynamic* loses significance under the restrictive condition of adding a lagged dependent variable. *Community dynamic* and *Contract dynamic* retain significance (online Appendix).

[17] We use algorithms developed by the Institute on Comparative Regional Integration Studies of the United Nations University in Bruges (UNU-CRIS) to calculate trade interdependence among an IO's members for a given year. Data are available from 1970.

[18] This analysis speaks to a rich international political economy literature that probes the connection between trade interdependence and institutional design. Haftel (2013) finds an effect of trade interdependence on spillover across subdomains of economic integration. Büthe and Milner (2014) turn the arrow around so that preferential trade agreements with supranational

Table 5.6. IOs by trade interdependence and trade policy

IO competence in trade	Data on trade interdependence		
	No	Yes	
No	34	0	34
Yes	8	34	42
	42	34	76

Note: 76 IOs in 2010; shaded IOs are included in the analysis of trade interdependence.

interdependence it makes sense to limit the sample to the thirty-four non-global IOs that have competence in trade on the intuition that if trade interdependence has an effect it will be evident in this subsample. Table 5.6 compares this subsample to the seventy-six IOs used elsewhere in this chapter.

The first column in Table 5.7 models *Community dynamic* and *Contract dynamic* under controls as a baseline.[19] For this subsample, as for the entire sample, the incompleteness of an IO's contract is positively associated with an expanding policy portfolio. The more distal estimate of *Community dynamic* loses significance. The next three models show that in bivariate fixed effects two of the three trade interdependence measures reach significance, though their explanatory power is weak. *Trade interdependence* loses significance in the presence of controls in model 5, while *Contract dynamic* retains significance in the fully specified model 6.

Although the analysis does not confirm that trade interdependence affects the growth of an IO's policy portfolio, it does suggest that an IO with competence in trade is likely to have a more dynamic policy portfolio than one without trade competence. However, this does not diminish the statistical power of incomplete contracting, nor that of community in the full sample. These results provide further confirmation that community expressed through incomplete contracting is a robust influence on an IO's policy portfolio and that the effect of community cannot be reduced to a confluence of economic interest among member states that have intensive trade relations.

---

dispute settlement mechanisms deepen economic interdependence because they attract more foreign direct investment. Baccini, Dür, and colleagues show that trade interdependence increases demand for deep and flexible preferential trade agreements (Baccini 2010; Baccini and Dür 2012; Baccini, Dür, and Elsig 2015; Dür, Baccini, and Elsig 2014). Gray finds a significant effect of trade and trade potential on the vitality of regional international organizations (Gray 2014, 2018; Gray and Slapin 2012).

[19] These results stand when controlling for *Trade policy* and for a lagged dependent variable.

Table 5.7. Community, contract, and trade interdependence

	DV = Change in policy scope					
	(1)	(2)	(3)	(4)	(5)[a]	(6)[a]
Community dynamic$_{t-1}$	0.022					0.023
	(0.026)					(0.026)
Contract dynamic$_{t-1}$	0.182**					0.179**
	(0.069)					(0.069)
Trade interdependence						
Intra-IO trade $_{t-1}$		0.266**				
		(0.129)				
Trade intensity $_{t-1}$			0.000			
			(0.000)			
Trade introversion $_{t-1}$				6.645***	0.947	0.522
				(1.698)	(1.522)	(1.488)
Controls	YES	NO	NO	NO	YES	YES
R² within	0.578	0.074	0.000	0.101	0.537	0.579
AIC	4,169	4,966	5,041	4,937	4,263	4,169

Note: 971 IO-years (N = 34 IOs); [a] Model with best Akaike information criterion (AIC) of the three trade models. Fixed effects estimation with standard errors clustered by IO. Controls (not shown) for democracy, power asymmetry, membership size, affluence, GDP dispersion, and year count.
*** $p < 0.01$, ** $p < 0.05$, * $p < 0.1$.

Exceptional Cases

It can be deeply instructive to examine cases that do not fit with one's hunches. Our theory makes two general claims. First, that incomplete contracting produces a more dynamic policy portfolio, and second, that community is required for incomplete contracting. The Council of Europe (CoE) is interesting because it has a highly incomplete contract but, contrary to our first claim, its policy portfolio has been static. The reason appears to be that the CoE has had to compete with several other IOs for policy space, including the European Union.

We then examine four IOs that challenge our core thesis that general purpose governance rests on community. The United Nations, the Commonwealth, the Organization of American States, and the African Union are general purpose IOs, yet encompass normatively diverse member states. These cases suggest how normative diversity can be finessed. One strategy is to disperse decision making horizontally across sub-organizations. Another is to decentralize the IO vertically so that regional groups take most decisions. Both strategies help to sustain a highly incomplete contract for governance among diverse peoples, either by breaking down the policy portfolio into smaller pieces or by clustering the member states into more coherent groupings.

The Council of Europe

The Council of Europe has an incomplete contract to "achieve a greater unity" in Europe, but today its policy portfolio, focused on human rights and cultural cooperation, is no wider than it was when it was founded in 1951. We observe four expansions of the CoE's portfolio, but we also detect two retrenchments producing a net change of zero. The initial reason for this lies in the conflict that plagued the organization at its inception. The French and Benelux governments, which conceived the CoE as a step towards federalism, were stymied by the British and Scandinavian insistence on a narrow intergovernmentalist organization (Grigorescu 2015: 235–7; Laffan 1992). Ernest Bevin, UK Foreign Secretary, demanded "a practical organism in Europe" which would, in effect, be a talking shop avoiding defense and economic issues (quoted in Schuman 1951: 729). The 1949 Statute of the CoE was an uneasy compromise between these conceptions. In the early 1950s the Council of Europe served as "the main forum for debate on European integration," but in the face of continued British resistance, federalists shifted their focus to the European Coal and Steel Community (Joris and Vandenberghe 2008: 4). A last-minute attempt by the British to assert the CoE's political authority over the European Coal and Steel Community failed, and the ECSC, guided by its more homogeneous membership which excluded Britain and Scandinavia, became the foundation for the expansive European Union. For its part, the CoE remained a niche organization concerned with human rights and cultural cooperation (Bond 2012).

Time and again, the CoE was outflanked by other international organizations (Alter and Meunier 2009; Brosig 2011; Panke and Stapel 2018). The CoE began discussing transport cooperation soon after its founding, but in 1953 sixteen states chose to set up the European Conference of Ministers of Transport under the umbrella of the OEEC (Patel 2013: 654). The chief culprit in the displacement of the CoE was the European Union, which used its supranational law-making capacity, superior financial resources, and its pragmatic focus on market integration to put the CoE's ideas into practice. In environmental policy, the CoE adopted a European Water Charter in 1967 which became a core policy of the European Union (Meyer 2017: 52). The CoE spearheaded cultural cooperation from the 1950s, but the European Community gradually adopted many of the CoE's ideas and policies, such as the notion of cultural heritage that framed its audiovisual policy (Patel and Calligaro 2017). The EU supplanted the CoE in regional development policy as networks of local and regional authorities shifted their attention from the CoE to the European Community which could provide them with substantial funding (Hooghe 1996; Wassenberg 2017). Most recently, the EU's foray into human rights, with the adoption of a Charter of Fundamental Rights in 2000 and the reform of the European Monitoring Centre for Racism and Xenophobia into a Fundamental Rights Agency, has "fueled perceptions that the Council of Europe [is] losing its role as the main European standard-setter in the field of human rights and fundamental freedoms" (Joris and Vandenberghe 2008: 18; Soriano 2017).

The CoE is a case in which competition appears to confound the dynamic properties of an incomplete contract. The CoE is a telling example of how a general purpose IO can play "the crucial role of... a laboratory for generating new policy ideas and an agenda-setter, as well as the equally important function of the various parliamentary assemblies as mechanisms by which policy ideas diffuse" (Risse 2017: 472). The chief quality of an incomplete contract is that it provides an IO with the flexibility to explore new avenues for cooperation as circumstances change. In the case of the CoE, its ideas were translated into policies by a more resourceful IO. Even the CoE's flag, a circle of yellow stars on a blue background, was adopted by the European Community in 1986, and today it is associated with the European Union rather than with the CoE (Patel 2013: 655–6).

United Nations

The United Nations has a broader policy portfolio than any other global IO, yet the organization has an extremely diverse membership. The tension between scale and community has shaped the UN's institutional development as a compendium of task-specific bodies.

The UN was conceived as potentially general purpose—"a center for harmonizing the actions of nations in the attainment of... common ends" (1946 Charter, Art. 1), although its core concern has always been peace and security. Over time, its responsibilities have expanded as international security came to encompass conflict within, as well as among, states. This has generated a wide array of subsidiary programs, funds, and institutes concerned with economic and social development, human rights, humanitarian aid, migration, and the environment. It makes the UN, or in practice, the UN *system*, the global site for general purpose governance.

The benefits of scale at the global level are vast, and normative diversity has not prohibited the creation of an interconnected web of global governance. However, the most significant organizational feature of the UN system is that it is fragmented in task-specific pillars which include the World Health Organization, the Food and Agriculture Organization, the International Labor Organization, the International Telecommunications Union, alongside eleven other specialized agencies (White 2000; UN website).[20] Each is a self-standing IO with its own constitution, decision-making bodies, and legal personality.

Whereas a general purpose IO grows by extension, as does a tree, UN organizations have spread in bamboo fashion, forming colonies of interlinked but self-standing organizations with common roots. The UN system has incorporated additional policies by emanating new organizations. This modular approach to global governance decomposes tasks to make them more amenable to technocratic problem-solving. Epistemic communities of experts frequently play a key role. International bureaucrats are often instrumental in designing an IO when it does not transparently engage domestic issues (Johnson 2014: 45).

Coordination is far denser within, than among, these organizations even though they are the "world's principal mechanism for international peace and security and for mobilizing international efforts to deal with global problems" (Childers and Urquhart 1999: 11). The UN system has been described as "a complex patchwork quilt" (MacKenzie 2010: 53); "an organizational hybrid, its many functions impossible to explain" (Hanhimäki 2015: 26); and a conglomerate where each agency "is primarily concerned to assert its unique competence" (Hurrell 1993: 49). As Ruggie (2003: 303) observes, the UN system "is not designed as a matrix at all but as a set of deeply rooted columns connected only by thin and tenuous rows. Nothing that has transpired since 1945 has transformed that fundamental reality."

Decomposing policy in separate organizations is always going to be tricky because so many problems are interrelated. Natural disasters almost always produce health, environmental, and financial problems alongside humanitarian challenges. Pacifying war-torn zones usually involves a host of development and financial issues alongside security and policing. After serving four years as Assistant Secretary General and senior adviser for strategic planning to the UN Secretary General, Ruggie (2003: 301) described coordination among UN organizations as his "paramount concern."

The Chief Executives Board for Coordination (CEB) is the regular meeting place for the executive heads of thirty-one UN programs, funds, specialized agencies, and related organizations. Its role is to bring "the disparate parts of a decentralized system of specialized bodies—each with its own constitution, mandate, governing bodies and budgets—into a cohesive and functioning whole."[21] However, the CEB has neither the resources nor the authority to

---

[20] United Nations, "Funds, Programmes, Specialized Agencies and Others," http://www.un.org/en/sections/about-un/funds-programmes-specialized-agencies-and-others/ (accessed February 28, 2019).

[21] UN, "United Nations System: Chief Executives Board for Coordination," https://www.unsystem.org/content/ceb (accessed February 28, 2019).

do the job effectively. As the CEB's website admits, the Charter instructs it merely to engage in "consultation and recommendation," which "underscores the decentralized nature of the UN system. No central authority exists to compel compliance by organizations of the system to act in a concerted manner. Coordination and cooperation are contingent upon the willingness of system organizations to work together in pursuit of common goals."

UN leaders have been acutely aware of how the diversity of members and peoples weakens the UN's standing. Dag Hammarskjöld, UN Secretary General from 1953 until 1961, worried that few people could relate to the United Nations because it was too distant from their daily lives. He hoped that, over time, "people, just people, [would] stop thinking of the United Nations as a weird Picasso abstraction and see it as a drawing they made themselves."[22]

The UN's response has been a combination of compartmentalization and decentralization. The UN General Assembly "comes closer than any other body to embodying 'the international community'" (Karns and Mingst 2010: 102; Kennedy 2007). It has spawned some forty boards, commissions, committees, councils, panels, or working groups as well as countless ad hoc bodies. Many of these bring together coalitions of the willing, which can make recommendations to the General Assembly for a non-binding resolution. The UN Economic and Social Council (ECOSOC) has also proliferated subsidiary bodies, beginning in 1946 with the Human Rights Commission; its resolutions too are non-binding. The only body in the compartmentalized headquarters with hard power and focus is the Security Council, a task-specific body that gives its most powerful members a veto and makes decisions binding on all UN members.

Beyond compartmentalizing decisions at the center, the United Nations has kept diversity in check by decentralizing programs.[23] The UN Charter envisaged a centralized organization, but the Economic and Social Council soon set up Economic Commissions in collaboration with regional groupings of member states in Europe, Latin America, Asia, and the Pacific (1947–8), followed by Africa (1958) and Western Asia (1973) (Graham and Felico 2006: 89; Jiménez 2010; Malinowski 1962). In 1998, the Economic and Social Council mandated each regional commission to hold regular inter-agency meetings to improve

---

[22] Interview with Hammarskjöld in *Time Magazine*, June 27, 1955.
[23] Regional groupings were conceived in terms of community and were intended to be general purpose, as a proposal by Egypt at the UN's founding San Francisco conference made explicit: "There shall be considered, as regional arrangements, organizations of a permanent nature grouping in a given geographical area several countries which, by reason of their proximity, community of interests or cultural, linguistic, historical or spiritual affinities make themselves jointly responsible for the peaceful settlement of any disputes which may arise...as well as for the safeguarding of their interests and the development of their economic and cultural relations" (UNCIO XII: 85, 857, June 8, 1945, quoted in Graham and Felico 2006: 87; see also Russett 1967).

coordination, and in 2006 a high-profile UN report conceived the commissions as vital for "a coherent regional institutional landscape" (Aziz, Diogo, and Stoltenberg 2006: 19; Graham 2012). No less than thirty UN funds, programs, and specialized agencies operate at the regional level (Fawcett 2012; Henrikson 1996; Lombaerde, Baert, and Felício 2012).

The postwar years spurred institutional creativity resulting in a heterogeneous, multilevel system of regional, global, multilateral, and bilateral arrangements rather than a coherent system of general purpose governance. "The initial American impulse was to urge upon other states the creation of a rather straightforward open and rule-based order," but the vision became increasingly differentiated. "[T]he order was not conceived in a singular vision and imposed on the world. It was cobbled together in a rolling political process" (Ikenberry 2011: 161). Among the definitive international settlements of the past four centuries, the post-World War II settlement is "both the most fragmented and the most far-reaching" (Ikenberry 2001: 163).

The Commonwealth

The Commonwealth of Nations is the oldest large-N general purpose organization, and one of its most heterogeneous. The Commonwealth encompasses fifty-two member states in five continents with a combined population of 2.4 billion. To the extent that the Commonwealth can draw on shared norms, these are rooted in the experience of existence in, and resistance to, the British Empire.

The Commonwealth reduces the tension between its relatively incomplete contract and normative diversity by minimizing the formal commitments of its member states and by fragmenting its activities among task-specific public–private bodies.

The Commonwealth has no single document that can be described as a constitution. An attempt to formalize the organization in 1926 was regarded by the Canadian prime minister, Robert Gordon Menzies, as "a misguided attempt to reduce to written terms things that were matters of the spirit and not of the letter" (quoted in Mansergh 2013 [1968]: 7). Jan Smuts, its most passionate defender, described the Commonwealth as the Cheshire cat in Lewis Carroll's *Alice in Wonderland*, which retains its grin after its body has disappeared. It is, in short, the epitome of an informal international organization operating chiefly on the basis of unwritten rules.

Informality in the Commonwealth has fostered a climate of voluntary cooperation and an emphasis on sovereignty, both of which are consistent with a normatively diverse membership (McKinnon 2005). Biannual meetings of government leaders in open and closed sessions produce pithy, but nonbinding, resolutions.

Human rights and good governance is the one field in which the Commonwealth has bared its teeth.[24] Several members have been threatened with suspension and have subsequently left the organization, including South Africa which was barred from 1961 until re-admission in 1994. Zimbabwe left the Commonwealth in 2003 after it was suspended, and the Maldives left in 2016 when it was threatened with suspension (Commonwealth CMAG 2016: Art. 9). Nigeria, Pakistan, and Fiji were suspended but came back in good standing, the latter two countries twice.[25]

A distinctive feature of the Commonwealth is its decentralization in numerous quasi-independent bodies. The "Commonwealth family" is a partnership between the intergovernmental Commonwealth Secretariat (ComSec) and the Commonwealth Foundation, a network of around two hundred professional and civic associations active in education, culture, and development, mostly run by non-state actors (Shaw 2005, 2008).

The Organization of American States

The Organization of American States (OAS), created in 1890 as the International Union of American Republics (Pan American Union from 1910) and revamped in 1948, is the largest international organization in the Americas with thirty-four members. The OAS has a confederal structure in which its constituent organizations are more authoritative than the center. Its charter and subsequent agreements cover democracy promotion, human rights, development, and conflict resolution, while its network of semi-autonomous intergovernmental institutions include the Pan American Health Organization, the Inter-American Commission of Women, the Inter-American Telecommunications Commission, and the Inter-American Development Bank.[26]

Contested community has hampered the organization from its early days (Bianculli 2016). The OAS likes to describe itself as the oldest regional organization and the heir of pan-Americanism. Nevertheless, it has had to contend with competing integration schemes such as the Latin American Integration Association (ALADI), the Latin American and Caribbean Economic System (SELA), the Community of Latin American and Caribbean States (CELAC),

---

[24] In 1971 the Commonwealth issued a stark condemnation of racial prejudice as "a dangerous sickness threatening the healthy development of the human race" (Commonwealth COMSEC 2004: "Harare Commonwealth Declaration, 1991").

[25] Zimbabwe applied to rejoin in May 2018, and the Maldives in December 2018.

[26] While the Inter-American Development Bank (IADB) is constitutionally independent of the OAS, only OAS members can become regional members. The Bank also has non-regional members (https://www.iadb.org/en/about-us/how-are-we-organized, accessed February 28, 2019).

and the Union of South American Nations (UNASUR), all of which exclude the United States and Canada.[27] Within the OAS, the Andean Community, the Central American Integration System, the Caribbean Community, and Mercosur are more cohesive general purpose IOs (Riggirozzi 2015; Thomas and Magloire 2000). The result is a patchwork of organizations with partially overlapping membership and policy agendas which has been characterized as "modular regionalism" (Gardini 2015) and "institutional elasticity" (Hofmann and Mérand 2012).

Institutional competition is motivated by the suspicion that the OAS has been an instrument for US interests.[28] In the late 1960s, Jerome Slater (1969: 52) observed that the "main function of the OAS has been to cloak essentially unilateral United States actions in a multilateral framework, thereby providing it with a measure of legitimacy." A recent US Congress report notes that "OAS decisions frequently reflected US policy during the twentieth century" and that there is "the lingering view of many in the region that the OAS is an institution dominated by the United States" (Meyer 2014: 1, 27).

The OAS has struggled to hold states to their promises. Cooperation appears most effective when issues can be hived off to task-specific arrangements or organizations operating under the OAS umbrella or one of its competitors (Gardini 2015; Riggirozzi 2015). The Inter-American Court of Human Rights (IACHR), a task-specific institution loosely associated with the OAS, has played an active role in pursuing human rights violations in Latin America (Alter 2014; Cavallaro and Brewer 2008; Sikkink and Booth Walling 2007). The IACHR can make binding rulings, authorize compensatory sanctions, and can admit cases from non-state parties referred to it by the Inter-American Commission on Human Rights. IACHR dispute settlement is optional for OAS members.[29]

---

[27] In its inaugural Caracas Declaration, CELAC appropriates the mantle of pan-Americanism in a direct challenge to the OAS: "CELAC, as the only mechanism for dialogue and consensus that unites the 33 countries of Latin America and the Caribbean, is the highest expression of our will for unity in diversity, where henceforth, our political, economic, social and cultural ties will strengthen on the basis of a common agenda of welfare, peace and security for our peoples, with a view to consolidation of our regional community (Art. 28)" (Caracas Declaration, December 3, 2011, http://www.pnuma.org/forodeministros/19-reunion%20intersesional/documentos/CARACAS%20DECLARATION.pdf, accessed February 28, 2019).

[28] This concern goes back to the Monroe doctrine. Article 25 of the 1948 Charter of the Organization of American States seemed to turn this around when it vested responsibility for fighting colonialism with all OAS members (Van Wynen Thomas and Thomas 1970). However, during the Cold War the US government used the new language to legitimize unilateral military intervention (Appleman Williams 1972: 18–58; Sexton 2011: 5–8). In November 2013 US Secretary of State Kerry declared that "the era of the Monroe doctrine is over."

[29] As of February 2019, only twenty-three of thirty-four OAS member states have ratified the American Convention on Human Rights.

The African Union

Among the four large-N heterogeneous general purpose IOs discussed here, the African Union (AU) has the most dynamic policy portfolio. Since its creation in 1963, it has added thirteen new policies to its initial five. The African Union comprises all fifty-five states in Africa with a combined population of more than one billion. The organization is chiefly concerned with security. A two-thirds majority of its member states in the Peace and Security Council can instigate coercive intervention, peacekeeping, sanctions, or expulsion, and this has happened several times in response to military coups. The AU has a prominent security role, having sent peacekeepers to Burundi, Sudan, South Sudan, and Somalia and to UN missions in the region. The African Union also monitors human rights, oversees economic integration, endeavors to build continental infrastructure from transport to telecommunications, coordinates health and educational initiatives, and represents African countries in several international fora.

The aspiration for a union of African peoples is rooted in the common experience of colonial domination. Independence struggles led peoples with disparate languages, religions, and cultures to a recognition that beyond their differences they shared a past and a future. The intellectual founder of the African Union, President Kwame Nkrumah of Ghana, stressed that "our strength lies in a unified policy and action for progress and development, so the strength of the imperialists lies in our disunity." Nkrumah conceived Africa as a community and dedicated his book *Africa Must Unite* (1963) to George Padmore, an early pan-Africanist, and to "the African Nation that must be." The first paragraph of the AU's Constitutive Act of 2001 reflects on "generations of Pan-Africanists in their determination to promote unity, solidarity, cohesion and cooperation among the peoples of Africa and African States."

The imagined African community has always existed in tension with its fractured self. Africa's emerging states were determined to prevent intervention in their own affairs (Elias 1965; Fredland 1973; Welz 2013). Most postcolonial states were themselves diverse and feared ethnic mobilization within their borders. The first attempt to create an African-wide general purpose IO, the Organization for African Unity (1963), foundered on superpower rivalries and on the insistence of newly independent countries for full national sovereignty (Packer and Rukare 2002). Its leaders "often behaved like a mutual preservation club" while advocating regime change in the white minority regimes of Angola, Mozambique, Rhodesia, Namibia, and South Africa (Makinda and Okumu 2008: 12). When these regimes were overthrown, it made less sense to equate human rights with ending white rule or to ignore abuses by domestic regimes. The OAU had condoned "a culture of impunity," but in

2006, the AU Assembly mandated Senegal "on behalf of Africa" to try Hissène Habré, the former president of Chad, for atrocities (Williams 2007: 269). For the first time, a former head of state was brought before an all-African court.[30] The idea that Africa's peoples form a community is challenged by dictators and by the sheer diversity of the peoples themselves, but it has provided a powerful normative basis for a general purpose international organization.

Although the African Union's aspirations are hardly less sweeping than those of today's European Union, its actual footprint is light. It has adopted a confederal approach inspired by the United Nations, but instead of farming out policies to task-specific organizations, it provides policy guidance and logistical support to Africa's subcontinental general purpose IOs.[31]

The experience of the United Nations, the Commonwealth, the Organization of American States, and the African Union reveals that an IO with weak community faces strong headwinds in pursuing general purpose governance. Although there is no solution, there are some ways in which this can be mitigated. The United Nations sits at the center of a family of organizations that decompose tasks into discrete, and therefore more manageable, pieces and which, in aggregate, amounts to something approaching general purpose global governance. The African Union and the Commonwealth decentralize functions to smaller-scale organizations that draw on more homogeneous memberships, including sub-regional general purpose IOs in the African Union, and voluntary professional and civic associations in the Commonwealth. Of the four organizations, the Organization of American States is the most constrained because it is challenged by an alternative conception of community which is Latin American or South American rather than pan-American.

Who is one of us? What does this mean for how we govern ourselves? The IOs discussed here reveal the open-textured nature of community among peoples who are diverse on just about any institutional measure. However, international governance is a terrain of human inventiveness and in diverse ways with varying degrees of success each of the IOs discussed here has sought to manage general purpose governance by decentralizing or decomposing its organization.

---

[30] The Extraordinary African Chambers, authorized by the AU, convicted the former president to life-long imprisonment in May 2016, and after appeal, the conviction was upheld in April 2017 (African Union press release of May 2, 2017, available at https://au.int/en/pressreleases/20170502/au-welcomes-appeal-outcome-hissene-habre-case-african-extraordinary-chambers, accessed February 28, 2019).

[31] The 1980 Lagos Plan signaled the intention to use regional organizations as stepping stones to African-wide integration. This became OAU policy with the 1991 Abuja Treaty and the 2001 AU constitutive Act. In 2008, the AU concluded a special protocol for cooperation with subcontinental IOs.

Conclusion

Policy scope is a key feature of an IO's basic set up. Some IOs have a highly dynamic and broad policy portfolio, whereas others have a static and narrow policy portfolio. What explains this variation?

We suggest two distinct, but complementary, causal paths. Incomplete contracting, which sets out the purpose of an IO in open-ended language, provides the flexibility necessary to adapt an IO's policy portfolio to new circumstances. Incomplete contracting is itself made possible by shared norms that underpin diffuse reciprocity, trust, and a reputation for keeping one's word. The combined effect of community and contract explains more than half of the variance in policy scope over time.

Our analysis reveals mixed support for the hypothesis that trade induces states to deepen international cooperation. While IOs with competence in trade are more likely to have a dynamic portfolio, the extent of trade interdependence does not appear to affect the growth of an IO's portfolio. Our inquiry finds no systematic effect for interest heterogeneity that might arise from power asymmetry, economic disparity, or foreign policy divergence.

Four cases defy the expectation that community and contract shape a policy portfolio: the United Nations, the Commonwealth of Nations, the Organization of American States, and the African Union. Each organization combines normative diversity, an incomplete contract, and a broad policy portfolio. Each is a testament to creativity in framing cooperation in the face of the tension between community and scale. Each makes the most of weak ties: the UN in its bamboo-like frame, the OAS and the AU in emphasizing continent-wide solidarity against imperialism and colonialism, and the Commonwealth in its shared colonial heritage. More sophisticated measures of community would do a better job of picking up these phenomena. What these cases do suggest, however, is that the effect of community appears to reach beyond our effort to test it quantitatively.

6

The Resistible Rise of International Authority

We detect a remarkable deepening of international authority in the postwar period. Sixty-one percent of the IOs that we observe saw an increase in both pooling and delegation (33 IOs) or in one or the other (13 IOs). No IO experienced a decrease in both pooling and delegation, and just seven underwent a decrease in either pooling or delegation and no increase in the other.[1]

Under what circumstances will states delegate authority to non-state actors? When will states pool authority in binding majoritarian voting? Our theory is that international authority reflects two contrary pressures, one functional and one social.

As an IO extends its policy commitments, it acquires the machinery of complex decision making. The intuition here is that the broader the range of an organization's policy portfolio, the greater the incentive to structure its agenda, marshal information, resolve disputes, and manage decision making. This is the idea that supranationalism arises as a functional adaptation to policy complexity. The IO retains its *inter*national character in that the member states negotiate its institutions, but in doing so states are induced to facilitate decision making by pooling authority among themselves and by turning over some key tasks to independent actors.

A functional logic explains both the overall trend towards greater IO authority over the past decades and the variation that we detect. However, functional adaptation is not the end of the story because international governance can generate a sharp political reaction among exclusive nationalists opposed to immigration, trade, and the loss of national sovereignty (Hooghe and Marks 2009b, 2018).[2] Functional pressures may meet intense resistance when an IO is politicized in domestic political conflict.

---

[1] We register change if there is an absolute shift of 0.01 or greater on a 0–1 scale from the first to the last year of an IO in the dataset. Twenty-three of the 76 IOs have the same score in their final year as in their first year.

[2] This argument builds on a growing literature that investigates the sources and consequences of politicization (Conceição-Heldt 2013; de Wilde, Leupold, and Schmidtke 2017; de Wilde et al.

The Resistible Rise of International Authority

The critique from the left is that international governance insulates globalization from democratic rules that protect jobs and the environment. The nationalist critique, and the most potent source of resistance today, is that international governance is illegitimate because it undermines national self-rule and national culture. Those who conceive their national identity in exclusive terms, as "us versus them," resist supranationalism as rule by foreigners. When an IO is politicized in domestic politics, a government may think twice about adapting policy to functional pressures. Politicization is arguably the chief reason why we do not live in a world of progressively deeper supranational governance.

The model we propose combines an analysis of the development of the policy portfolio laid out in Chapter 5 with the effects of the policy portfolio and politicization for IO authority in this chapter. Figure 6.1 summarizes these expectations by placing policy scope in a causal chain beginning with community. Community—the extent to which an IO encompasses normatively similar participants—underpins diffuse reciprocity and provides the basis for member states to engage in highly incomplete contracting. Highly incomplete contracting opens the door to an expanding policy portfolio, which leads to the pooling and delegation of IO authority. Rather than conceiving norms and functional pressures as alternative explanations of international governance, we theorize a sequential process in which the normative basis of contracting among states determines the growth of the policy portfolio, and the functional pressures arising from the policy portfolio determine the course of IO authority. Finally, IO authority evokes politicization because it enhances supranational shared rule at the expense of national self-rule.

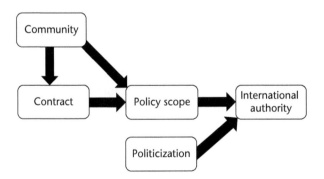

Figure 6.1 A model of international authority

2019; Ecker-Ehrhardt 2014; Kriesi et al. 2008; Hooghe and Marks 1999, 2009b; Hurrelmann and Schneider 2015; Hutter and Grande 2014; Kay 2015; Mansfield and Mutz 2012; Morgenstern et al. 2007; Rathbun 2012; Rixen and Zangl 2013; Schmitter 1969; Solingen 2008; Zürn 2004; Zürn, Binder, and Ecker-Ehrhardt 2012).

Policy Expansion

Chapter 5 demonstrates that community—shared norms that undergird diffuse reciprocity—are vital for the incomplete contracting that facilitates policy expansion. Here we take the argument one step further to theorize how policy expansion affects the authority of an international organization. As the policy portfolio of an IO expands, so there are pressures to empower non-state actors and facilitate majoritarian decision making among the member states. This hypothesis is a special case of the more general claim that "More prevalent and complex political activity places growing demands on decision makers [...] and [enhances] the need to delegate decisions" (Pierson 2000: 483). There is abundant evidence for this functional logic in the development of national states and the expansion of civil services, courts, and agencies. Summarizing the findings of the literature on delegation within the state, Moe (2012: 17) observes that "In complex policy areas, the value of agency [...] will tend to be higher, and the optimal level of independence higher."

We hypothesize a functional logic of empowerment in four mechanisms:

- *Moral hazard.* Pooling authority in majoritarian decision making alleviates a moral hazard—veto blackmail—that becomes more severe as an IO's policy scope expands.
- *Issue cycling.* Delegation of agenda setting to non-state actors constrains issue cycling under majority voting as the dimensionality of the policy space increases.
- *Information.* The informational benefits of independent non-state expertise increase with the diversity of an IO's policy portfolio.
- *Dispute settlement.* Policy expansion increases the demand for institutionalized monitoring of state compliance.

The argument that pooling authority responds to moral hazard begins with the observation that the more things a group must decide, the more troublesome is the rule that nothing can be decided without the consent of each participant. A major problem with unanimity is that it allows each participant to threaten to block a decision unless they receive a side payment. It is sometimes argued that an IO handling more policies will generate more opportunities for logrolling in which votes can be traded across policies in an effort to gain the support of every legislator. However, logrolling is no panacea if veto players are willing to cloak their true preferences to gain blackmail potential. Empirical studies of voting in the European Union confirm this: "Multidimensional legislation creates opportunities for logrolling and legislators' veto power under the unanimity rule enables them to exploit these opportunities" (Aksoy 2012: 538, 543). Several studies suggest that fear of this moral hazard was instrumental in leading EU member states to limit the national veto as the organization extended its competences (Sandholtz and Zysman 1989: 115; Keohane and Hoffmann 1991: 21). It is instructive that where unanimity has been retained, as in the EU's 2012 compact to coordinate fiscal policy, agreement was achieved not by logrolling, but by limiting the dimensionality of the policy space: "Time limits and political disagreements made it easier to achieve agreement by eliminating provisions as opposed to adding new ones" (Tsebelis and Hahm 2014: 1405; see Hug and König 2002 for earlier episodes). Rather than easing the potential for gridlock, expanding the policy scope of an IO appears to replicate the problem of decision making under unanimity in a wider range of issue areas. This grounds the expectation that the functional benefit of (super)majority voting increases as an IO's policy agenda expands.

The flipside of majority rule is that it produces instability unless there is some institutional constraint on agenda setting. As an IO's policy portfolio expands, so the number of possible reforms that could gain majority support increases. If agenda setting is unconstrained, every proposal can be defeated by another proposal that is majority preferred.[3] This has been intensively studied in the formal analysis of legislative choice: "Simply expanding the dimensionality of the choice space from one to two has profound disequilibrating consequences.... Consequently, majority rule theoretically can wander anywhere" (Krehbiel 1988: 267). Hence, pooling authority in majority voting has the knock-on effect of making it necessary to constrain majority cycling. Delegating agenda setting power to a non-state actor is one possible solution. In the field of international organization, this usually involves an independent secretariat with the power and, in some cases, the exclusive power to draft legislative proposals (Hawkins et al. 2006a; Müller, Bergman, and Strøm 2003; Pollack 2003).

As an IO's policy portfolio broadens, so does the need for unbiased information. Arrow (1974: 53–6) points out that while an organization can acquire vastly more information than can any individual, this information must be carefully structured to be of use in decision making. Non-state agents may be valuable in retrieving, filtering, and disseminating information that would be expensive for a state to produce (Bradley and Kelley 2008; Koremenos 2008; Pollack 2003). Non-governmental organizations (NGOs), for example, may have a comparative advantage in providing local knowledge and in publicly monitoring member state commitments (Tallberg et al. 2014: 754–5). Moreover, a reputation for detachment from any one country—cultivated by an

---

[3] Tsebelis (2002: 154) observes that increasing the dimensionality of decision making adds to the number of voters who have the deciding vote in an otherwise tied outcome.

independent IO secretariat—may be useful in gaining the trust of national interlocutors and in retrieving unbiased information (Beyers and Trondal 2004; Egeberg 1999; Hooghe 2005). For each of these reasons, independent non-state actors may have informational access and expertise that becomes more valuable as an IO's policy portfolio grows.

Finally, policy expansion intensifies the problem of monitoring and enforcement. The more complex the policy environment, the greater the scope for contending interpretations of whether a particular behavior is a rule violation. Jurisdiction to interpret the meaning of the law is a basic court function. "Since the principals themselves disagree on what the contract implies, they cannot instruct the agent on exactly how to decide on the issue(s) under dispute. Principals, therefore, go to considerable lengths to select (or create) impartial agents with relatively high autonomy" (Hawkins et al. 2006a: 18; Kono 2007; Koremenos 2008: 168–9). Correspondingly, there is a functional logic in empowering an independent panel or standing court to arbitrate disputes and enforce its rulings by fine, sanction, or retaliatory measure (Alter 2008; Carrubba and Gabel 2017; Dworkin 1988; Franck 1988: 741).

These mechanisms suggest that as an IO comes to have a broader policy footprint its member states will be induced to extend majority voting and empower non-state actors. There is no subterfuge involved. International authority in this theory results from the decisions of the member states themselves, not merely from the efforts of non-state actors to work around member states or extend "agency slack."

Politicization

Politicization—the salience and divisiveness of debate over an IO—can constrain international authority even in the face of functional pressure.[4] Functional pressures are most effective where decision making is sheltered from political conflict, and where as a result, it is shaped by efficiency rather than power. International authority touches a human nerve—who rules our community—and this may generate political conflict that can overpower the benefits of scale. When push comes to shove, domestic politics can trump economic efficiency.

An individual's attitude over international authority depends on how they consider themselves in relation to others. How do they conceive the communities to which they belong? Who is included; who is excluded; who has a

---

[4] The notion that politicization implies contestation as well as rising salience and widening involvement is well established (de Wilde, Leupold, and Schmidke 2017; Hutter, Grande, and Kriesi 2016).

right to rule? The functional virtue of international governance can be a domestic political liability because it challenges the claim that the state alone has legitimacy to exercise authority within its domain. This can cause resentment on the part of those who experience economic insecurity, who are fearful of immigration, and who regard international authority as rule by foreigners.

The politicization of international governance is, in principle, agnostic about whether it promotes or depresses supranationalism. In the early years of European integration, it was possible to believe that mass publics would press for more supranational integration as its benefits filtered into their lives (Inglehart 1970; Schmitter 1969). However, the observed effect of politicization has been negative.[5] The predominant response has been a reaction on the part of those who feel that they suffer the consequences of jurisdictional shocks that challenge established loyalties and ways of life.

As the setting for the most far-reaching jurisdictional reform, the European Union has been in the forefront of politicization.[6] The first clear signs of this came with the Maastricht Treaty (1993) which extended the competences of the EU into areas that had previously been monopolized by states, including currency, immigration, and citizenship. The treaty was written as an epiphany to the benefits of scale, but it was perceived as a shock to national self-rule. Referendums in Denmark, where the treaty was rejected, and France, where it narrowly passed, hastened the rise of nationalist parties opposing European shared rule. Over the past quarter century, twenty-two referendums were initiated by national governments seeking legitimacy for European reform. Eleven went down in defeat.

Faced with resistance from nationalist political parties, governments thought twice about taking further steps even when the functional pressures were undeniable. This was sharply evident in the response to the Eurozone crisis from 2008. Responding to public opinion which was vehemently opposed to

---

[5] Grande and Kriesi (2016: 297, 299) observe that "the political consequences of the most recent waves of politicisation are neither positive nor open-ended but negative." Zürn (2018: 137–69) characterizes politicization as "a double-edged sword" which may upgrade participation but intensify demands.

[6] On politicization in the EU, see Bartolini 2005; Bornschier 2018; Börzel 2016; Börzel and Risse 2018; Curtice 2017; De Vries 2018; De Vries and Hobolt 2018; De Wilde, Leupold, and Schmidtke 2016; Evans 1999; Evans, Carl, and Dennison 2017; Grande and Hutter 2016; Grande and Schwarzbözl 2017; Green-Pedersen 2012; Hobolt 2016; Hobolt and Tilley 2016; Höglinger 2016; Hooghe and Marks 1999, 2001, 2009b, 2018b; Hurrelmann, Gora, and Wagner 2015; Hutter 2014; Hutter, Grande, and Kriesi 2016; Kleider and Stoeckel 2019; Kriesi et al. 2008; Kuhn 2015; Kuhn and Stoeckel 2014; Kuhn et al. 2016; Laffan 2016a, 2016b; McNamara 2015; Marks 1999; Marks and Wilson 2000; Marks and Steenbergen 2004; Piattoni 2010; Polk and Rovny 2017; Polyakova and Fligstein 2016; Prosser 2016; Risse 2010; Rohrschneider and Whitefield 2016; Saurugger 2016; Schimmelfennig 2014, 2018a, 2018b; Van Elsas, Hakhverdian, and van der Brug 2016; Van Kersbergen and De Vries 2007; Webber 2019; Zürn 2012.

Eurozone bailouts, Chancellor Merkel recommitted her government to Article 125 of the Maastricht Treaty, the anti-bailout clause prohibiting shared liabilities or financial assistance. Other northern European governments followed suit. The result was a series of incremental reforms that staved off disaster while prolonging austerity (Copelovitch, Frieden, and Walter 2016). Above all, Eurozone governments sought to avoid reform that would intensify politicization. The European Stability Mechanism was based on a treaty modification which, ingeniously, avoided referendums by requiring only a two-line amendment to the Treaty on the Functioning of the EU. The European Central Bank, a technocratic institution insulated from popular pressures, became instrumental in providing liquidity from 2012. Eurozone governments reverted to conventional diplomacy which had the intended effect of empowering national executives and, at least temporarily, bypassing EU institutions (Genschel and Jachtenfuchs 2018; Jones, Kelemen, and Meunier 2016). The EU was trapped in a postfunctionalist dilemma: on the one side, Eurozone governments were impelled by an unrelenting functional logic toward fiscal union; on the other, they were unnerved by tenacious domestic resistance (Börzel and Risse 2018; Schimmelfennig 2018a; Hooghe and Marks 2019).

Politicization is starkly evident in the European Union, but the phenomenon appears to be more general. Its effects have been detected in the United States, Latin America, and in several global IOs. Solingen and Malnight (2016) make the argument that how government leaders respond to globalization depends on their domestic support. Where an "inward-looking" coalition of nationalist or religious movements with import-competing industries is predominant, government leaders will tend to oppose regional cooperation.

Politicization around the North American Free Trade Agreement (NAFTA) appears to have had a powerful anticipatory effect in constraining subsequent international governance. At the time it was negotiated, from the summer of 1991, NAFTA became a major political issue (Mayer 1998: 5; Cameron and Tomlin 2001). Organized labor and environmental NGOs pressured Democratic party candidates, and populist conservatives supporting Buchanan pressured Republicans (Bow 2015: 41). NAFTA was precisely contracted to minimize delegation to non-state actors, and to deflect the accusation that it was "part of a skeletal structure for world government" (Buchanan 1993). Both the Clinton and Bush administrations trod carefully on an issue that divided their supporters: "large scale politicization in the late 1980s and early 1990s had the effect of discouraging political elites from pursuing further integration initiatives, and this in turn made politicization recede" (Hurrelmann and Schneider 2015: 255).

In Latin America, Mercosur, the Andean Community, CARICOM, and SICA have seen bouts of politicization (Hoffmann 2015). This has been linked to a shift to "intergovernmental agreements rather than institutionalized treaties or supranational institutions" (Riggirozzi 2015: 240). Recent agreements in energy, food security, culture, finance and banking, social development, healthcare, and education are relatively complete contracts that involve little or no pooling or delegation.

Several global international organizations have contended with politicization, inducing them to alter their legitimation narratives, adjust policy, or adopt institutional reforms. The World Bank, the International Monetary Fund, and particularly the World Trade Organization (WTO), have been targeted (Ecker-Ehrhardt 2018). Criticism from the radical left has focused on democracy and the environment, as in Seattle in 1999 when tens of thousands of activists chanting "no globalization without representation!" broke up a ministerial WTO meeting (Munck 2007: 60). In recent years, however, opposition has been most intense on the part of nationalists, particularly in the US, who believe that the WTO's appellate body encroaches on national sovereignty, and that "member states rather than unelected appeal judges should decide ambiguous or contentious issues and that it is wrong for the appellate body to establish precedents for future cases" (Elliot 2018).

Key Variables

This section describes how we estimate the building blocks of our explanation—delegation, pooling, policy scope, and politicization.

Delegation

Delegation is an annual measure of the authority of independent non-state bodies in an IO's decision-making process. Figure 6.2 summarizes the change in an IO's score from its first to last year in the dataset. Delegation has increased overall, but the trend is far from uniform. Forty-seven (62 percent) of the seventy-six IOs experienced an increase, twenty-four saw no change, and five saw a decline, with UNESCO as outlier.[7] Seven IOs move more than 0.3 points on the 0–1 scale, and all are general purpose IOs. This is what one might expect to find if change in delegation is sensitive to expansion of the

---

[7] UNESCO's Executive Board was originally composed of experts who served "on behalf of the Conference as a whole and not as representatives of their respective governments" (UNESCO 1946, Art. V.A.2). Beginning in the 1950s, member states implemented reforms that progressively restricted the independence of board members, and by 1991, the Board was composed exclusively of national delegates (Finnemore 1993; Sewell 1975).

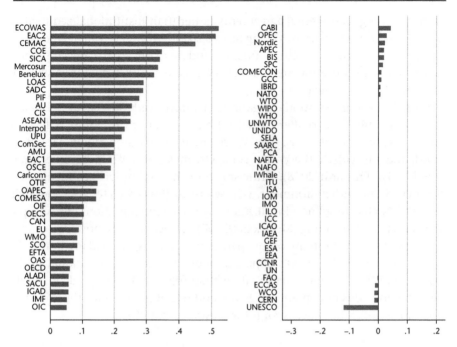

Figure 6.2 Change in delegation by IO

Note: N = 76 IOs for 1950–2010. The boxes show for each IO how much delegation has changed from the first to the last year. The left panel shows IOs for which delegation has increased by 0.05 or more; the right panel shows IOs for which delegation has increased marginally, remained unchanged, or decreased.

policy portfolio. As Chapter 5 shows, a general purpose IO, that is, an IO with an incomplete contract, tends to have an expanding policy portfolio.[8]

Figure 6.3 provides a disaggregated picture of delegation. Forty-one IOs (54 percent of the total) begin with a secretariat having no agenda powers or agenda powers in just one of five key decision areas (panel A). By the last year in the dataset, this shrinks to nineteen (or 25 percent). Conversely, the number of IOs with a secretariat that can set the agenda in three or more decision areas doubles from twelve to twenty-four. The sharpest increase is in the budget and policy making. By 2010, fifty-four of seventy-six IOs have a secretariat that both drafts the annual budget and initiates policy, compared to thirty-four at the start.

Dispute settlement has become much more supranational (Figure 6.3, panel B). Forty-seven IOs (or 62 percent) lack third-party dispute settlement at the beginning, falling to twenty-nine (or 38 percent) at the end. At the start, the

---

[8] By 2010 or the final year in the dataset, general purpose IOs had, on average, competence in 14.2 policies.

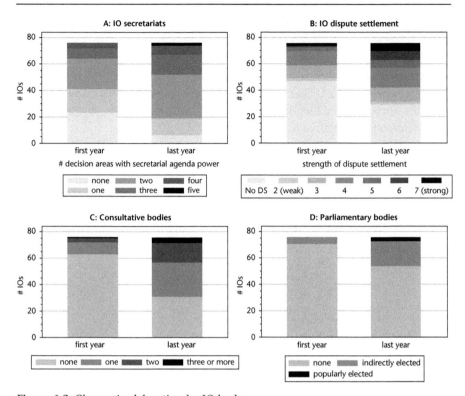

Figure 6.3 Change in delegation by IO body
A *Note*: N = 76 IOs. The bars stack the number of IOs according to the strength of their secretariat: from IOs with a secretariat without agenda power (white stack at bottom) up to IOs with a secretariat that has agenda powers in five decision areas (black stack at top). The bars compare the distribution among IOs in their first (left) and last (right) year in the dataset.
B *Note*: N = 76 IOs. The bars stack the number of IOs according to the strength of their dispute settlement: from IOs without third party dispute settlement (white stack at bottom) to IOs with a strong supranational dispute settlement (black stack at top). The bars compare the distribution among IOs in their first (left) and last (right) year in the dataset.
C *Note*: N = 76 IOs. The bars stack the number of IOs according to the incidence of standing consultative bodies composed of non-state actors: from IOs without consultative bodies (light gray stack at bottom) to IOs with three or more such bodies (black stack at top). The bars compare the distribution among IOs in their first (left) and last (right) year in the dataset.
D *Note*: N = 76 IOs. The bars stack the number of IOs by the incidence of a parliamentary assembly composed of elected politicians: from IOs without assembly (light gray stack at bottom) to IOs with an indirectly elected assembly, to IOs with a directly elected assembly (black stack at top). The bars compare the distribution among IOs in their first (left) and last (right) year in the dataset.

median IO scored zero on a seven-point scale for dispute settlement. By 2010, this had risen to four on the same scale. This is commensurate with a standing tribunal that (a) makes binding rulings, (b) provides automatic access (i.e. a litigant does not need prior consent by some political body), and (c) is an integral part of the contract for all member states rather than a subset.

Our data on consultative bodies (Figure 6.3, panel C) are consistent with data collected by Tallberg et al. (2014: 741–2), who detect "a shift toward forms of governance that involve transnational actors [as] policy experts, service providers, compliance watchdogs and stakeholder representatives." While at their creation just thirteen IOs (or 17 percent) had one or more formally recognized consultative bodies of non-state actors, by 2010, this had increased to forty-five (or 59 percent).

The bodies that have the least delegation are IO assemblies. There appears to be little functional pressure to transform a member-state dominated assembly into a directly or indirectly elected legislature or to supplement an IO's decisional apparatus with a second chamber. Where this has happened it has been part of an effort to legitimize IO decision making (Lenz, Burilkov, and Viola 2019).[9] Nineteen IOs have done so, of which the European Union, the Central American Integration System, and the Andean Community have directly elected parliamentary bodies (Figure 6.3, panel D).[10]

Pooling

Pooling taps the extent to which authoritative control is taken out of the hands of individual states by majoritarian voting in collective state decision making. We weight *Pooling* by the bindingness of decisions and the extent to which a ratification procedure allows individual states to escape a collective decision.

Figure 6.4 shows the net change in pooling. Overall, pooling is less dynamic than delegation. Thirty-seven IOs experienced an increase in pooling, twenty-eight did not change, while eleven IOs saw a decrease, including the World Health Organization (−0.14), the International Civil Aviation Organization (−0.06) and the International Monetary Fund (−0.06). Five IOs move up more than 0.3 points on the 0–1 scale, and an additional ten grow by 0.15 or more. All but two of the fastest growing IOs are general purpose.

Majority voting has become almost the norm in budgetary allocation and policy making (Figure 6.5). Majority voting has also become more common in the remaining decision areas, though consensus or unanimity remains the mode. As one might expect, the incidence of majority voting is much greater in day-to-day decision making than on constitutive decisions

---

[9] Legitimacy pressures have been well documented in the ratcheting up of the European Parliament's authority in response to the criticism that the EU weakens national parliaments and weakens democracy (Goetze and Rittberger 2010; Rittberger 2005, 2012; Schimmelfennig 2010).

[10] In 2005, Mercosur agreed to introduce direct elections for the Mercosur Parliament. By February 2019, only two member states—Argentina and Paraguay—had held direct elections (Comisión de Juristas para la Integración Regional 2019).

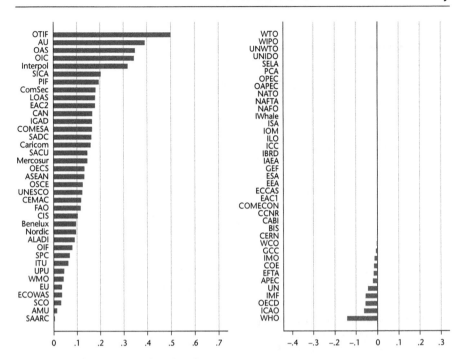

Figure 6.4 Change in pooling by IO

Note: N = 76 IOs for 1950–2010. The boxes show for each IO how much pooling has changed from the first to the last year. The left panel shows IOs for which pooling has increased; the right panel shows IOs for which pooling has remained unchanged or decreased.

relating to membership accession, suspension, compliance, and constitutional reform.

An IO can weaken majority voting by making collective decisions conditional on opt-in, or at least by allowing states to opt out. As Table 6.1 indicates, IOs have in general clamped down on escape routes from binding IO decisions. An IO is coded as making a binding decision when there is no legal opt-out and no possibility of circumventing the decision through domestic ratification. Bindingness is the norm for budgetary allocation: the proportion of IOs having binding budgets rose from 64 percent to 85.5 percent. Policy making is still primarily only partially binding or non-binding, though the number of IOs with binding policy making increased from twenty-two (29 percent) to twenty-eight (37 percent).

Ratification can provide individual states with a back-door veto. The last three rows of Table 6.1 show the change in ratification requirements for accession, constitutional reform, and policy making. Binding voting on accession and policy making is the least ring-fenced, with most IOs not requiring ratification. By contrast, most IOs do require ratification on constitutional reform, and the proportion has increased. As in domestic politics, the

A Theory of International Organization

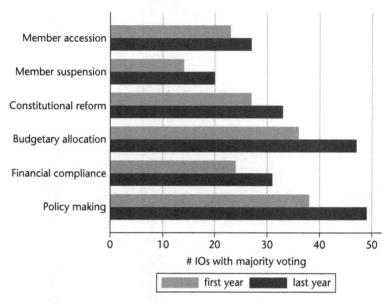

Figure 6.5 Change in majority voting in 76 IOs

Note: N = 76 IOs in their first and last year in the dataset. An IO exercises majority voting when the most conservative state-dominated body uses simple majority or supermajority to reach a final decision.

Table 6.1. Change in bindingness and ratification in 76 IOs

	First year		Last year	
Decision is unconditionally binding				
Budget	49	(64.0%)	65	(85.5%)
Policy (at least one stream)	22	(29.0%)	28	(36.8%)
Decision comes into force without ratification				
Accession	49	(64.5%)	58	(76.3%)
Constitutional reform	13	(17.1%)	11	(14.5%)
Policy (at least one stream)	39	(51.3%)	46	(60.5%)

Note: 76 IOs.

incidence of veto points is greatest when it comes to changing the rules of the game.

Policy Scope

Policy scope estimates the legal, financial, and organizational basis of an IO's policy portfolio assessed for each of twenty-five policies. We use eight indicators outlined in the Appendix.

Politicization

Politicization estimates the salience and divisiveness of debate over an IO. It refers to "a process whereby the technocratic behind-the-closed-doors logic of decisions and decision-making processes in and about international institutions...is challenged" (Zürn 2012: 52). Media coverage of protests directed at an IO is an accessible indicator for contestation about an IO, and it is plausible that such coverage indicates politicization (Beyeler and Kriesi 2005; Tarrow 2005). We use an algorithm developed by Tallberg et al. (2014) for annual media coverage of protests/demonstrations directed at an IO in the LexisNexis database.[11]

Controls

We control for several variables that are hypothesized to affect delegation or pooling:

- *Democracy* on the hypothesis that democratic rulers are less fearful of supranational authority than are authoritarian rulers (Risse-Kappen 1995; Simmons 2009).
- *Power asymmetry* on the ground that powerful states can be expected to oppose international authority because they prefer informal, "me-first," arrangements in which they can impose their preferences (Abbott and Snidal 2000: 448; Grieco 1990; Krasner 1976; Mattli 1999).
- The *number of IO member states* because the incentive to delegate and pool authority can be expected to increase as the growth of an IO's membership impedes decision making (Hawkins et al. 2006a; Koremenos, Lipson, and Snidal 2001: 789; Pollack 2003).
- *Affluence* because more affluent populations transact more across national borders and may have a greater incentive to empower an IO.
- *GDP dispersion* on the hypothesis that the more economically heterogeneous the member states of an IO, the greater the benefit of empowering the IO to mediate conflicts (Carnegie 2014; Martin 1995; 2006: 145).[12]
- *Core state powers* on the expectation that member states will be less willing to cede authority in defense and security (Genschel and Jachtenfuchs 2016; Haftel 2011; Kono 2007; Martin 1992; Snidal 1985; Stein 1982).

---

[11] *Politicization* is calculated as a three-year moving average of the number of mentions that combine the word *protestor* or *demonstrator* with the IO name (see Appendix). The measure is quite strongly correlated with an estimate of the salience of an IO derived from a count of references to the IO in Google (r = 0.75).

[12] Hawkins et al. (2006a: 21) and Snidal (1994: 63–6) discuss alternative hypotheses.

- A *year count* to pick up the effect of an omitted variable that might produce an incremental increase in IO authority over time.[13]

Evidence

We analyze seventy-six international organizations from the year they were set up (or 1950) to 2010. All models estimate fixed effects to gauge change over time using one-year lags for independent variables. Table 6.2 begins with base models predicting delegation and pooling, respectively, by the number of IO policies in the previous year and a three-year moving average of politicization. All models have the full range of controls and a year count to address pressures of time in an unbalanced panel.

Policy scope and *Politicization* are robust predictors of *Delegation* and *Pooling* over time. We find this under all combinations of controls including the fully specified models.[14] The models in Table 6.2 account for around 41 percent of the variance in change in *Delegation* and 25 percent of the variance in change in *Pooling*. *Pooling* is more sluggish than *Delegation*, and it is cross-sectionally dominated.[15] Both functionalist and postfunctionalist pressures appear to shape international authority within IOs over time. An expanding policy portfolio induces states to increase delegation and pooling, while politicization operates in the opposite direction. The estimate for the effect of an increase in the number of policies handled by an IO is significant at the

Table 6.2. Explaining change in delegation and pooling

	DV = Change in delegation	DV = Change in pooling
Policy scope$_{t-1}$	0.015***	0.010***
	(0.003)	(0.003)
Politicization$_{t-1}$	−0.011**	−0.018***
	(0.005)	(0.006)
R^2 within	0.412	0.256
AIC	−10,858	−10,269
F-statistic (sign. at 0.0001 level)	6.19	5.81

Note: N = 3,199 IO-years (76 IOs) for 1950–2010. The dependent variables *Change in delegation* and *Change in pooling* vary between −1 and +1.
*** $p < 0.01$, ** $p < 0.05$, * $p < 0.1$. Fixed effects estimations with standard errors clustered by IO and under controls (democracy, members, power asymmetry, affluence, GDP dispersion, core state powers, year count).

---

[13] Models using a fractional polynomial instead of year count produce essentially the same results (see online Appendix).
[14] *Democracy* is significant at the 0.1 level in the base model for *Pooling*, but not for *Delegation*. None of the remaining controls, except the year count, reaches statistical significance.
[15] Chapter 7 accounts for cross-sectional variance in *Pooling*.

0.01 level in predicting change in *Delegation* and *Pooling*. *Politicization* has a negative effect that is significant at the 0.05 level for *Delegation* and at the 0.01 level for *Pooling*.

The substantive effects of a changing policy portfolio are sizeable. Holding all controls at their means, a shift in an IO's policy portfolio by five policies (one standard deviation) changes delegation by 0.08 and pooling by 0.05 on a 0–1 scale. A 0.08 increase in delegation is equivalent to the introduction of an independent and compulsory arbitration system with authority to make binding judgments unless a collective state body overrules. The same increase would result if the general secretariat's agenda power was extended to two additional decision areas. A 0.05 increase in pooling is equivalent to introducing a binding budget adopted by simple majority at the agenda-setting stage and by consensus at the final stage.[16]

It is worth stressing that we are modeling reform negotiated among the member states themselves. Hence, our findings do not encompass the possibility that IO bureaucrats slip from state control to extend their own agency (Johnson 2014). This makes what we do find all the more consequential for it is one thing to say that supranationalism grows because non-state actors informally escape state control, and quite another to find that states agree to convey authority to non-state actors and pool authority in binding majoritarian decision making. The authority estimated in our models is formally negotiated, explicitly contracted, and consequently costly to change. It does not arise merely as an unintentional gap in state control.

Our theory conceives IO authority as the result of a two-step process in which the scope of an IO's policy portfolio is both a predictor and an outcome (see Figure 6.1). In the first step, change in the policy scope of an IO reflects normative commonalities among its members and the incompleteness with which they contract governance. The premise is that community shapes the possibilities for international governance which one can observe when states contract an IO and as the policy portfolio changes over time. In the second step, the authority of the IO depends on its policy scope and the extent to which the IO is caught up in public contestation. The claim here is that the normative basis of an IO has functionalist consequences for pooling and delegation which are tempered by the unwillingness of a government to empower an IO targeted in domestic political contestation.

---

[16] We test alternative explanations for IO design in the online Appendix. We find some support for the hypothesis that states are less willing to cede authority to IOs concerned with core state powers. We also find that IOs having an epistemic community tend to experience lower politicization, though the effect is small (Haas 1992). Finally, we detect no robust effect for power asymmetry or GDP dispersion. Separate models that test for foreign policy divergence and for trade interdependence find no significant effect. In all models, policy scope and politicization are robustly significant.

A Theory of International Organization

Table 6.3. A two-stage model explaining change in delegation and pooling

	DV = Change in delegation	DV = Change in pooling
Policy scope$_{t-1}$ instrumented	0.026***	0.018***
(instruments: community, contract)	(0.006)	(0.006)
Politicization$_{t-1}$	−0.014*	−0.021***
	(0.007)	(0.006)
R^2 within	0.331	0.205
AIC	−10,445	−10,060
F-statistic (sign. at 0.0001 level)	6.28	5.23

Note: N = 3,199 IO-years (76 IOs) for 1950–2010. The dependent variables *Change in delegation* and *Change in pooling* vary between −1 and +1.
*** $p < 0.01$, ** $p < 0.05$, * $p < 0.1$. Two-stage fixed effects resulting from a two-stage model in which community dynamic and contract dynamic explain policy scope, and policy scope (instrumented) explains international authority; standard errors clustered by IO and full controls.

We model this in a two-stage fixed effects regression, in which *Contract* and *Community* explain *Policy scope*. Table 6.3 reports the second-stage results for delegation and pooling. In both equations, *Instrumented policy scope* is significantly associated with change in both *Delegation* (p = 0.0001) and *Pooling* (p = 0.007). Two-stage estimation is almost always less efficient than ordinary least squares estimation (Bartels 1991), but here the loss in statistical power is negligible. The F-statistics for the two-stage models in Table 6.3 (6.28 and 5.23, respectively) are only slightly weaker than the F-statistics for the fixed effects models in Table 6.2 (6.19 and 5.81, respectively).

Illustrative Cases

The development of ASEAN provides a telling example of how member states may empower a secretariat as the policy breadth of cooperation grows. ASEAN was founded as a security organization by Indonesia, Malaysia, Philippines, Singapore, and Thailand in 1967 as a response to the threat of Communist subversion. The normative foundation of the organization was described as the "ASEAN way"—an informal style of cooperation, consultation, consensus, non-interference, and weak institutionalization (Acharya 2001; ASEAN 1967, 1976a). Decision making was sparse and intergovernmental (Jetschke and Katada 2016: 233–4). It was not until ASEAN took on regional development and energy cooperation in the mid-1970s that it came to have an independent secretariat tasked with framing the budget and developing "plans and programs" (ASEAN 1976b: Art. 3.2.viii). This was still a bare bones operation with just seven staff, all seconded from national ministries.

Following the member states' decision to move toward market integration in 1992, the role of the secretariat and its secretary general was considerably strengthened. The position of secretary general was elevated to ministerial status, its tenure was extended to five years, and it was empowered to "initiate, advise, co-ordinate and implement ASEAN activities." The secretary general was also charged to "serve as spokesman and representative of ASEAN on all matters" (ASEAN 1992: Arts. 2.1.4 and 2.1; Jetschke 2012). The secretary general was now assisted by a deputy, four bureau directors, eleven assistant directors, and eight senior officers, plus front-line staff. An executive of "Senior Economic Officials" was set up which could take decisions by consensus (i.e. with abstentions not counting), "a break with ASEAN traditional insistence on effective unanimity" (Kahler 2000: 554).

This was just the beginning of a functional process in which expanding policy commitments led to the creation of resourceful IO bodies. In the 1990s, ASEAN member states signed a Framework Agreement on Services, an Industrial Cooperation Scheme, and a plan for an ASEAN Investment Area, followed in the 2000s by a series of formal agreements for cooperation in preferential tariffs, financial regulation, energy, and the environment. In 1996, the member states set up dispute settlement to monitor compliance and in 2004 they weakened political control by referring adjudication to a body of senior economic officials which could reverse a decision only by consensus (Alter 2014: 153; Hooghe et al. 2017: 441). Over the past two decades, the trail of documents detailing the rules of the organization and powers of its bodies has considerably thickened, and the bodies themselves are accorded a larger role in agenda setting, providing information, resolving disputes, and managing decision making.[17] ASEAN has retained its reputation for informal negotiation and consensus, but this takes place within an increasingly institutionalized context in which written rules are, not surprisingly, useful in providing explicit guidelines (Khong and Nesadurai 2007).

The negative effect of politicization on change in delegation and pooling is robust across alternative specifications.[18] These include analyses limited to the fifty-three IOs that have experienced politicization and analyses restricted to the post-1989 period which has seen the most intense politicization. The finding is robust also in models that use two- and three-year time lags for politicization.[19]

---

[17] The 1996 Protocol on Dispute Settlement Mechanism, Art 7 (ASEAN 1996); the 2004 Protocol for Enhanced Dispute Settlement Mechanism, Arts. 9.1 and 12.13 (ASEAN 2004).
[18] The Appendix discusses the limitations of LexisNexis for estimating politicization.
[19] *Politicization* is significant and negative at the 0.05 level or better for all but one of ten robustness analyses. The exception is change in *Pooling* for the post-1989 period, where the coefficient for *Politicization* has a negative sign but is not significant.

Politicization, as we estimate it here, is mainly a Western phenomenon. The IOs that are mentioned in the LexisNexis database alongside the terms "protestor" and "demonstrator" are chiefly those that are contested in Western societies—e.g. the WTO, the UN, the EU, and NATO. However, populist nationalism, which in recent years underpins much politicization, is more general.

The Southern African Development Community (SADC) experienced a sharp drop in delegation in 2013 after six years of intense politicization. The target of contention was SADC's Tribunal which became operational in 2006 (Lenz 2012). Modeled on the European Court of Justice, it provided automatic third-party access and binding rulings, and importantly, it offered preliminary rulings to national courts and litigation access to private persons (SADC 2001a). The Tribunal claimed jurisdiction over the principles formulated in the SADC Treaty, including member state adherence to "human rights, democracy, and the rule of law" (SADC 2001b: Art. 4). All this made the Tribunal "in theory even more politically intrusive than the ECJ" (Alter 2012: 140; Lenz 2012).

The Tribunal ran into trouble with its first major case in 2007, when a Zimbabwean white farmer filed against the Mugabe land redistribution reform (Alter, Gathii, and Helfer 2016). Other farmers joined the suit and the Tribunal made a series of judgments condemning the land reform as a violation of landowners' rights on the grounds that it denied access to justice, discriminated on the basis of race, and failed to provide fair compensation. This directly challenged President Mugabe's land redistribution program and was met by intensified efforts to kick the farmers off their farms. Mugabe defended the program as an act of national self-rule: "We have courts here in this country that can determine the rights of people. Our land issues are not subject to the SADC tribunal."[20] SADC member states were reluctant to come to the defense of the Tribunal because postcolonial land reform has deep emotional resonance in their own societies (Achiume 2018: 125, 136–40). In August 2010, the SADC Summit hired an outside consultant to review the Tribunal and did not reappoint judges whose terms had expired. In effect, the Tribunal was suspended, and in 2013 it was officially dissolved (Alter, Gathii, and Helfer 2016: 312–13; Nathan 2013). The result in terms of *Delegation* is a decline from 0.35 in 2010 to 0.08 from 2013.[21]

---

[20] Quoted in Chinaka (2009) and Alter, Gathii, and Helfer (2016: n. 99), available at https://mg.co.za/article/2009-02-28-mugabe-says-zimbabwe-land-seizures-will-continue.

[21] In 2014, the Summit agreed a protocol for a new tribunal without private access or preliminary ruling. Member states would be permitted to withdraw from the tribunal's jurisdiction, making coverage optional (SADC 2014). The protocol requires ratification by two-thirds of the member states, which by February 2019 had not happened. In December 2018, the South African Constitutional Court ruled that the new SADC Protocol is unconstitutional because it bars private litigants.

Conclusion

Most of the IOs observed in this book experienced an increase in delegated authority to non-state actors or took on majoritarian voting rules in member state decision making. The period 1950 to 2010 was an era of international governance.

This chapter explains how this happened, why some IOs deepened their authority while others did not, and how this process has been curbed. Our explanation ties together the normative conditions of international cooperation, the subsequent development of the policy portfolio, the effects of this for international governance, and the political resistance that has ensued.

The evidence presented confirms that an IO's authority is responsive to two forces: a functional pressure arising from change in an IO's policy portfolio, and a political reaction in which IO authority is swept up and constrained in public debate. Our expectation about the portfolio effect is grounded in a literature on decisional complexity and organizational design. It argues that a growing policy portfolio produces an incentive to limit the ability of any one actor to exercise a veto and an incentive to delegate authority to independent actors who can frame the agenda, provide information, and adjudicate conflicts.

Functionalist theory, for all its power, leads one to expect increasing supranationalism among general purpose IOs which tend to have expanding policy portfolios. However, we hypothesize a contending effect arising from the politicization of international governance and the mobilization of demands for national self-rule. Politicization can strip away the protective blanket of permissive consensus which exists when domestic publics trust their governments to do the right thing. It thrusts international governance into domestic politics and so challenges the causal priority of functional pressures.

Fixed effects models confirm the effect of both change in an IO's policy portfolio and politicization. In addition, two-stage models support the broader claim that IO authority depends on the growth of the policy portfolio which in turn depends on the incompleteness of an IO's foundational contract and the normative coherence of its member states.

In concluding, it is worth considering the scope conditions. The evidence here engages international organization in the six decades following World War II. From a long-historical perspective this might be an N of 1. Since 2010 politicization has gathered strength. It has come to structure political conflict in several Western and non-Western societies. A core claim of postfunctionalist theory is that the demand for national self-rule may challenge international governance even when the benefits of scale are considerable.

7

Why States Pool Authority

The pooling of authority in binding majoritarian decision making among states is a puzzling phenomenon. By ceding the national veto, individual member states put themselves at the mercy of the majority of their peers. Why and under what circumstances are states willing to do this?

We can begin by putting aside two possible answers. One is that states agree to majoritarian voting only when they can avoid implementing decisions they don't like. However, we find that states consent to pool authority in binding decision making. Our measure of pooling encompasses not only the voting rules, but also the possible escape routes by which a majoritarian decision can be finessed by a member state, including ratification. Another possible answer is that states pool authority only on less important topics, and specifically avoid it on security matters. We find evidence for this, but it explains only a small share of the variation.

We start from the premise that in choosing a decision rule participants face a trade-off between facilitating decision making and avoiding exploitation. Majority voting eases decision making but introduces the risk of exploitation for a voter on the losing side. Unanimity eliminates that risk but opens the door to decisional blockage by allowing any voter to demand a side payment for their consent to a proposal.

Our argument is that the trade-off between the costs of decisional blockage and the risk of exploitation is sensitive to the scale of an IO's membership. Whereas the risk of exploitation under majority voting rises only slightly in an IO with a larger membership, the decisional cost of unanimity increases sharply. So a large membership IO will be more sensitive than a small membership IO to the decisional cost of unanimity, and this will induce it to pool authority in majoritarian decision making.

This implies that international governance is embedded in a trilemma. Effective governance, national sovereignty, and large-scale membership are prohibitively difficult to have at one and the same time. Effective governance is compatible with the national veto only if an IO has few member states.

National sovereignty is compatible with a large membership only by emasculating decision making. Effective governance is compatible with large membership only by sacrificing the national veto.

Hence, pooling is an adaptation to the threat of decisional blockage in an IO with a large membership. This functional logic is embedded in sociality because the transnational community, or its weakness, sets the parameters for the basic set-up of an IO, including the incompleteness of its contract, the breadth of its policy portfolio, and whether a large membership is feasible. One consequence is that many global bads remain ungoverned or governed only by thin agreements that have little or no capacity to adjust to changing conditions. However, where cooperation among many is feasible, the trilemma induces states to finesse the national veto by pooling authority in (super)majoritarian decision making.[1] In the next sections we set out the logical basis of the argument and then turn to the evidence.

The Scale Hypothesis

An extensive literature conceives a state's preference over the voting rule in an IO as the result of a trade-off between the risk of exploitation and the cost of decision making (Buchanan and Tullock 1962; Miller and Vanberg 2013; Posner and Sykes 2014). A state is exploited when it is harmed by a collective decision. The risk diminishes with the size of the majority required for a collective decision, until at unanimity, it disappears entirely. This is represented in Figure 7.1 where the risk of exploitation is highest under simple majority and decreases to zero as the voting rule approaches unanimity.

Decision costs run in the opposite direction. As the decision rule approaches unanimity, a progressively smaller minority may block a proposal. Under unanimity any single voter can thwart a decision. As the size of the majority required for a decision increases, so side payments become vital in getting voters to agree. This can be both time-consuming and difficult in situations where the value of a side payment is contested. So the more closely a decision rule approaches unanimity, the larger the role of negotiation over side payments, the longer the expected delays, and the greater the incentive for voters "to 'act tough' and bargain for a larger share of the surplus created by an efficient action" (Miller and Vanberg 2013: 376). This is represented by the

---

[1] It is worth noting that this does not imply that decisions will actually be made by a majority in the presence of a dissenting minority. A majoritarian rule may facilitate decision making by casting a shadow over negotiation prior to the vote. There are good reasons to believe that the effect of a majority voting rule far exceeds the incidence of majority voting.

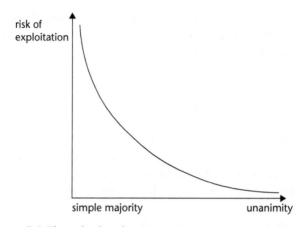

Figure 7.1 The risk of exploitation
Note: Based on Buchanan and Tullock (1962); Miller and Vanberg (2013).

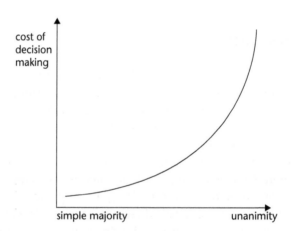

Figure 7.2 The cost of decision making
Note: Based on Buchanan and Tullock (1962); Miller and Vanberg (2013).

curve in Figure 7.2 depicting increasing decision costs as the voting rule goes from simple majority to unanimity.

This raises the question of how the risk of exploitation and the cost of decision making vary with the scale of IO membership. How sensitive is the trade-off to the number of member states?

There are strong grounds for thinking that the cost of decision making is very sensitive—and increases considerably—in a larger membership IO, whereas the risk of exploitation is insensitive and does not much increase at all. If so, this provides a basis for solving the puzzle of when states pool authority.

The risk of exploitation in an IO is the risk of being repeatedly on the losing side, of facing an entrenched majority of winners. This depends primarily on the distribution of preferences over the policy portfolio of the IO and the fixity of winning and losing coalitions.[2] It is not much affected by the sheer number of voters. A group as small as three may produce a durable coalition of two against one, and stable coalition building becomes no more likely as the size of a group increases. Hence, the effect of the decision rule on the risk of exploitation is not much greater in a large-N IO than in a small-N IO.

The same cannot be said for the cost of decision making. The effect of unanimity is intensified in an IO with a larger membership. The larger the number of veto players, all else equal, the smaller the size of the win-set and the more difficult it is to depart from the status quo (Koremenos, Lipson, and Snidal 2001: 30; Shubik 1982; Tsebelis 2002). The more voters under unanimity, the greater the number of potential veto wielders who have to be mollified and the greater the opportunities for blackmail. The problem is exacerbated because information about the true preferences of voters across alternative proposals is private rather than public. This opens the door to strategic deception. Acting honestly would be good for the group as a whole, but it is not in the self-regarding interest of individual voters. Whereas the decision rule makes only a small difference for the cost of decision making when there are just a few voters, it becomes increasingly influential in a large membership IO.

Unanimity always imposes greater decision costs and less risk of exploitation than majoritarianism, but the costs arising from unanimity increase more steeply than the costs from the risk of exploitation with progressively higher numbers of member states. Figure 7.3 visualizes this hypothesis by graphing the risk of exploitation divided by the cost of decision making on the Y-axis and the number of member states on the X-axis. As the number of members increases, the cost of decisional blockage increases faster than the risk of exploitation. If pooling authority in majoritarian decision making responds to these concerns, then one would expect more pooling in larger IOs.

The *scale hypothesis* is not the only explanation that has been suggested to explain voting rules in an IO. An alternative—*the homogeneity hypothesis*—seems plausible on a priori grounds. This is the conjecture that majoritarian voting systems will be found in smaller, rather than larger, groups because organizations with smaller memberships are likely to be more homogeneous. This builds on the idea that homogeneous groups will be more willing to vote

---

[2] On this logic, during the negotiations that led to the foundation of the United Nations in 1944, the United States and Britain were reconciled to majority voting in the UN Assembly on the accession of new members: "[M]agnanimity...was essentially cost-free, for it was understood that the United States and Britain would command comfortable majorities of friends and clients in the General Assembly for the foreseeable future" (Hoopes and Brinkley 1997: 144). On the other side, the Soviet Union demanded broad-ranging veto powers in the Security Council because it feared permanent minority status (Hilderbrand 1990: 95).

A Theory of International Organization

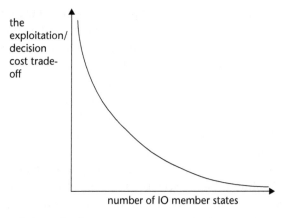

Figure 7.3 The scale hypothesis

Note: The exploitation/decision cost trade-off is the cost of the risk of exploitation divided by the cost of decisional blockage.

by majority because the preferences of their members will be more closely aligned.

The idea that majoritarianism is rational only in homogeneous groups comes out of a literature on optimal voting systems. Maggi and Morelli (2006) argue that majority voting in IOs can be expected only where member state preferences are aligned. On the assumption that an IO cannot make a member state implement a collective decision, the authors conclude that "a nonunanimous rule is more likely to be adopted in more homogeneous organizations" (Maggi and Morelli 2006: 1138). That is to say, the larger and more heterogeneous the membership of an IO, the less likely it will adopt majoritarian voting—an expectation that is exactly contrary to the scale hypothesis.

The homogeneity hypothesis reverses the causal arrow from voting system to organizational formation. Renou (2011) has a model in which the choice of the voting rule leads a group to decide how large the organization should be. Because larger groups will tend to have members with a greater diversity of preferences, Renou (2011: 595) argues that majoritarian voting rules will produce small IOs and, conversely, that "unanimity favors the formation of larger groups."

Both the scale hypothesis and the homogeneity hypothesis are logically coherent, so one must turn to the evidence to assess their validity.

Evidence

Member states pool authority when they agree to relinquish the national veto in (super)majority voting rules while binding themselves to their collective decisions.[3] The variable *Pooling* is a weighted aggregate that taps the decision rule (majority, supermajority, consensus/unanimity) in each IO body across six decision areas: membership accession, membership suspension, constitutional reform, budgetary allocation, financial compliance, and up to five streams of policy making. Further, we assess whether and to what extent majoritarian decisions are (a) binding and (b) not subject to a back-door veto through ratification. A score of zero indicates that agenda setting and the final decision in all six decision areas are subject to member state veto. At the opposite end of the scale, a score of one indicates that agenda setting and the final decision in all six decision areas are determined by simple majority and the decision is binding and not subject to subsequent ratification by member states.

The bulk of the variance in *Pooling*—around ninety percent—is cross-sectional.[4] While the membership of many IOs has increased by leaps and bounds as the number of independent states around the world has risen, the distribution of membership size across IOs remains rather static.[5] The average membership of an IO in 1950 or at founding is twenty-eight.[6] This more than doubles to sixty-seven by 2010. However, the number of member states when an IO is established is a good predictor of its future membership. The association is 0.875.[7] Hence it is possible that the growth in the membership of an IO is anticipated by its founders. This would explain why *Pooling* is exceptionally sluggish over time.

We can test this by comparing the association between *Pooling* in 1950 (or an IO's founding year, if later) and (a) IO membership in that year; (b) IO membership in 2010; and (c) average IO membership from 1950 (or an IO's

---

[3] Examining voting rules for IOs at their founding, Blake and Lockwood Payton (2009: 23; 2015: 398) find that the predicted probability of majority voting in an IO's supreme body increases from around 50 percent for an IO with five or six member states to 90 percent for an IO with forty or more member states. Haftel and Thompson (2006: 269) compare thirty regional organizations and find no significant association between the number of member states and majoritarian voting. However, the effect of scale on voting rules will be less apparent in samples of IOs with relatively small memberships.

[4] A Hausman test indicates that fixed effects and random effects yield dissimilar coefficients and so we model *Pooling* over time in Chapter 6 and cross-sectionally in this chapter. Our prior is that the growth of membership in an IO is far more predictable than the future course of an IO's policy portfolio. Hence the effect of membership growth is best explained in a cross-sectional analysis while the effect of the growth of an IO's policy portfolio is best explained in a fixed effects analysis.

[5] IO membership is scaled logarithmically in the analyses that follow because the expected effect of an additional member state declines as the absolute number of members increases. Using an absolute measure produces the same pattern of statistical significance (see online Appendix).

[6] Of the seventy-six IOs, twenty-four were founded before 1950.

[7] This is the association between the number of member states at an IO's inception (or in 1950 if the IO is established earlier) and the number of member states in 2010 (or in the year of an IO's demise if earlier). As high as it is, the figure of 0.875 may underestimate the association because the initial membership of an IO in our data encompasses only states that ratified membership by the end of an IO's first year of existence and it excludes states that were in process to ratify membership.

Table 7.1. Cross-sectional models for pooling

	Pooling 1950		
Members 1950	0.224***		
	(0.048)		
	t = 4.64		
Members 2010		0.212***	
		(0.035)	
		t = 5.97	
Members 1950–2010 mean			0.224***
			(0.039)
			t = 5.74
Controls	YES	YES	YES
R^2	0.484	0.555	0.542
N	76	76	76

Note: OLS regressions for pooling in 1950 or an IO's first year in the dataset. The number of IO member states is logarithmic (log10) because the expected effect of an additional member state declines as the number of members increases, though the results are robust when using raw membership numbers (online Appendix). All models include controls for policy scope, core state powers, politicization, democracy, power asymmetry, affluence, and GDP dispersion.
*** $p < 0.01$, ** $p < 0.05$, * $p < 0.1$.

founding year, if later) to 2010. Table 7.1 models *Pooling 1950* as the dependent variable and the number of members as the predictor with controls for democracy, power asymmetry, affluence, policy scope, politicization, GDP dispersion, and core state powers. Interestingly, anticipated membership is a stronger predictor of pooling in 1950 (or at founding) than the membership of an IO in 1950 (or at founding). The first column shows that the coefficient for *Members 1950* is highly significant with a t-value of 4.64. The t-value for *Members 2010* increases to 5.97 and the model accounts for 56 percent of the variance.[8] The t-value is 5.74 for the average membership of an IO from 1950 to 2010.[9]

There is reason to believe that the direction of causality is from the scale of membership in an IO to its level of pooling. It is implausible to argue that the causality is in the reverse direction, i.e. that more pooling in an IO will encourage states to join. It seems reasonable to presume that member states like having a veto and will sacrifice this in pooling arrangements only when they are induced to do so. Member states join an IO because it provides them with the capacity to problem solve and they pool authority because this is an

---

[8] Calculating marginal effects in this model and holding controls at their means, a one standard deviation increase in *Members* (adding fifty-four states to an IO's membership) is associated with an increase of 0.12 in *Pooling*. This is equivalent to shifting from non-binding to unconditionally binding budgets or policy, or from supermajority to simple majority in two decision areas.

[9] *Core state powers* is significant and negative at the 0.05 level in the model with *Members in 2010*, and it is significant at $p < 0.1$ in the other two models (see online Appendix).

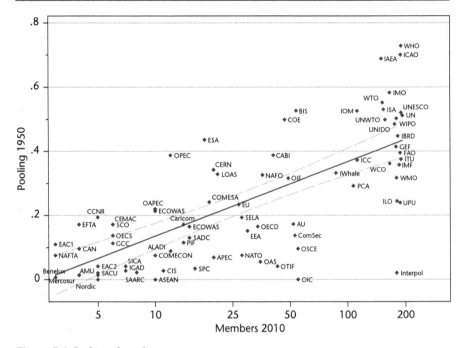

Figure 7.4 Scale and pooling

Note: 76 IOs. The X-axis indicates the size of membership in 2010 on a log 10 scale; the Y-axis indicates pooling in 1950 or when the IO was established (r = 0.72).

acceptable compromise when the problem involves a large number of member states.

The first two models in Table 7.1 suggest indeed that the size of an IO's membership can be anticipated by its founders, and they build this into their initial design. The causality, here as elsewhere in this study, is that of *deliberatively produced regularities*, that is, regularities that are produced by actors who contemplate the consequences of their actions (Pearl 2009).

Figure 7.4 plots the bivariate relationship between *Pooling 1950* and *Membership 2010* for seventy-six IOs. The simple association is 0.72. As much as half of the variance in the rules for collective decision making in 1950—majority voting, bindingness, and ratification—can be predicted by IO membership in 2010, despite the fact that, on average, IO membership more than doubles from the first to the last year.

Interpol is a major outlier in the bottom right corner of the Figure. Interpol's pooling in 1950 is poorly predicted by its membership of 179 states in 2010. That is because, until 1956, the International Criminal Police Commission (ICPC)—later renamed Interpol—was not a conventional intergovernmental organization, but it was composed of national police representatives who hoped to sideline national governments. During the war, the organization had been taken over by Nazi Germany, and the police forces that revived the organization in 1946 wished to build an independent crime-fighting organization (Barnett and Coleman 2005: 605; Deflem 2002). They went so far as to apply to the United Nations and the Council of Europe for non-governmental status (Fooner 1973). This was granted by the UN in 1949, but needing funding and access to state resources, the organization became intergovernmental in 1956. From that time, Interpol's pooling score falls in line with the Universal Postal Union and the International Labour Organization.

It is worth noting that the IOs with high levels of pooling do not appear to be following a common template. All ten IOs that have an aggregate pooling score of 0.50 (±0.04) in 1950 (or at founding) vote by majority on the budget. They each have extensive pooling, including supermajority voting on whether to suspend a member state in financial arrears.[10] Beyond this there are interesting and sometimes wide differences. The World Trade Organization is exceptionally supranational in monitoring trade barriers and it is exceptionally intergovernmental in deciding whether a member state can join. The Council of Europe can suspend, by a two-thirds majority, any member state that has violated "human rights and fundamental freedoms" in Article 3 of its statute. In contrast, the Bank for International Settlements has no written rules on suspension.

Even within the UN family, which is sometimes thought to follow a template, there is wide variation (Magliveras 1999: 131–55). For example, the UN Industrial Development Organization (UNIDO) has full control over which states become a member, but no control over suspension. Any member suspended by the United Nations is automatically suspended from UNIDO, and UNIDO cannot suspend a member on its own initiative. By contrast, UNESCO has no control over who becomes a member. All states acceding to the UN automatically accede to UNESCO, but it has full control over suspension: while the United Nations may request a suspension, UNESCO can refuse. The International Atomic Energy Agency is yet different: it has full control over accession and suspension, but it cannot expel a member. In short, there seems little evidence that pooling in large member IOs is the blanket result of a common template. Instead one observes the adaptation of pooling to the particular purpose of the IO in question.

It is now time to examine the contending hypothesis that the incidence of majoritarian decision making depends on the homogeneity of the group. The homogeneity in question refers to homogeneity of interests, and so it is not the same as the shared norms that are measured with the variable *Community*.

---

[10] Even here there are minor variations which include, in the Bank for International Settlements, simple majority for suspension of a member in financial arrears.

The *Affinity of Nations* dataset provides estimates of the homogeneity of the foreign policy preferences of an IO's member states, which it taps by the extent to which two states vote similarly in the UN assembly (Bailey, Strezhnev, and Voeten 2017). Homogeneity in an IO can be calculated as an inverse function of the average distance between *Ideal points* for all member state dyads.[11] When we replace *Members* with this variable in models accounting for *Pooling* under controls, it is significant at the 0.05 level, but with the wrong sign. The greater the homogeneity of foreign policy preferences of an IO's member states, the *weaker* its pooling. An IO with a larger membership tends to encompass states with *less* homogeneous *Ideal points*, and it is the size of an IO's membership, not its preference homogeneity that appears to drive pooling. A model with *Members* alongside *Ideal points* shows the robust predictive power of *Members*.[12]

However, there is an intuitive feel to the homogeneity hypothesis that is not easily dismissed. Would one not expect a group of like-minded voters to be less reluctant to dispense with unanimity than a group of contentious voters? One can examine this with the help of a variable which taps the existence of a network of expert professionals who share priors in a particular field of policy. *Episteme* has a value of 1 if an IO explicitly requires professional or expert qualifications for those who sit on its executive. This allows an indirect test of the homogeneity hypothesis on the premise that an IO with an epistemic community has some operational equivalence to an IO where member states' interests are aligned.[13]

Episteme is strongly and positively associated with *Pooling* in the bivariate model in the first column of Table 7.2, and just retains significance under

Table 7.2. Epistemic community

	Pooling 1950		
Episteme	0.177***	0.101*	0.006
	(0.053)	(0.053)	(0.047)
Members 1950–2010 mean			0.225***
			(0.039)
Controls	No	Yes	Yes
R^2	0.131	0.315	0.542

Note: N = 76 IOs. Policy scope is not included as a control because all epistemic IOs have narrow policy scope.

---

[11] Since the variable estimates distance, higher values indicate heterogeneity.
[12] Analyses in the online Appendix.
[13] The first IOs that adopted majority voting from the late 1800s onward were those in which epistemic communities of experts set technical standards on communications, sanitation, health, and navigation (Zamora 1980: 574–5).

controls in the second column. However, it is insignificant in a model with *Members* in the third column of Table 7.2. Perhaps a more refined measure of interest homogeneity might pick up a stronger effect, though it is worth stressing that the evidence to this point is more in line with the scale hypothesis than with the homogeneity hypothesis.

Illustrative Cases

The history of governance in IOs provides strong backing for the idea expressed by Cromwell Riches in 1940 that "[T]oo frequently unanimity in large gatherings is obtained only at the expense of accomplishment. To obtain the consent of all, the conference resorts to the adoption of mere platitudes on which all are, of course, in agreement, or to formulas so evasive in their wording as to be susceptible to a variety of interpretations" (14). Majority voting was first adopted in technical task-specific IOs, including the International Telegraph Union, the Universal Postal Union, the International Wine Office, the International Office of Chemistry, and the International Institute of Agriculture (Zamora 1980). The membership of these IOs at their founding included the major European empires controlling numerous dependent colonies, though the number of independent voting members still ranged from twenty to forty-one.[14]

Majority voting went beyond technical IOs to other large member IOs, including the Hague conferences which had forty-four members in 1907, and which permitted the passage of resolutions by majority vote. Inis Claude (1956: 31) remarks that the

> very size [of the Hague conferences] conduced to the adoption of innovations in conference technique. Experimental use was made of the apparatus of chairmen, committees, and roll calls, even though 'It seemed extraordinary to those not accustomed to it to see Governments, as ordinary individuals, responding to a roll call.' Although the rule of unanimity formally prevailed, this traditional practice, resting upon the fundamental respect for sovereignty which characterized international law, was mitigated to the extent that *voeux*, or recommendations, of the conference were passed by a mere majority vote.

In 1919, the International Labour Organization made simple majority a default rule in its assembly. Unanimity in the League of Nations was subject to "numerous and important exceptions," including the admission of new members and amendments to the Covenant which required a three-quarters

---

[14] The International Telegraph Union was founded with twenty members; the International Institute of Agriculture had forty-one.

Table 7.3. Membership and majority rule

# decision areas under majority rule	Membership size		
	Small (< 25 members)	Medium (25–55 members)	Large (> 55 members)
Zero	18	3	0
One	11	2	0
Two	5	3	1
Three	1	4	5
Four	0	2	10
Five	0	1	8
Six	0	1	1

Note: N = 76 IOs in final year in dataset. Pearson chi^2(10) = 57.8 (p < 0.000). The decision areas are accession, suspension, constitutional reform, the budget, financial compliance, and policy making. A decision area is majoritarian if, in the final decision, the decision rule is simple majority or supermajority, the decisions in that area are binding, and they are not subject to ratification.

majority in the Assembly and unanimity in the Council (Ellis 1929: 124; Riches 1933).[15] After World War II, "the steady lifting of the dead hand of the unanimity rule" was evident in many newly created IOs with potentially large memberships (Claude 1956: 121).

Table 7.3 provides another line of sight into the data by breaking down the distribution of decision areas under majority rule for IOs having small, medium, and large memberships in 2010. In the table, a decision area under majoritarian rule meets three criteria: the decision rule in the final decision stage is simple majority or supermajority; decisions are binding; and they are not subject to any form of ratification. There are two breaks in the data. The modal decision rule among IOs with fewer than twenty-five members is the national veto in all six decision areas. No small IO has binding majority rule in more than three areas. At the other extreme, the modal decision rule for IOs with more than fifty-five members is majority rule in four areas. No large member IO has the national veto in more than two areas. The intermediate category, which includes less than one-quarter of the IOs in our sample, is indeterminate and spans the entire range.

The Permanent Court of Arbitration (PCA) is the only large-membership IO (107 states in 2010) with binding majority in just two decision areas: accession and the annual budget. Its chief policy output consists of non-binding rules for arbitration which are decided by simple majority. By making its arbitration rules optional, the PCA sidesteps the trade-off between decision costs and

---

[15] The failure of the League of Nations is often attributed to its decision rule of unanimity. Franklin Delano Roosevelt certainly thought so. In 1923, he wrote an essay, "Plan to Preserve World Peace," in a competition for the American Peace Award in which he proposed to eliminate the League's use of unanimity in decisions involving sanctions and collective force. During the negotiations of the UN Charter two decades later, the Roosevelt administration sought to limit the use of the veto for the permanent members in the Security Council (Hoopes and Brinkley 1997).

exploitation risk that is the dilemma of a large-N IO. At its inception at the Hague Conference in 1899, the PCA was the first global mechanism for interstate dispute settlement and states wanted to tread carefully (Romano 2011: 263). The PCA has no provisions for suspending members or revising its founding document. It organizes interstate and public–private arbitration by setting out "procedures enabling states to choose arbitrators from a group of people identified in advance as potential candidates" but it does not itself engage in arbitration (Posner and Yoo 2005: 9).

With six members, the Economic and Monetary Community of Central African States (CEMAC) is exceptional in having binding supermajority voting in three decision areas: the budget, financial compliance, and policy making. The Central African Customs and Economic Union (UDEAC), the predecessor of CEMAC, began life with the national veto across the board (Mytelka 1974). This paralyzed the organization during the economic crisis from 1985 to 1993 (Zafar and Kubota 2003). UDEAC had inherited a common currency from French colonial times, but the member states were unable to agree on how to manage it. UDEAC was forced to suspend operations when its member states reneged on their contributions (Awoumou 2008: 112; Godwin Bongyu 2009: 389–90). Despite its small membership, unanimity produced gridlock. In the mid-1990s, a new leadership, the return of economic growth, and a favorable international climate set the conditions for an institutional overhaul in which CEMAC's Council of Ministers can pass the budget, suspend a non-paying member, and pass legislation on the common market, currency, and trade on a vote by five of its six members.

The scale hypothesis that pooling increases with the size of membership holds for general purpose IOs and task-specific IOs separately.[16] This is so even though the basic set-up of these types constrains membership in contrasting ways. A task-specific IO provides a contractually specified policy for a flexible membership. A general purpose IO makes an open-ended commitment for a relatively inflexible community of states. General purpose IOs tend not to expand their membership nearly as much as task-specific IOs (see Chapter 4). However, states in close proximity to a general purpose IO may feel the attraction of success and may be induced to seek membership to avoid trade diversion (Mattli 1999: 32). The founders of the IO may not anticipate that surrounding member states will clamor to join, and if the IO grows in membership we expect pressure for pooling to intensify.

The European Union is a fascinating case for precisely these reasons. Its founders had little expectation that the organization would grow much beyond the original six. The most likely additional member was the United Kingdom

---

[16] In separate equations for task-specific and general purpose IOs, the t-value for *Members (log10)* is 3.89 and 3.68, respectively.

which at first rejected the organization and, having changed course, was itself rejected in 1961 and 1967. The quadrupling of the membership of the EU from six to twenty-eight would have stunned its founders. One result has been prolonged and intense debate about majority rule. Fears of rising decision costs and blockage have mounted with each enlargement, yet defense of the national veto has been persistent. In an effort to preempt the introduction of majority voting in 1966, President de Gaulle imposed a blockage of his own by withdrawing France from the community's bodies. The Luxembourg Compromise, which resolved the dispute, stated that, where "very important interests of one or more partners are at stake," member states would "endeavor, within a reasonable time, to reach solutions which can be adopted by all the members of the Council" (Council of Ministers 1966: 5). While the text stopped short of saying that discussions should continue until a unanimous decision was reached, the French delegation interpreted it so (Teasdale 1993).

The challenge to the national veto was motivated by the ambition to get rid of obstacles to trade. What was to stop any state from using the veto to leverage side payments on the roughly three hundred anticipated legislative acts? "For this reason, it has been painfully difficult to extend the Community's authority, to change the rules of finance, or to proceed with the creation of a unified market and change the rules of business in Europe" (Sandholtz and Zysman 1989: 115). As a direct response, the Dooge Committee, tasked with making reform proposals, argued that "more use will need to be made, especially in the context of the enlarged Community, of the majority voting provisions laid down in the Treaties" (Dooge Committee 1985: 14). At the opening session of the 1985 intergovernmental conference leading to the Single European Act, Commission president Jacques Delors stated the conundrum bluntly: "[A]ny searching appraisal of the decision-making process or, more accurately, the all-too-frequent non-decision-making process shows the cause of our predicament to be 'unanimity,' the dead weight which is crushing the whole Community system. Its menacing presence, even when decisions may be taken by qualified majority, is producing paralysis" (Delors 1985: s.p.). When British Prime Minister Thatcher was faced with the choice between majority voting in the Council of Ministers or protecting the principle of the national veto, she went with majority voting. Virtually no one was more committed to national sovereignty than Mrs. Thatcher, but she acquiesced because she feared that the decision costs associated with unanimity would grind market reform to a halt (Keohane and Hoffmann 1991: 21). When asked in the House of Commons on May 16, 1989, whether she wished she had not used a three-line whip to put through the Single European Act, Margaret Thatcher replied "No, I do not. We wished to have many of the directives under majority voting because things which we wanted were being stopped by others using a single vote" (Thatcher 1989: s.p.).

Fear of decisional blockage re-emerged with Eastern enlargement. In its position paper to the European Council in 1992, the European Commission observed that

> In the perspective of enlargement, and particularly of a Union of 20 or 30 members, the question is essentially one of efficacy: how to ensure that, with an increased number of members, the new Union can function?...In the case of Council decisions to be adopted by unanimity, it is manifest that each new accession will increase the difficulty of reaching consensus.
> (Commission of the European Communities 1992: 13, 15)

In December 2001, the Laeken Declaration of the European Council launched a Constitutional Convention to overhaul EU decision making. How, it asked, can we "improve the efficiency of decision making and the workings of the institutions in a Union of some thirty Member States? How could the Union set its objectives and priorities more effectively and ensure better implementation? Is there a need for more decisions by a qualified majority?" (European Council 2001). The 2003 Nice Treaty responded by extending majority voting to policy areas outside the single market.

After the Nice Treaty, hardly anyone contested that unanimity voting compounded decision costs. The Luxembourg Compromise was dead, and majority voting was conceded in principle. The precise conditions were set out in the 2009 Lisbon Treaty as the battle lines shifted from the principle of majoritarianism to its application. A literature has emerged to illuminate the potential risks of exploitation under alternative voting systems (Hosli, Mattila, and Uriot 2011; Kirsch and Langner 2011).

As majority voting was introduced in more areas, so member states sought to specify the shrinking conditions under which they could avoid an unwelcome decision. The Ioannina compromise of 1994 and the emergency brake provisions of the 1999 Treaty of Amsterdam, the 2003 Treaty of Nice, and the 2009 Lisbon Treaty permitted a minority of member states to request the Council to do "everything in its power" to arrive at a solution acceptable to an enhanced supermajority. While this raised the bar, it did not reintroduce the veto and, in any case, the provisions were rarely activated (Hayes-Renshaw, van Aken, and Wallace 2006: 164). Since 2017, a minority of member states can ask for extended negotiations, but if the Council fails to compromise, the decision rule falls back to the standard qualified majority.

Studies show that, between 1994 and 2011, on average around 20 percent of legislative acts subject to qualified majority were contested by a negative vote or abstention (Novak 2013: 1092; van Aken 2012). And majority voting casts a long shadow over Council negotiations. The Council presidency, which rotates every six months among the member states, appears chiefly concerned with identifying and eliminating blocking minorities early in the game.

Its aim is not to achieve the broadest support for a measure but rather the minimum votes needed for qualified majority—irrespective of whether there will be a formal vote (Novak 2013: 1096).

These examples suggest that pooling of international authority is a rational response to the cost of decision making under the national veto. In most cases, the growth of an IO's membership can be anticipated, and it would be foolish for its founders not to consider this while negotiating the IO's institutions. However, the growth of an IO's membership cannot always be predicted, and then one would expect to see a process of ongoing reform, as in the European Union.

Conclusion

The basic set-up of an IO has powerful consequences for collective decision making among its member states. A large membership IO can exploit economies of scale and allow states to cooperate over problems that would otherwise confront them individually or that might not be dealt with at all. But at the same time, cooperation brings the danger of decisional blockage as the number of veto players rises. The most plausible explanation for why member states pool authority in international organizations appears to be the simplest: they do so in response to the number of potential veto players in the organization.

States have grounds to fear exploitation under majority rule. Unanimity cuts out this risk entirely while preserving national sovereignty, the principle that states have the exclusive right to exercise legitimate authority over those living in their territory. However, the trade-off between the cost of decision making and the risk of exploitation is sensitive to the scale of an IO's membership. The risk of exploitation does not increase much as the number of voters increases, while the costs of decision making rise substantially. We test this argument in cross-sectional analysis using a measure that taps gradations of majority rule across six decision areas and that takes into account the extent to which a decision is binding. Inferential tests lend strong support to the hypothesis that the scale of an IO's membership is the decisive causal factor. Surprisingly, the most powerful predictor of pooling is the *anticipated* scale of membership for an IO rather than the membership at the time the IO is established. When states set up an IO, they appear to make a reasonable estimate of the course of membership over time and build accordingly. This appears to be a deliberatively produced regularity on the part of actors who anticipate the consequences of their choices.

We fail to find support for the hypothesis that pooling is facilitated by more homogeneous state interests. We do find some evidence suggesting that epistemic authority can reduce the risk of exploitation in a large-scale IO, though the statistical results are not robust.

The causality of pooling is an exceptionally clear example of how functional pressure may displace a well-established normative principle, national sovereignty expressed in the national veto. Our analysis suggests that while states are reluctant to give up the national veto, they do so when the threat of decisional blockage looms large. To handle a worldwide problem, it makes sense for an IO to have an inclusive membership. But to escape inertia, it is induced to circumvent the national veto. This is a response to a trilemma of international governance. It is not possible to have a large membership, the national veto, and effective decision making at one and the same time. A distinctive characteristic of the postwar epoch is that in IOs with serious standing in the international domain, it is the national veto that has yielded.

8

Five Theses on International Governance

This book is concerned with formal IOs—rule-based cooperation among three or more states. IOs are the principal source of political authority and the strongest expression of the rule of law in the international domain, yet they are extremely diverse in their organizational set-up, what they do, and how they make decisions. This book seeks to explain this variation.

Two premises undergird the analysis. The first is that to make progress in explaining the form and substance of international organization one should pay close attention to written rules. When states establish an IO they do so by explicit contract, that is, by using written symbols to specify how the bodies of the IO are constituted, what they are mandated to do, and how they make decisions. There is every reason to believe that states care a lot about what these contracts say and consequently negotiate their content with intent. This is why our first step in coming to grips with international governance is to assess the rules that govern IOs (Hooghe et al. 2017).

The second premise is that international organizations as diverse as the European Union, NAFTA, the United Nations, the Organization of Islamic Cooperation, and the Economic Community of West African States, can be studied as units of a single population. The processes theorized by postfunctionalism take place within all IOs, and we conjecture that a given value on an independent variable (for example, the size of an IO's membership) produces the same outcome on the dependent variable (for example, the pooling of authority) for any IO. We examine the implications of postfunctionalism by observing a wide range of IOs over an extensive period of time.

Two logics—one functionalist and one social—motivate postfunctionalist theory. The functionalist logic considers international authority an adaptation to the benefits of governance among states. So, for example, we find that states pool authority in response to the decisional blockage that would occur in an IO with a large number of veto-wielding member states. On the same functionalist logic, delegation to non-state actors facilitates decision making as an IO's policy portfolio expands.

However, socio-political factors explain the incidence of functionalist pressures. The number of member states in an IO reflects a design choice between general purpose and task-specific governance. The expansion of an IO's policy portfolio takes place in IOs that have the normative coherence to sustain a highly incomplete contract. Only if the member states have the expectation that they can draw on diffuse reciprocity will they be willing to make an open-ended commitment for broad and flexible governance. Hence, postfunctionalism conceives functionalist and social factors as interacting to produce observable outcomes.

To conclude this study, we summarize the argument in five theses:

- International governance is formal and informal;
- International governance is contractual;
- International governance is functional;
- International governance is social;
- International governance is politicized.

International Governance is Formal and Informal

Postfunctionalism theorizes how informal norms constrain an IO's formal shell of written rules. Informal understandings facilitate convergent interpretation of behavior, and diminish the fear of exploitation under incomplete contracting. Hence, we argue that an IO's basic set up—its membership, policy portfolio, and contract—depends on the norms of the participants.

The idea that formal and informal rules are complementary runs counter to everyday usage in which informality is considered a virtue and formality a fault. The Latin *forma*—form, contour, figure, shape, outward appearance—is the root of the term *formal* which came to imply "mere ceremony" based on the notion that the outward appearance of a thing is no guide to its true nature.[1] In current usage,[2] *formal* is a pejorative term for "accordance with convention or etiquette," "strictly conventional," "a style...characterized by...elaborate grammatical structures," "officially sanctioned," "concerned with outward form," and "having the form or appearance without the spirit." The term *informal*, by contrast, has positive connotations: "having a relaxed, friendly, or unofficial style, manner, or nature," "denoting the grammatical structures, vocabulary, and idiom suitable to everyday language and conversation rather than to official or formal contexts."

---

[1] https://www.etymonline.com/word/formal; https://www.etymonline.com/word/form (Accessed April 27, 2019).

[2] The definitions of formal and informal are from the *Oxford English Dictionary*: https://en.oxforddictionaries.com/definition/formal; https://en.oxforddictionaries.com/definition/informal (Accessed April 27, 2019).

When applied to international governance these connotations point in the wrong direction, and it takes a positive effort to escape them. The formal in international governance refers, at its core, to the substitution of the rule of law for anarchy. The rule of law is the principle that those who wield power are constrained by explicit, generally applicable, and prospectively enforceable rules of behavior.[3] The international organizations described in this book express the rule of law in the international domain. International rules both empower and constrain the mighty. They entrench vested interests, but they also impose costs on raw power by setting out a legal framework for who makes decisions, how decisions should be made, and how disputes over the interpretation of these rules should be resolved. Formal rules in international governance, then, are no different from other types of formal institutions: they reduce uncertainty by prescribing and proscribing behavior.[4]

Table 8.1 lays out three ways in which formal and informal governance connect. In the first image, informal norms underpin formal rules. The formal rules are contracted among the member states. However, in the absence of norms about how states interpret and act on these rules, the formal rules are mere scraps of paper. Another way of putting this is to say that no set of formal rules is self-enforcing. This is the message of Lewis Carroll's famous dialogue between Achilles and the tortoise.[5] "Why," the tortoise asks Achilles, "should a state abide by the rules of the contract you are designing?" Achilles responds by adding a legal protocol stating that all must obey the rules in the contract.

Table 8.1. Formal and informal governance

	First image	Second image	Third image
How do formal and informal connect?	informal norms underpin formal organization	informal norms facilitate cooperation in areas formal organization does not reach	informal norms supplant formal organization
What is the virtue?	rule of law	flexibility	national sovereignty
What is the disadvantage?	national resistance	cheating	warfare

[3] Locke summarized the virtue of the rule of law in five words: "Wherever law ends, tyranny begins" (1728 [1690]: Section 202 of ch. XVIII "Of Tyranny" in Book II). "It is better," Aristotle remarked in *Politeia*, "for the law to rule than one of its citizens, so even the guardians of the laws are obeying the laws." "The hallmarks of a regime which flouts the rule of law are, alas, all too familiar: the midnight knock on the door, the sudden disappearance, the show trial, the subjection of prisoners to genetic experiment, the confession extracted by torture, the gulag and the concentration camp, the gas chamber, the practice of genocide or ethnic cleansing, the waging of aggressive war" (Bingham 2011: 9).

[4] Koremenos 2016; Moe 2005.   [5] Carroll 1895. The rendition of the dialogue is our own.

The tortoise responds, "Now that is solved, but you must add another protocol saying that states must obey the first protocol." When Achilles adds a second protocol to this effect, the tortoise asks for a third which says that states must obey the second protocol. This infinite regress makes the point that the rules of an international organization are obeyed because those subject to them are willing to accept that they are committed to their commitments. They may try to bend or escape from rules that they find burdensome, but in doing so, they recognize that a willingness to play by the rules is essential for cooperation in an IO.[6]

No organization can operate entirely without informal norms. Rules are guides to subsequent interpretation, but no set of rules can interpret themselves. The moment a rule is specified in language, it calls for interpretation that lies outside the rule. This has a crucial implication for a postfunctionalist theory of international governance because it requires that one consider not only the difficulty of implementing rules, but of interpreting them. Different forms of international governance make contrasting demands on whether the participants share informal norms that can limit contending interpretations. This provides an opening to contract theory and the idea that the more incomplete a contract for international governance, the greater the scope for divergent interpretations of whether a particular behavior is in fact a rule violation. Incompleteness increases the importance of behavior consistent with the *spirit* of the contract alongside behavior consistent with the *letter* of the contract (Hart and Moore 2008: 3; Williamson 1975: 69).

This has empirically testable implications. The greater the incompleteness of a contract, the greater the reliance on informal norms. The informal norms in question relate to how the participants regard each other. Do they share overarching norms that lead them to perceive cooperation and defection in the same way? Or do they conceive collective shared rule as rule by foreigners? Answers to these questions are expressed in the nature of the contract that underpins their cooperation. The absence of overarching norms by no means exhausts human creativity in devising international cooperation but, in the absence of overarching community, the possibilities for cooperation lie in task-specific governance, that is, governance on a narrow policy front.

The causal effect runs chiefly from norms to contract. Norms are deeply rooted and are not easily manipulated, whereas contracts are the product of strategic choice. However, the experience of cooperation within formal institutions can change how actors regard each other in ways that facilitate highly

---

[6] This is another way of saying that "consent cannot itself create an obligation; it can do so only within a system of law which declares that consent duly given, as in a treaty of a contract, shall be binding on the party consenting. To say that the rule *pacta sunt servanda* (treaties are binding on the parties) is itself founded on consent is to argue in a circle" (Clapham 2012: 51).

incomplete contracting. Several IOs with some overarching community start modestly and deepen as the participants gain confidence in the reciprocity of their cooperation. The European Union, for example, grew by stages from its authoritative but narrow origins in the European Coal and Steel Community. In the revived East African Community, the members took on an incomplete contract for political federation after six years of experimentation with limited cooperation. Discovering community by practicing cooperation can reinforce the "we-feeling" that made the initial step possible. In the medium term, international governance appears to be a dynamic phenomenon in which the experience of cooperation may enhance diffuse reciprocity.

The second image in Table 8.1 regards informal rules as a substitute for formal rules. This can provide a basis for cooperation among states that reject formal rules (Abbott and Snidal 2000; Kleine 2013; Lipson 1991; Stone 2011; Vabulas and Snidal 2013; Westerwinter 2016). An informal agreement may be easier to negotiate than a formal agreement because it bypasses domestic ratification, avoids public posturing, and can be interpreted to suit each party (Linos and Pegram 2016). "In informal organizations, the meta-organizational rules of participation, agenda-setting, and proposal-making are typically not codified. Indeed, even fundamental principles such as voting rules, monitoring, and enforcement are often poorly specified" (Westerwinter 2016: 6). Examples include the G-groups (G7, G8, G20, etc.) alongside less influential bodies, such as the Alliance of Small Island States and the Visegrad Four. The 2002 World Summit on Sustainable Development was typical. Rather than attempting to negotiate new legally binding rules for states or strengthening environmental IOs, it encouraged the formation of private–private and public–private partnerships to pursue sustainable development (Abbott et al. 2015: 13). One virtue of such bodies is that they are more flexible than contracted organizations; another is that they do not impinge on state sovereignty.

Even if the participants are good-willed, they may have contending interpretations of what was, or was not, agreed. A feeling that others are cheating can fester when expectations are not put in writing and there is no agreement on how to settle disputes:

> Formal governance may have its flaws, but among the reasons for its existence is a well-recognized ability to confront cheating.... How can an arrangement that tolerates cheating be a solution to the high costs and inefficiencies of formalism, given that the reason why formalism has high costs and inefficiencies in the first place is to enable participants to deter the risk of cheating? (Verdier 2015: 198)

As Verdier shows, cheating in an informal agreement is difficult to contain unless the initiator of the agreement has alternative options if its partners defect. Of course, if the purpose of an informal meeting is simply to exchange information, set benchmarks, and build trust, then cheating may be immaterial. In this second image, informality is not conceived as superior to formal organization, but rather as a form of governance that can reach places that formal governance cannot (Abbott et al. 2016: 729). Informal norms supplement formal organization and may serve a path to formality (Abbott and Snidal 2004; Avant and Westerwinter 2016; Pollack and Shaffer 2012; Shelton 2000; Trubek and Trubek 2005).

There is a third possibility, the replacement of formal organization by informal relations among states because formal organization is regarded as overly rigid and impervious to power. This critique is two-sided. On one side, there is the view that IOs are too constraining. Formal rule—i.e. hard law—is inflexible because it is too high a hurdle for leaders who find the rule of law oppressive. On the other, there is the view that IOs are ineffective. Since IOs cannot really exercise hierarchical authority, they may be dismissed as dysfunctional because they cannot deliver the rule of law in the international domain. This perceives the limitations of informality—its lack of precision, weakness of obligation, unequal access, limited accountability, and susceptibility to cheating—as strengths.

This third image of formality–informality is part of a nationalist reaction against international law and formal international organization. Radical populist leaders, including President Trump, Marine Le Pen, Matteo Salvini, and Geert Wilders oppose formal organization in principle. In a speech launching her campaign for the 2017 presidential race, Le Pen promised to regain "our territorial sovereignty" by pulling France out of the Eurozone and NATO. President Trump is similarly committed to regaining national sovereignty, as in his first major policy speech where he explained that "The nation-state remains the true foundation of happiness and harmony. I am skeptical of international unions that tie us up and bring America down. And under my administration, we will never enter America into any agreement that reduces our ability to control our own affairs."[7] There is not a single IO described in this book that does not exert some authority and thereby reduces the ability of its member states to control their own affairs. Those who prefer the third image reject external constraints on national sovereignty, preferring informality and anarchy to formal organization and the rule of law.[8]

---

[7] President Trump speaking on foreign policy in his address to the Center for the National Interest, Washington DC, April 25, 2016.

[8] Speaking to the Central Intelligence Agency, President Trump openly questioned the rule of international law when he suggested that the spoils of war belong to the victor (see also Patrick 2017): "When I was young, we were always winning things in this country. We'd win with trade. We'd win with wars. At a certain age, I remember hearing from one of my instructors, 'The United States has never lost a war.' And then, after that, it's like we haven't won anything. We don't win anymore. The old expression, 'to the victor belong the spoils'—you remember. I always used to say, keep the oil. I wasn't a fan of Iraq. I didn't want to go into Iraq. But I will tell you, when we were in,

This book brings the third image into focus by analyzing the effects of politicization. The mobilization of nationalism may erode shared rule among peoples. Two decades of research on the European Union has illuminated how exclusive national identity can constrain cooperation—even if the functional pressures are greater than ever (Hooghe and Marks 2019).

International Governance is Contractual

We conceive an IO as a contractual agreement among states. The idea that governance can be understood as a contract among autonomous actors is perhaps the chief contribution of Western philosophy to the study of politics. It is particularly appropriate to international governance because the state of nature, the hypothetical condition prior to the contract, speaks directly to the nature of states in international relations. The dilemma confronting a state in the international domain is similar to that confronting a citizen within the state. Each participant would like to have full freedom of action, but if all had this, collective problem solving would be possible only where individual and social rationality converged.

Within states, the dilemma finds a rational solution in an imaginary contract in which each citizen agrees to sacrifice their individual autonomy to an overarching authority. *Among* states, the dilemma has a rational solution in an actual contract in which states agree to sacrifice some freedom of action in collective decision making. National sovereignty—the supreme power by which a state is governed—is limited by states themselves as they come to grips with problems that they cannot solve independently. Each state retains sovereignty in the decision to join or leave an IO, but within the organization they pool and delegate authority.

We adapt contract theory by relaxing the assumption that the contract is all or nothing. Contract theorists from Hobbes to Rawls conceive a founding contract as one that bundles public goods in a single regime for a single society, "a more or less self-sufficient association of persons" (Rawls 1999: 4). Early postwar theorists of international relations shared the view that authority is indivisible.[9] Our premise, by contrast, is that governance can be contracted in

---

we got out wrong. And I always said, in addition to that, keep the oil." Full text: "Trump, Pence remarks at CIA Headquarters on January 23, 2017," http://www.cbsnews.com/news/trump-cia-speech-transcript/.

[9] Morgenthau (1948: 259) stresses that "If sovereignty means supreme authority, it stands to reason that no two or more entities—groups of persons, agencies—can be sovereign within the same time and space" (see also Hinsley 1966; Vernon 1971).

parts at different scales (Hooghe and Marks 2003, 2009a; Lenz et al. 2015). The world we have in mind is one of multiple levels of governance among overlapping societies at diverse scales. At each level one can ask who has the right to form a jurisdiction, what should be decided, how, and by whom. IOs are embedded in a wider authoritative architecture that structures human cooperation.

This conception of international governance rejects the demarcation criterion, the claim that politics among and within states are distinct causal domains.[10] The allocation of authority across subnational, national, and international levels is better conceived as a matter of choice and of degree. There are many instances in which independent states have formed federations, leagues, or other multilevel forms of governance in which authority is dispersed across jurisdictions at different scales. The demand for public goods that arises as humans interact has produced a variety of political forms, of which IOs are one. Hence anarchy in the international domain is conditional rather than universal. Our claim is that these conditions are both functional and social.

International Governance is Functional

International governance is an exercise in human ingenuity under incentives and constraints. A fundamental incentive for governance arises from interdependence. The functional imperative for rule-based cooperation has its intellectual roots in social contract theory, and it is carried through with increasing sophistication in contemporary public choice theory. The idea that governance is functional is also well established in international relations. Simply put, states use international organization to reduce the costs of solving collective action problems (Keohane 1984; Koremenos 2016; Koremenos, Lipson, and Snidal 2001; Sandler 2004). Cooperation is difficult, however, because in many cooperative situations the incentives of individual countries and those of the group are misaligned. International organizations can help states overcome the collective action dilemma by lowering the transaction costs of negotiating mutually beneficial agreements, providing information, framing the agenda, and punishing defectors.

Functionalist theory can explain how the basic set-up of an IO—its membership, portfolio, and contract—shape the pooling and delegation of

---

[10] The demarcation criterion gets domestic politics wrong as well as international politics when it claims that "domestic systems are centralized and hierarchic" (Waltz 1979: 88).

authority. Two mechanisms appear decisive. The first connects the sheer number of member states in an IO with their willingness to sacrifice the national veto. On the one hand, the national veto can lead to decisional blockage; on the other, relaxing the national veto introduces the risk that a state will be exploited in majority voting. Our reasoning is that the decision costs increase more than the risk of exploitation in an IO with a larger number of members. Decision making in an IO with a few member states may be efficient even if states retain the national veto, whereas the potential for decisional blockage increases sharply as the number of veto-wielding member states increases. By contrast, the risk of exploitation under majority voting is not much greater in a large membership IO than in one with just three members. Hence, a larger membership changes the terms of the trade-off between decision costs and the fear of exploitation.

This functionalist logic accounts for more than half of the variance in pooling across the seventy-six IOs we observe. Surprisingly, the most powerful predictor of pooling at the foundation of an IO is its membership decades into the future. We suspect that the founders of an IO build expectations about future membership into their design. If so, this is an example of a deliberatively produced regularity in which actors take into account the anticipated consequences of their choices.

A second functional mechanism explains how delegation and pooling in an IO change over time in response to the policy portfolio. An organization that comes to handle a swathe of problems places growing demands on its decisional framework. As decision making becomes more complex there is an incentive to formally structure who can set the agenda, improve the retrieval of information, and institutionalize dispute settlement. Independent agents can be useful in each respect. An independent secretariat with the power to draft legislative proposals can structure the agenda and limit issue cycling as the dimensionality of the choice-space increases. Independent consultative bodies may have access to policy-relevant information. Lowering the threshold for passing legislation by introducing majoritarian voting reduces the blackmail potential of individual legislators. Standing courts of qualified judges with authority to impose penalties reduce uncertainty by regularizing dispute resolution. In line with the literature on public bureaucracy within states, we find evidence that delegation and pooling are functional adaptations to growing complexity produced by the expansion of an IO's policy portfolio.

Observational analysis suggests that functional pressures flowing from the scale of an IO's membership and the scope of its policy portfolio are causally powerful. However, the incidence of these functional pressures depends on prior decisions about an IO's membership and its policy portfolio. What leads states to expand an IO's policy portfolio? What brings states to limit the membership of an IO to a select group of states or to open membership to most states around the world? To answer these questions one needs to theorize the effect of sociality.

International Governance is Social

Cooperation requires more than a confluence of interests. Do the participants share perceptions about what counts as cooperation? Are they able to cooperate on the basis of diffuse reciprocity?

Shared norms increase the accuracy of communication and reduce ambiguity in social interaction. A group that shares norms will have more convergent interpretations of what counts as cooperation and defection and will be better able to monitor and punish the behavior of its members. That cushions fears of exploitation and enhances tolerance for ambiguity. Perceptions come sharply into play when one has to decide whether a member state is actually cheating and, more generally, whether one can tolerate the uncertainty of an open-ended contract.

A community is a normative setting in which a participant may internalize the effects of their choices over time. There are strong grounds for believing that the core characteristics of community—shared norms, an overarching identity, a sense of common fate—exist in tandem and provide a group with the ability to sustain diffuse reciprocity.

Communities both facilitate and impede the provision of public goods. These positive and negative effects are expressed by the term parochial altruism (Bernhard, Fischbacher, and Fehr 2006). The social solidarity that facilitates governance within communities can constrain governance among them. Communities are parochial in that they divide the social world into us and them, into insiders and outsiders.

This is the darker side to community. Communities may, and often do, demarcate sharply between members and non-members. Social psychologists have long diagnosed "in-group favoritism" and "out-group hostility" in association with how individuals conceive themselves in relation to their communities (Tajfel 1981; Tajfel and Turner 1986). Those who identify exclusively with a nation are likely to think of international authority as illegitimate rule by foreigners.[11]

In both respects, community provides a key to the provision of governance, and hence to the possibilities for international organization. Transnational

---

[11] What appears to be decisive is how these attachments fit together. Does an individual conceive of national identity as one among a set of attachments or as an exclusive attachment (Cram 2012; Díez-Medrano 2003; Díez-Medrano and Gutiérrez 2001; Herrmann and Brewer 2004; Hooghe and Marks 2005; Risse 2010)? And how intensely does an individual favor her in-group over other groups (Mutz and Kim 2017; Sidanius et al. 2007)?

community almost always exists alongside more powerful national and subnational identities, yet some meeting of the minds among the peoples encompassed in an IO is necessary for broad, continuous, and open-ended cooperation. General purpose governance places a considerable burden on the participants to have a common understanding of each other's behavior. There are many possible courses of action; the linkages among them are multiplex; the costs and benefits for individual member states are difficult to estimate; and cooperation and defection are opaque. Such incompletely contracted cooperation is vulnerable to mistakes, wrong moves, and ambiguity. Specific reciprocity is insufficient. A strategy of tit-for-tat is impressively robust against exploitation in an iterated prisoners' dilemma, but just a single mistake will kill cooperation. If members of a group interpret cooperation and defection differently, this can have similarly adverse effects.

Hence, in the absence of community, contracting is constrained to greater specificity by fear of exploitation. This does not exclude international governance, but it is governance of a particular kind. An IO may serve as a forum for non-binding interaction or it may exploit a more limited form of reciprocity based on specific exchange. The basic set-up of such IO will be contractually pinned down to minimize ambiguity.

This has dynamic implications for the growth of an IO's policy portfolio and beyond that for its authority. Community and incomplete contracting facilitate the expansion of an IO's policy portfolio, and by doing so, they enhance the complexity of decision making in an IO. This induces states to finesse the national veto by introducing majority voting and to delegate powers to non-state actors, including supranational courts, independent assemblies, and agenda-setting secretariats. So while the functional pressure resulting from decisional complexity provides a powerful proximate explanation of an IO's pooling and delegation, it does so within the possibilities of incomplete contracting, and behind that, the extent to which the participants share normative understandings.

In cross-sectional time-series models, variables tapping community and contract are much stronger predictors of change in an IO's policy portfolio and authority than variables consistent with alternative explanations, including trade interdependence, power asymmetry, democracy, affluence, and GDP dispersion.

For these reasons, we argue that one must engage sociality to explain the conditions under which international organizations provide public goods. Community produces a propensity for general purpose governance. It loads the dice, but it does not point-predict. Moreover, cooperation can develop over time, as suggested by the expansion of the policy portfolios of general purpose IOs. Incomplete contracting opens up a space for the discovery of cooperation as the participants interact.

International Governance is Politicized

Community facilitates cooperation, but it can also motivate political backlash. Authoritative international governance challenges the claim that only states should exercise authority within their territory, and so as IO authority deepens, it can generate a reaction that mobilizes national conceptions of community against collective shared rule.

International organizations have served as a bedrock of the liberal international order established after World War II (Hooghe, Lenz, and Marks 2018; Lake 2018). Regional integration in Europe, Latin America, and Africa sought to realize scale in public goods provision on a basis of equality among member states. Bretton Woods institutions—the International Monetary Fund, the World Bank, and the General Agreement on Tariffs and Trade—sustained the principle of non-discrimination in an effort to avoid mutually exclusive economic blocs and beggar-thy-neighbor policies. The system legitimated economic intervention at the national level—a grand political bargain that Ruggie (1982) termed "embedded liberalism." After the Cold War this bargain was recast in a wave of institutional reform that facilitated international economic exchange and migration by empowering IOs that extended the rule of law among states.

Transnationalism was hugely successful in diminishing the costs of communication and exchange across national borders, and its aggregate effect was to increase human welfare and spread liberal norms. However, this has generated a profound cultural and economic reaction that appears most intense in Europe and the United States, the heartlands of the liberal global order.

Contestation over international governance is prominent in party political programs; it influences national elections; and it has structured political conflict in both Europe and the United States. At the forefront stand nationalist political parties and candidates who oppose international organization in principle as well as in practice. In the March 2018 elections, the Italian Northern League competed on the slogan "Slaves of Europe? No, thanks!" In its first year, the Trump administration pulled the United States out of the Paris Climate Change Agreement, withdrew from UNESCO, reigned in immigration from non-Western countries, and renegotiated NAFTA. Subsequently, the Trump administration unilaterally imposed tariffs on allies and competitors, pulled the rug from under a nuclear disarmament deal with Iran that was jointly negotiated with the EU, and declared the International Criminal Court (ICC) "already dead to us" because it "unacceptably threatens American sovereignty and U.S. national security interests."[12]

---

[12] National security advisor John Bolton in a speech to the Federalist Society, September 10, 2018, in Washington (Lee 2018).

The expression of popular resentment against immigration, trade-exacerbated economic inequality, and the loss of national sovereignty has transformed the politics of Western democracies. The delegitimation of IOs, and of international governance more generally, is more than a clash of ideas. It takes the form of a cleavage pitting the cultural and economic losers of transnationalism against its supporters (de Wilde et al. 2019; Kriesi et al. 2006; Mutz 2018; Zürn, Binder, and Ecker-Ehrhardt 2012). In Europe, this cleavage has as its core a political reaction against European integration and immigration (Hooghe and Marks 2018).[13] In the United States, the reaction against transnationalism has intensified partisan polarization, corroded the legitimacy of democratic institutions, and elected a president deeply critical of international governance. The revolt against international governance is socially rooted. Partisans are sharply distinguished by gender, occupation, rural–urban location, and above all, education (Becker, Fetzer, and Novy 2017; Evans and Tilley 2017; Hobolt 2018; Marks et al. 2018; Maxwell 2019; Stubager 2010; Van Elsas, Hakhverdian, and van der Brug 2016).

Politicization has gathered sufficient momentum to constrain IO authority across the board. Several IOs have attempted to push back by engaging social groups, creating consultative parliamentary bodies, strengthening access for civil society stakeholders, and by making their decision making more transparent (Dingwerth et al. 2015; Zürn 2018). However, it is not possible for an IO to placate those who reject it in principle. Critics aim their sharpest barbs at general purpose IOs because they are the nearest thing in the international domain to government, the exercise of authority across a wide, incompletely contracted policy portfolio. General purpose IOs are anathema for those who conceive national and transnational identity in zero-sum terms.

International organizations have been a conspicuous anchor of international governance over the past seven decades. In place of conquest and coercion, IOs are based on contractual agreement; instead of hierarchy, their organizing principle is equality among states and peoples; and instead of exploitation as the chief mode of engagement, international organization routinizes interstate bargaining. However, there are signs that international organization, as we have known it, is under duress. An era of relatively benign transnationalism based on a permissive consensus seems to be drawing to a close.

---

[13] For radical nationalist and radical left parties these issues relate to the defense of national community against transnational shocks (on Europe, see De Vries 2018; Häusermann and Kriesi 2015; Hobolt and Tilley 2016; Inglehart and Norris 2016; Rydgren 2013; Teney, Lacewell, and de Wilde 2013; Van Elsas, Hakhverdian, and van der Brug 2016. On Brexit, see Hobolt 2016; Hobolt, Leeper, and Tilley 2018).

The most direct challenge to international governance seems to come from within the liberal core. To understand the tensions arising from transnationalism, we need to broaden our point of view beyond relations among countries to conflict within them. Politicization plays on a parochial conception of community. Who is one of us, and what does this mean for our ability to solve the problems generated by interaction among communities? Contrasting conceptions of community have come, ever more transparently, to shape international governance.

Appendix

The Appendix describes the dependent and independent variables. Part I summarizes operationalization, shows descriptives, and contains a list of IOs in the MIA dataset. Part II provides detail on the conceptualization and operationalization of key variables of interest. The online Appendix has model specifications and robustness checks for Chapters 5, 6, and 7.[1]

Part I: Operationalization

This section provides a short description of how we define and operationalize delegation, pooling, policy scope, community, contract, politicization, and trade interdependence (Table A.1). This is followed by descriptive statistics for dependent and independent variables (Table A.2). The section finishes with a list of the seventy-six IOs, arranged by geographical location, that make up the Measure of International Authority (MIA) (Table A.3).

Table A.1. Operationalization of variables

Affluence	Annual mean GDP per capita for the member states of an IO using Penn World Tables 7.3. Missing observations in early years are derived from Maddison's Statistics on World Population, GDP and Per Capita GDP. Missing observations for countries that ceased to exist after 2005 (and are not included in the 7.3 version of Penn World Tables) are derived from Penn World Tables 5.6. Values are divided by 1000 to facilitate interpretation. *Sources*: Penn World Tables (Feenstra, Inklaar, and Timmer 2013); Maddison Historical Data 2013 (Bolt and van Zanden 2014).
Community	This factor represents the cultural, geographical, political, and institutional commonality among the member states of an IO in a given year using five indicators of diversity, which are reversed to express community: • *Diversity in geographical location* is Rae's index of fractionalization $1 - \sum_{i=1}^{m} s_i^2$ where s_i is the share of a region in an IO's membership, and m refers to the number of regions (out of nine) represented in the IO (*Source*: Jacobson 1998: V2001 IN; Shanks, Jacobson, and Kaplan 1996). • *Diversity in religion* is a Rae index, where s_i is the share of a religion among an IO's membership, and m is the number of religions represented in the IO. A state is assigned the religion that has the largest number of followers in the country (from a list of eleven religions). *Source*: CIA World Factbook (n.d). • *Diversity in civilization* is a Rae index, where s_i is the share of a civilization in an IO's membership, and m is the number of civilizations (out of nine) represented in this IO. *Sources*: Huntington (1996); Russett, Oneal, and Cox (2000).

(continued)

---

[1] Available at the authors' websites.

Appendix

Table A.1. Continued

	• *Diversity in political regime* is the standard deviation of the Polity2 score (rescaled from 1 to 21) among the individual members of an IO. We use the POLITY IV dataset. *Source*: Marshall, Gurr, and Jaggers (2017). • *Diversity in legal tradition* is the Rae index, where s_i is the share of a legal tradition in an IO's membership, and m is the number of legal traditions (Islamic law, civil law, common law, mixed law) represented in this IO. *Source*: Mitchell and Powell (2009, 2011). Table 5.2 in Chapter 5 reports a principal components factor analysis. Factor scores are normalized and reversed so that higher values indicate greater commonality. See the section on *Community* in this Appendix.
Contract	This dichotomous variable estimates the extent to which an IO contract is complete. • A contract is *complete* (value = 1) if its purpose is to achieve a fixed objective under clearly specified conditions. Relatively complete contracts identify the means to cooperate in given policy areas. • A contract is *incomplete* (value = 2) if its purpose is to attain broad-ranging cooperation among governments or peoples under weakly specified conditions. Incomplete contracts focus on the process rather than the outcome. *Source*: own coding of foundational documents (with intercoder reliability tests); see the section on *IO Contract* in this Appendix.
Core policy	A core policy meets three or more of eight criteria that capture a tangible legal, financial, or organizational footprint. *Core policy* is a count of the number of core policies that an IO is estimated to have out of a list of twenty-five policies. Annual estimation. *Source*: own coding; see the section on *Policy scope* in this Appendix.
Core state powers	An IO scores 1 if, in a given year, the IO has one or several of the following core policies: foreign policy, diplomacy, political cooperation; military cooperation, defense, military security; justice, home affairs, interior security, police, anti-terrorism; migration, immigration, asylum, refugees; welfare state services, employment policy, social affairs, pension systems; financial regulation, banking regulation, monetary policy, currency; taxation, fiscal policy coordination, macro-economic policy coordination. *Source*: MIA data on core and flanking policies, to which we apply Genschel and Jachtenfuchs' (2016: 44) conceptualization of policies that are directly related to a state's monopoly of coercion ("core state powers"); see the section on *Core State Powers* in the online Appendix.
Delegation	Delegation is a 0–1 scale that estimates, on an annual basis, the allocation of authoritative competences by member states to non-state bodies in an IO's decision-making process. Delegation is assessed (a) within one or more IO bodies (assemblies, executives, consultative bodies, general secretariats, dispute settlement bodies), that are (b) partially or wholly composed of non-member state actors, and that (c) exercise or co-exercise authority over agenda setting or final decision making in (d) one or more of six decision areas: membership accession, membership suspension, constitutional reform, budgetary allocation, financial non-compliance, and up to five streams of policy making. *Source*: Hooghe et al. (2017: ch. 3); see the section on *Delegation* in this Appendix.
Democracy	Annual mean score for the member states of an IO using the Polity2 scale of the Polity IV dataset. Scores are transformed to a 1–21 scale. *Source*: Marshall, Gurr, and Jaggers (2017).
Enlargement	Change in the number of IO member states from the first observation of the IO in the dataset to its final year divided by the number of observation years. *Source*: Correlates of War IGO v2.3 (Pevehouse, Nordstrom, and Warnke 2004), complemented by own research for years after 2005 and for missing IOs.
Epistemic community	A dichotomous variable that takes the value of 1 if the IO has a provision in its constitution, treaty, regulations, or bylaws that (a) requires states to select representatives with recognized professional expertise to represent them in the IO assembly or an IO executive, and (b) mandates that these representatives have some decisional autonomy. *Source*: own coding for 76 IOs over time; see the section on *Episteme* in the online Appendix.

Appendix

GDP dispersion	Annual coefficient of variation of the GDP per capita for the member states of an IO using Penn World Tables 7.3. Missing observations are derived from Maddison's Statistics on World Population, GDP and Per Capita GDP, and from Penn World Tables 5.6. The coefficient of variation shows the extent of variability in relation to the mean of the population. *Sources*: Penn World Tables (Feenstra, Inklaar, and Timmer 2013); Maddison Historical Data 2013 (Bolt and van Zanden 2014).
Historical ties	Dichotomous variable that takes on a value of 1 if two-thirds of an IO's founding members (1) share a history of membership within a federation, or (2) share experience of membership within—and resistance to—a colonial empire. *Source:* own coding for 76 IOs; see the section on *Community* in this Appendix.
Historical ties extended	Dichotomous variable that takes on a value of 1 if two-thirds of an IO's founding members (1) share a history of membership within a federation, or (2) share experience of membership within—and resistance to—a colonial empire, or (3) host a pan-national movement that champions transnational political union and has substantial elite support. *Source:* own coding for 76 IOs; see the section on *Community* in this Appendix.
Ideal points	Estimate of congruence among the members of an IO in voting in the UN General Assembly. Voting is arrayed on a single dimension that reflects state positions toward the US-led liberal order. Votes are aggregated by UN session. The unit is the absolute distance between country *A* and country *B*'s posterior mean ideal-point estimates. The measure *Ideal points* is an IO's annual average of the absolute distance between ideal points for all dyads of an IO's member states between 1950 and 2010. Annual measure. *Source*: the variable *absidealdiff* as calculated by Bailey, Strezhnev, and Voeten (2017).
Membership	The number of states that are formal members of the IO. Unless otherwise stated, we use the logarithm (log10) in analyses. *Source*: Correlates of War IGO data, v. 2.3 (Pevehouse, Nordstrom, and Warnke 2004), and own updates for years after 2005 and for missing IOs.
Policy scope	Policy scope is a discrete variable for the range of policies for which an IO is responsible from a list of twenty-five non-exclusive policies. The list was initially developed by Lindberg and Scheingold (1970) and adapted by Schmitter (1996) and Hooghe and Marks (2001). Policy scope is assessed at each reform moment of an IO, i.e. at the time of a treaty revision, a new protocol or convention, the passing of framework legislation, or the creation of a new IO body or instrument (e.g. a fund) by applying eight criteria that capture a tangible legal, financial, or organizational footprint. Policy scope is an annual measure. *Source*: own coding; see the section on *Policy scope* in this Appendix.
Politicization	Raw count of mentions that combine "PROTESTOR" or "DEMONSTRATOR" with the IO name or acronym in "Major World Publications" in LexisNexis. We use an equally weighted three-year moving average of year t, t_{-1}, and t_{-2}. Raw counts are divided by 100 to ease interpretation. *Source*: own calculations; see the section on *Politicization* in this Appendix.
Portfolio change	Average annual change in *Policy scope* from the first to the final year of observation of the IO in the dataset.
Pooling	Pooling is a 0–1 scale that estimates the extent to which member states share authority through non-unanimous voting in decision making. Pooling is assessed by (a) examining the voting rule in interstate IO bodies, (b) for agenda setting and for the final decision, (c) in six decision areas: membership accession, membership suspension, constitutional reform, budgetary allocation, financial non-compliance, and (up to five streams of) policy making, and then (d) assessing the extent to which a decision is binding on member states and/or requires domestic ratification. *Source*: Hooghe et al. (2017: ch. 3); see the section on *Pooling* in this Appendix.
Power asymmetry	The ratio in material capabilities of the largest member state to the sum of all member states of the IO. *Source*: Composite Index of National Material Capabilities

(continued)

Appendix

Table A.1. Continued

	(CINC) v.5.0 (Singer 1987; Singer et al. 1972), which summarizes military expenditure, military personnel, energy consumption, iron and steel production, urban population, and total population annually from 1950 to 2010.
Security	A dichotomous variable that takes the value of 1 if an IO's sole mandate is estimated to be collective (military) security. The IO must focus exclusively on security and may not be estimated to have concurrent mandates in economic, multi-issue, or "other" areas. Cross-sectional coding based on an estimation in the early 2000s. *Source:* Boehmer, Gartzke, and Nordstrom (2004), complemented with own coding for IOs not included in the BGN dataset.
Trade policy	A dichotomous variable that takes on a value of 1 from the first year in which trade becomes an IO competence (core or flanking), and 0 if trade is not an IO competence. *Source:* own coding; see section on *Policy scope* in this Appendix.
Trade interdependence	Three variables that tap the relative importance of trade among IO members compared to trade with the world outside the IO. Three measures with increasing complexity: • *Intra-IO trade share*, which estimates an IO's intra-IO trade (i.e. trade interdependence among member states) as a percentage of the overall trade of an IO's members. • *Trade intensity*, which estimates the ratio of an IO's intra-IO trade share and its share of world trade. • *Trade introversion*, which estimates the relative size of an IO's internal trade to the relative size of an IO's external trade. *Sources:* measures adopted from Iapadre and Plummer (2011); algorithm provided by Philippe de Lombaerde, the Institute on Comparative Regional Integration Studies of the United Nations University in Bruges (UNU-CRIS). See the section on *Trade interdependence* in this Appendix.

Table A.2. Descriptives

	Mean	Median	Min	Max	N
Delegation	0.183	0.175	0	0.652	3292
Pooling	0.291	0.285	0	0.728	3292
Policy scope	5.687	3	1	24	3292
Affluence	8.091	5.473	0.186	59.923	3290
Community	0.000	−0.280	−2.403	3.570	3279
Contract	1.3704	1	1	2	3292
Core policy	2.002	2	1	10	3292
Core state powers	0.420	0	0	1	3292
Democracy	13.615	13.773	1.333	21	3279
Enlargement	0.937	0	−3	72	3216
Episteme	0.243	0	0	1	3295
GDP dispersion	0.718	0.212	0.002	46.640	3290
Historical ties	0.173	0	0	1	3292
Historical ties extended	0.243	0	0	1	3292
Ideal points	0.711	0.670	0.003	2.347	3281
Members	54.789	24	3	192	3292
Members log	1.433	1.380	0.301	2.283	3292
Politicization (moving)	0.065	0	0	5.650	3288
Portfolio change	0.079	0	−7	14	3222
Power asymmetry	0.352	0.292	0.086	1	3286
Security	0.030	0	0	1	3292
Trade policy	0.492	0	0	1	3292
Intra-IO trade share	15.916	9.93	0.040	72.120	1013
Trade intensity	56.470	5.13	0.250	5228.300	1013
Trade introversion	0.680	0.76	−0.600	5.360	1013

Table A.3. IO population in MIA

Africa (10 IOs)
African Union (AU) (1963–2010)
Economic and Monetary Community of Central African States (CEMAC) (1966–2010)
Common Market for Eastern and Southern Africa (COMESA) (1982–2010)
East African Community I (EAC 1) (1967–76)
East African Community II (EAC 2) (1993–2010)
Economic Community of Central African States (ECCAS–CEEC) (1985–2010)
Economic Community of West African States (ECOWAS) (1975–2010)
Intergovernmental Authority on Development (IGAD) (1986–2010)
Southern African Customs Union (SACU) (1950–2010)
Southern African Development Community (SADC) (1981–2010)

Americas (9 IOs)
Andean Community (Andean/CAN) (1969–2010)
Caribbean Community (CARICOM) (1968–2010)
Latin American Integration Association (LAIA/ALADI) (1961–2010)
Common Market of the South (MERCOSUR) (1991–2010)
North American Free Trade Agreement (NAFTA) (1994–2010)
Organization of American States (OAS) (1951–2010)
Organization of Eastern Caribbean States (OECS) (1968–2010)
Latin American and Caribbean Economic System (SELA) (1976–2010)
Central American Integration System (SICA) (1952–2010)

Asia-Pacific (5 IOs)
Association of Southeast Asian Nations (ASEAN) (1967–2010)
Pacific Islands Forum (PIF) (1973–2010)
South Asian Association for Regional Cooperation (SAARC) (1986–2010)
Shanghai Cooperation Organization (SCO) (2002–2010)
Pacific Community (SPC) (1950–2010)

Europe (12 IOs)
Benelux Union (BENELUX) (1950–2010)
Central Commission for the Navigation of the Rhine (CCNR) (1950–2010)
European Organization for Nuclear Research (CERN) (1954–2010)
Commonwealth of Independent States (CIS) (1992–2010)
Council of Europe (CoE) (1950–2010)
Council for Mutual Economic Assistance (COMECON) (1959–1991)
European Economic Area (1994–2010)
European Free Trade Association (EFTA) (1960–2010)
European Space Agency (ESA) (1980–2010)
European Union (EU) (1952–2010)
Nordic Council (NORDIC) (1952–2010)
Organization for Security and Cooperation in Europe (OSCE) (1973–2010)

Middle East (4 IOs)
Arab Maghreb Union (AMU) (1989–2010)
Gulf Cooperation Council (GCC) (1981–2010)
League of Arab States (LOAS) (1950–2010)
Organization of Arab Petroleum Exporting Countries (OAPEC) (1968–2010)

Multi-regional (11 IOs)
Asia-Pacific Economic Cooperation (APEC) (1991–2010)
Bank for International Settlements (BIS) (1950–2010)
Centre for Agriculture and Bioscience International (CABI) (1987–2010)
Commonwealth of Nations (COMSEC) (1965–2010)
North Atlantic Treaty Organization (NATO) (1950–2010)
International Organization for la Francophonie (OIF/ACCT) (1970–2010)
Northwest Atlantic Fisheries Organization (NAFO) (1979–2010)

(continued)

Appendix

Table A.3. Continued

Organization for Economic Co-operation and Development (OECD) (1950–2010)
Organization of Islamic Cooperation (OIC) (1970–2010)
Organization of Petroleum Exporting Countries (OPEC) (1960–2010)
Intergovernmental Organization for International Carriage by Rail (OTIF) (1950–2010)

UN organizations (15 IOs)
Food and Agriculture Organization (FAO) (1950–2010)
International Civil Aviation Organization (ICAO) (1950–2010)
International Labour Organization (ILO) (1950–2010)
International Maritime Organization (IMO) (1960–2010)
International Monetary Fund (IMF) (1950–2010)
International Telecommunication Union (ITU) (1950–2010)
United Nations (UN) (1950–2010)
UN Educational, Scientific and Cultural Organization (UNESCO) (1950–2010)
UN Industrial Development Organization (UNIDO) (1985–2010)
Universal Postal Union (UPU) (1950–2010)
World Bank (IBRD) (1950–2010)
World Health Organization (WHO) (1952–2010)
World Intellectual Property Organization (WIPO) (1970–2010)
World Meteorological Organization (WMO) (1950–2010)
World Tourism Organization (UNWTO) (1975–2010)

Global (10 IOs)
Global Environmental Facility/Fund (GEF) (1994–2010)
International Atomic Energy Agency (IAEA) (1957–2010)
International Criminal Court (ICC) (2002–2010)
International Criminal Police Organization (INTERPOL) (1950–2010)
International Organization for Migration (1955–2010)
International Seabed Authority (ISA/ISBA) (1994–2010)
International Whaling Commission (IWhale) (1950–2010)
Permanent Court of Arbitration (PCA) (1950–2010)
World Customs Organization (1950–2010)
World Trade Organization (WTO) (1995–2010)

Part II: Variables

International Authority

We conceive IO authority as comprised of delegation and pooling. States may *delegate* authority to independent non-state bodies which set the agenda, oversee implementation, and monitor compliance. The extent of delegation depends on (a) the degree to which an IO body is independent of member states, (b) its role in the decision-making process, and (c) the range of decision areas in which there is delegation.

States may *pool* authority in a collective body that makes joint decisions on behalf of its members. The extent of pooling depends on (a) how majoritarian decision rules are in interstate bodies, (b) the bindingness of their decisions, (c) the conditions under which they come into effect, and (d) the range of decision areas that are pooled.

Appendix

Delegation and pooling along with their components are explained in the Measure of International Authority (MIA) dataset (Hooghe et al. 2017: ch. 3). The time series ranges from 1950 (or the date of creation) to 2010 (or date of abolition).[2]

Measuring Delegation

The variable *Delegation* is an annual measure of the allocation of authoritative competences to non-state bodies in an IO's decision-making process. We distinguish between political delegation in agenda setting and final decision making, and judicial delegation in dispute settlement.

Political delegation is assessed

- in one or more IO bodies (assemblies, executives, general secretariats, consultative bodies) that are
- partially or fully composed of non-member state actors, which
- exercise or co-exercise authority over agenda setting or final decision making
- in one or more of six decision areas: membership accession, membership suspension, constitutional reform, budgetary allocation, financial non-compliance, and up to five streams of policy making.

Judicial delegation is the conditional transfer of authority to courts, arbitrators, or tribunals. It is assessed with items that tap how obligatory and independent third-party dispute settlement is, how binding it is, whether there is a standing tribunal, who has access, whether there is a remedy for non-compliance, and whether the tribunal can make compulsory preliminary rulings.

Scoring an IO on Delegation is as follows:

1. Each IO body receives a composition score for the degree to which it is non-state (on a zero to 1 scale). This is assessed using explicit criteria for the extent to which the body is partially or wholly composed of representatives who are (a) not part of the national executive (e.g. national parliaments, trade unions, indigenous groups, courts), or (b) operate under an explicit norm of independence.
2. Agenda setting. Composition scores are averaged for all non-state bodies that participate in agenda setting in each decision area. This produces an *agenda-setting score* for each of six decision areas.
3. Final decision. Composition scores are calculated for all non-state bodies that participate in the final decision in each decision area. The *final decision score* for each decision area is the score of the body with the highest (i.e. most non-state) composition score.[3]
4. Dispute settlement. If an IO has more than one dispute settlement mechanism, we select the one with the highest composition score.

---

[2] An update with estimates through 2020 will be released in 2021.
[3] Whereas delegation in agenda setting is estimated as an average effect, scoring for final decision making is targeted at the most supranational body.

Appendix

5. We now have three scores for each decision area: an *agenda-setting score*, a *final decision score*, and a *dispute settlement score*. The average of these scores is the delegation score for a decision area.
6. The *delegation score* for an IO is the average of the delegation scores across the six decision areas.

Measuring Pooling

Pooling estimates the extent to which member states share authority in collective decision making. We assess pooling

- in one or more IO assemblies and/or IO executives,
- in which member states collectively set the agenda and make final decisions
- by jointly deciding under some voting rule with some degree of bindingness and/or requiring some form of ratification
- in one or more of six decision areas: membership accession, membership suspension, constitutional reform, budgetary allocation, financial compliance, and up to five streams of policy making.

Scoring an IO on Pooling is as follows:

1. IO bodies whose membership is chiefly or fully selected by member states are identified as state-dominated bodies at the agenda-setting stage and the final decision-making stage for each decision area.
2. Each of these state-dominated bodies receives a voting score in agenda setting and in the final decision for each decision area. Scores range from 0 (national veto) to 1 (simple majority).
3. A weighting factor for bindingness and for ratification is calculated for each decision area and applied to the voting score.
4. Agenda setting. For each decision area weighted voting scores are averaged for all state-dominated bodies that participate in agenda setting. This produces an *agenda-setting score* for each decision area.
5. Final decision. In each decision area the body with the lowest (i.e. least majoritarian) weighted voting score is identified. This produces a *final decision score* for each decision area.[4]
6. We now have two scores for each decision area: an *agenda-setting score* and a *final decision score*. The average of these scores is the pooling score for each decision area.
7. The *pooling score* for an IO is the average of the pooling scores across the six decision areas.

---

[4] Whereas we identify all bodies that are involved in agenda setting, we identify the most intergovernmental body in the final decision as the barrier over which decision making must pass.

Appendix

Discussion

Delegation and pooling can be estimated as summated rating scales or as latent factors. Summated rating scales have the virtue of being unaffected by the composition of the sample. Factor analysis uses the available information more efficiently by weighting each indicator according to its contribution to the score for a given IO.

Table A.4 reports a principal components analysis (PCA) yielding two latent variables with eigenvalues greater than unity corresponding to delegation and pooling. These latent variables capture the bulk of the variance, 61 percent, in twelve indicators. There is no meaningful statistical difference between using factors or additive scales. The additive index is very highly correlated with the comparable predicted components from the PCA analysis. Table A.5 reports the correlation matrix for these factors and additive scales for delegation and pooling across the six decision areas. The Cronbach's alpha for the additive scale for pooling is 0.80 and for delegation it is 0.92, indicating high internal consistency. Tables A.6 and A.7 provide summary statistics for the components of delegation and pooling for the seventy-six IOs in the dataset from 1950 to 2010.

Table A.4. Principal components factor analysis of delegation and pooling

Components	Two-factor solution	
	Delegation	Pooling
Delegation in accession	**0.421**	−0.035
Delegation in suspension	**0.380**	0.043
Delegation in constitutional reform	**0.440**	−0.031
Delegation in budgetary allocation	**0.413**	−0.026
Delegation in financial compliance	**0.343**	0.063
Delegation in policy making	**0.421**	−0.022
Pooling in accession	0.003	**0.421**
Pooling in suspension	0.061	**0.376**
Pooling in constitutional reform	−0.007	**0.405**
Pooling in budgetary allocation	−0.127	**0.443**
Pooling in financial compliance	−0.021	**0.471**
Pooling in policy making	0.027	**0.301**
Eigenvalue	4.31	3.04
Explained variance (%)	0.36	0.25

Note: Principal components factor analysis, promax rotation, listwise deletion. N = 3,292 IO-years (all 76 IOs between 1950 or establishment to 2010). The highest score for each dimension is in bold.

Table A.5. Correlation matrix of delegation and pooling

	Delegation (additive)	Delegation (PCA)	Pooling (additive)	Pooling (PCA)
Delegation (additive scale)	1			
Delegation (PCA)	0.999	1		
Pooling (additive scale)	0.243	0.253	1	
Pooling (PCA)	0.235	0.275	0.997	1

Note: N = 3,292 IO-years.

Appendix

Table A.6. Descriptives for delegation

Indicator	Mean	Median	Coefficient of variation	Min	Max	Q25	Q75
Delegation by decision area							
Delegation on accession	0.140	0.143	1.147	0	0.778	0	0.191
Delegation on suspension	0.108	0.119	1.133	0	0.643	0	0.167
Delegation on constitutional reform	0.128	0.119	1.131	0	0.644	0	0.167
Delegation on budgetary allocation	0.318	0.333	0.626	0	1	0.167	0.443
Delegation on financial compliance	0.132	0.143	1.138	0	0.667	0	0.179
Delegation on policy making	0.270	0.254	0.641	0	0.933	0.167	0.364
Delegation by decision stage							
Agenda setting	0.231	0.208	0.642	0	0.708	0.139	0.333
Final decision	0.047	0	2.301	0	0.550	0	0
Dispute settlement	0.270	0.286	1.085	0	1	0	0.500
DELEGATION	0.183	0.175	0.731	0	0.652	0.061	0.260

Note: N = 3,292 IO-years.

Table A.7. Descriptives for pooling

Indicator	Mean	Median	Coefficient of variation	Min	Max	Q25	Q75
Pooling by decision area							
Pooling on accession	0.351	0.330	0.697	0	1	0.125	0.500
Pooling on suspension	0.169	0	1.513	0	1	0	0.330
Pooling on constitutional reform	0.200	0.165	0.985	0	0.750	0.041	0.330
Pooling on budgetary allocation	0.442	0.330	0.715	0	1	0.165	0.660
Pooling on financial compliance	0.299	0.165	1.099	0	1	0	0.580
Pooling on policy making	0.312	0.250	0.691	0	1	0.165	0.375
Pooling by decision stage							
Agenda setting	0.253	0.221	0.749	0	0.749	0.083	0.375
Final decision	0.338	0.304	0.617	0	0.790	0.179	0.540
POOLING	0.295	0.292	0.631	0	0.728	0.138	0.447

Note: N = 3,292 IO-years.

Both delegation and pooling are lowest in membership suspension, constitutional reform, and financial compliance—three decision areas in which national sovereignty is deeply implicated. Conversely, delegation and pooling are strongest in budgetary allocation and relatively strong in policy making, the two decision areas most closely related to day-to-day operations. The sole marked difference concerns membership accession, where pooling among member states is relatively high but delegation to non-state bodies is relatively low.

Overall, there is slightly more variation in delegation than in pooling, as the coefficient of variation in the third column reveals. The coefficient of variation is a more useful measure of spread because it summarizes variability relative to the mean of the

Appendix

distribution. Interestingly, decision areas and decision stages with the lowest mean tend to have the largest coefficients of variation. Variation among IOs is relatively large for those components of authority which affect national sovereignty most severely.

Policy Scope

The policy scope of an IO—its policy portfolio—is a key element of an IO's basic set-up (see Chapter 4). We seek to understand what drives change in the policy portfolio over time in Chapter 5. This, in turn, affects an IO's international authority, as explained in Chapter 6.

Our measure of an IO's policy scope is annual, and distinguishes between core and flanking policies. The data are available in the MIA dataset.

The scope of an IO's portfolio is assessed across a list of twenty-five policies (Table A.8). This is more fine-grained than classifications of an IO's mandate, such as the three-way distinction between economic, security, and multi-issue IOs in the Correlates of War dataset (Boehmer, Gartzke, and Nordstrom 2004). It covers more IOs, and includes more policies than measures developed for regional organizations (see e.g. Balassa 1961; Haftel 2013), security IOs (Haftel and Hofmann 2017), or IO legislative output (Lundgren, Squatrito, and Tallberg 2018).

In constructing a dictionary for policy categories, we draw from extant policy dictionaries (such as the Comparative Agenda project), case studies of international organizations and agreements, and IO documentation.

Table A.8. Policy categories

1. Agriculture
2. Competition policy, mergers, state aid, antitrust
3. Culture and media
4. Education (primary, secondary, tertiary), vocational training, youth
5. Development, aid to poor countries
6. Financial regulation, banking regulation, monetary policy, currency
7. Welfare state services, employment policy, social affairs, pension systems
8. Energy (coal, oil, nuclear, wind, water, solar)
9. Environment: pollution, natural habitat, endangered species
10. Financial stabilization, lending to countries in difficulty
11. Foreign policy, diplomacy, political cooperation
12. Fisheries and maritime affairs
13. Health: public health, food safety, nutrition
14. Humanitarian aid (natural or man-made disasters)
15. Human rights: social & labor rights, democracy, rule of law, non-discrimination, election monitoring
16. Industrial policy (including manufacturing, SMEs, tourism)
17. Justice, home affairs, interior security, police, anti-terrorism
18. Migration, immigration, asylum, refugees
19. Military cooperation, defense, military security
20. Regional policy, regional development, poverty reduction
21. Research policy, research programming, science
22. Taxation, fiscal policy coordination, macro-economic policy coordination
23. Telecommunications, internet, postal services
24. Trade, customs, tariffs, intellectual property rights/patents
25. Transport: railways, air traffic, shipping, roads

Appendix

An IO policy meets two general criteria. First, it is a multilateral policy administered by the IO rather than an aggregation of bilateral policies among the member states. The Association of South East Asian Nations (ASEAN) provides an example. From 2000, ASEAN countries began to coordinate their management of regional short-term liquidity problems by setting up bilateral swap arrangements—the so-called Chian Mai Initiative. We consider "financial stabilization and lending to countries in difficulty" as part of the policy portfolio of ASEAN only from March 2010, when the Chiang Mai Initiative Multilateralization (CMIM) Agreement became a multilateral policy administered by ASEAN.

The second criterion is that the policy is institutionalized. This requires a tangible legal, financial, or organizational footprint—not merely declarations of intent—evidenced in documentation, e.g. treaties, protocols, declarations, constitutions, framework legislation, budgetary documents, or white papers.

Policy scope is assessed at each reform moment of an IO, i.e. at the time of a treaty revision, new protocol or convention, the passing of framework legislation, or the creation of a new IO body or instrument.

The following eight indicators are designed to tap whether there is tangible evidence that an IO's portfolio encompasses a particular policy:

- The policy features in the name of the organization;
- The policy is highlighted as a central purpose of the IO in the opening paragraphs of its foundational contract;
- The policy is the primary subject of a separate treaty section;
- The policy is the primary subject of an annex, a protocol, a convention, or an agreement;
- The policy is explicitly tied to budgetary resources in a convention, constitution, protocol, annexes, or ancillary document;
- The policy is the primary subject of an (actually existing) IO instrumen: agency, fund, directorate, or tribunal;
- The policy is the primary subject of an (actually existing) IO intergovernmental committee, council, working group or equivalent;
- The policy features as the functional specialization of the national representatives who sign the IO's foundational document.

These indicators assess policy scope at foundation and following institutional reform. For recent decades, in particular, one can often find valuable information on the IO's website, from NGOs, and from academics monitoring the IO.

In estimating the portfolio, we distinguish between core policies and flanking policies. Table A.9 provides descriptives.

- A policy is conceived as *core* when it meets three or more of the above criteria. A core policy is very often prominent in the name of the organization or in the opening paragraphs of the foundational contract.
- A policy is considered *flanking* when it meets two criteria. *Policy scope* is the unweighted sum of core and flanking policies.

Appendix

Table A.9. Descriptives for policy scope, core, flanking policies

Indicator	Mean	Median	Coefficient of variation	Min	Max	Q25	Q75
Policy scope (core + flanking)	5.689	3	0.875	1	24	2	9
Core policies	2.002	2	0.642	1	10	1	3
Flanking policies	3.685	2	1.072	0	16	1	6

Note: N = 3,292 IO-years.

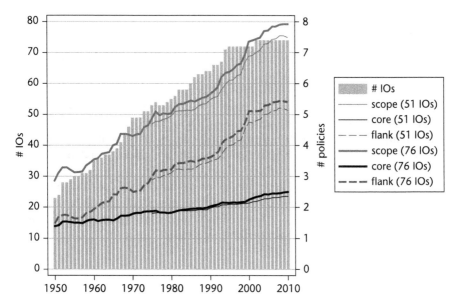

Figure A.1 Policy scope over time

Note: Thin lines trace the development of the average IO in the dataset since 1975 (N = 51); thick lines trace the development of the average IO in a given year (with a varying number of IOs from an overall sample of 76 IOs).

The coding was a joint exercise by the three authors of this book. We began by coding a subset of IOs for the year 2010 before revising the coding scheme for all seventy-six IOs at the time of an IO's establishment or 1950 (if later) and 2010 (or the final year the IO appears in the dataset). We then identified intervening reform moments (treaty revisions, framework legislation, creation of new organizations such as a fund, court, or major council or committee). The coding procedure can be described as "interpretation through dialogue" (Hooghe et al. 2016: 27–30 and Hooghe et al. 2017: 31–2).

Figure A.1 displays policy scope over time. The thin lines plot average policy scope, average core policies, and average flanking policies for the fifty-one IOs for which we have continuous data since 1975. The thick lines track average scope, core, and flanking policies for all IOs in the dataset in a given year. The number of IOs varies from twenty-three in 1950 to fifty-three in 1975 and seventy-four in 2010. The shaded bars track the growth in the number of IOs over time.

Appendix

Three patterns can be discerned. First, IOs have seen a secular expansion of their policy portfolios, from an average of 2.9 policies in 1950 to eight policies in 2010 (light-gray solid line). Second, there is less movement in IOs' core policies over time, from an average of 1.4 core policies in 1950 to 2.5 in 2010. Third, and by implication, the dynamism in an IO's policy portfolio derives mostly from adding flanking policies, as revealed by the broken line in the figure. Interestingly, these trends are relatively similar for both the overall sample of seventy-six IOs and for the consistent sample of fifty-one IOs since 1975.

Community

Community is operationalized as the extent to which the member states of an IO have similar or dissimilar cultural, political, and legal institutions.[5] This follows Deutsch's (1966 [1953]) pluralistic understanding of community as expressed across diverse social, cultural, and political fields. Hence it would make sense to tap community with a range of factors, including individual and elite perceptions; the extent of networking within a group; its boundedness; territorial cohesion; the ways of life of group members; their cultural, religious, and linguistic homogeneity; and the history of conflict between the group and others.

Data limitations are severe. Public opinion surveys have partial coverage and are not available over the entire period of this study. Surveys of elite norms are yet more limited. However, we can draw on institutional, cultural, and geographical indicators to estimate overarching norms across IO member states.

Indicators for Community

Community is composed as follows:

- *Culture*: To what extent do the IO's member states belong to the same civilization? A state is categorized in one of nine civilizations according to the largest share of its population: Western, Latin American, Hindu, Slavic Orthodox, Islamic, African, Sinic, Buddhist, or lone culture (Huntington 1996, applied by Russett, Oneil, and Cox 2000).

- *Religion*: To what extent do the populations of an IO's member states share a religious affiliation? A state is categorized in one of eleven categories following the religious affiliation of the largest share of its population as atheist, Buddhist, Catholic, Hindu, indigenous/animist, Jewish, Orthodox, Protestant, Shia, Sunni, or Taoist (CIA World Factbook).[6]

---

[5] We treat indicators of economic interest and foreign policy position separately as alternative explanations. These include *GDP dispersion*, measured as the coefficient of variation in GDP among an IO's members in a given year; three measures of trade interdependence (discussed below); and *Ideal points*, measured as the average absolute distance between dyads of IO members in how they vote in the UN assembly in a given year. The correlation of *Community* with *GDP dispersion* is 0.15; with *Ideal points* it is −0.72; and with measures of trade interdependence it ranges between −0.18 and −0.01 for the relevant subset of IOs. *Community* is robustly significant in models that control for these variables.

[6] Available at https://www.cia.gov/library/publications/resources/the-world-factbook/index.html.

- *Political regime*: How similar are the political regimes of an IO's member states? The *Polity2* measure scores the democratic and authoritarian character of a regime by assessing the competitiveness and regulation of political participation, the competitiveness of executive recruitment, and constraints on the chief executive (Marshall, Gurr, and Jaggers 2017). Scores are annual.
- *Legal tradition*: To what extent do an IO's member states have a common legal tradition? A state's domestic legal system is categorized as civil, common law, Islamic, or mixed (two or more systems coexist) (Mitchell and Powell 2009, 2011).
- *Geography*: To what extent are an IO's member states located in the same world region? A state is located in one of nine regions: Africa, Middle East, South Asia, East Asia, Oceania, Europe, North America, Central America, or South America (Shanks, Jacobson, and Kaplan 1996).

Political regime is estimated as the standard deviation among member states of an IO in a given year. All other indicators apply Rae's index of fractionalization, which was developed to estimate the extent to which a parliament is fragmented into political parties (Rae 1967).

$$1 - \sum_{i=1}^{m} s_i^2$$

where S_i is the share of a group in a population, and m refers to the number of groups represented in the population. The measure takes into account the relative size as well as the number of parties. Hence a parliament divided into nine groups with one group holding 50 percent of the seats has a smaller fractionalization index (0.72) than one with nine equally sized groups (0.89).

We use principal components analysis to estimate the common component, *Community*, and multiply by −1 to achieve commonality. Table A.10 shows that these indicators are highly correlated. The standardized alpha is 0.943, and the common factor accounts for 79 percent of the variance of the indicators (see Table 5.2). Dropping one or several criteria does not meaningfully weaken the alpha or the index.[7]

Table A.10. Correlation matrix of indicators of community

	Community	Culture	Religion	Political regime	Legal tradition
Community (factor)	1.000				
Culture	0.953	1.000			
Religion	0.890	0.859	1.000		
Political regime	0.795	0.709	0.576	1.000	
Legal tradition	0.920	0.836	0.842	0.642	1.000
Geography	0.885	0.817	0.678	0.678	0.766

Note: N = 3,279 IO-years.

---

[7] Our results are robust across alternative operationalizations that (a) merge Catholic and Protestant in the *Religion* variable; (b) allocate mixed systems of *Legal tradition* to its nearest substantive equivalent (civil, common law, or Islamic); or (c) combine the three American regions (North, Central, South) into a single region and the two Asian regions (East and South) into a single region.

Appendix

Historical Ties

We operationalize community along a second track using indicators of a common political history. A common political history can leave a residue of shared norms that survive the break-up of the polity even if divorce comes through war.

Historical ties is a dichotomous variable where an IO has a value of 1 if at least two-thirds of its founding member states share a history of membership within a federation or within a colonial empire that meets the following criteria: the political (con)federation or colonial empire endured for at least twenty years, and it was in existence no more than fifty years prior to the creation of the IO. Table A.11 lists the fifteen IOs that meet one of these criteria.

Table A.11. Historical ties among IO founding members

IO name	End of ties	IO creation	Description of historical ties
Arab Maghreb Union (AMU)	±1960	1989	4 of 5 founding members are former French colonies
Benelux	1839 ongoing	1944	federation between 1815 and 1839; BLEU: Belgium-Lux economic & monetary union (from 1922)
CABI international	±1960	1987	former British colonies
Caribbean Community (CARICOM)	1962	1968	former British colonies; former West Indies Federation (1958–62)
Central American Integration System (SICA)	1922	1952	Federal republic of Central America (1823–41); five short-lived attempts, most recently the Federation of Central America (1921–2)
Commonwealth of Independent states (CIS)	1991	1992	former members of the Soviet Union federation
Commonwealth of Nations	±1960	1965	former subjects of the British colonial empire
Common Market for Eastern and Southern Africa (COMESA)	±1960	1982	8 of 12 founding members are former British colonies
East African Community I (EAC1)	1961–7	1967, 1993	former British colonies (until 1961); East African High Commission (EAHC) (1948–61); East African Common Services Organization (EACSO) (1961–67)
East African Community II (EAC2)	1961–7	1993	see EAC1
Economic and Monetary Union of Central African States (CEMAC)	1958	1966	former French colonies; Federation of Equatorial French Africa (AEF) (1910–58)
Gulf Cooperation Council (GCC)	1971	1981	4 of 6 founding members are former British colonies
Intergovernmental Authority on Development (IGAD)	±1960	1986	4 of 6 founding members are former British colonies
Nordic Council	1905	1952	colonial/confederal ties: Sweden–Finland (1150–1809); Norway–Denmark (1524–1814); Norway–Sweden (1814–1905); Denmark–Iceland (1524–1944)
Organization of Eastern Caribbean States (OECS)	1962	1968	former British colonies; former West Indies Federation (1958–62)
Pacific Islands Forum (PIF)	±1965	1973	5 of 7 founding members are former British colonies (2 other founding members are former colonies of New Zealand, itself founding member)

Appendix

A more inclusive operationalization of historical ties, *Historical ties extended*, adds a third criterion inspired by idealist theories of international cooperation: the presence of a pan-national movement that champions transnational political union and which has substantial support in at least two-thirds of the founding members of an IO. This applies to four additional IOs: the European Union (pan-Europeanism), the Organization of American States (pan-Americanism), the African Union (pan-Africanism), and the League of Arab States (pan-Arabism).[8]

Community and *Historical ties* are alternative measures of the institutional fabric of a community and produce similar results (see online Appendix).

IO Contract

An IO's contract is a key element in its basic set-up (see Chapter 4) and affects the development of the IO's policy portfolio (see Chapter 5) and, indirectly, the IO's authority (see Chapter 6).

All international organizations are incomplete contracts, but their degree of incompleteness varies. Whereas some IOs, such as NAFTA, spell out a narrow range of commitments in considerable detail, others, such as the European Union or the Economic Community of West African States, entail diffuse commitments for general purpose governance. An IO with a highly incomplete contract can more easily adjust to the uncertainties of the world, but incomplete contracting also increases the scope for contending interpretation and this can fester into non-compliance (Ostrom 1990: 88). A relatively complete contract impedes an IO's capacity to adapt to changing circumstance, but it also draws explicit boundaries around its member states' commitments. Hence, an IO's contract tells one something important about how an IO may develop over time, which we test in Chapters 5 and 6.

Contract is a dichotomous variable where a *complete* contract for a fixed purpose for inter-state cooperation under clearly specified conditions takes the value of 1, and an *incomplete* contract expressing an open-ended purpose among governments and peoples takes a value of 2. Some examples clarify the coding.

A contract that specifies a free trade agreement normally falls into the first category. For example, the Dickinson Bay agreement establishing the Caribbean Free Trade Organization (CARIFTA) specifically limits cooperation to free trade: "AWARE that the broadening of domestic markets through the elimination of barriers to trade between the territories is a prerequisite to [full employment and improved living standards]; CONVINCED that such elimination of barriers to trade can best be achieved by the immediate establishment of a Free Trade Economic Community for all the countries who so desire" (Preamble). The Latin American Free Trade Association also articulates a specific goal: "By the present Treaty, the Contracting Parties establish a free-trade-zone" (Art. 1, 1960 Montevideo Treaty). It delineates a program of trade

---

[8] Whereas the coding for *Community* and *Historical ties* relies on well-established facts, that for *Historical ties extended* is contestable. Perhaps the most contestable decision is the exclusion of the Council of Europe (CoE). Pan-Europeanism was present in the immediate postwar period in several CoE countries, though only among influential minorities.

151

Appendix

liberalization requiring periodic negotiations between member states, the removal of tariffs based on national and common lists, and detailed flanking measures in industry, tax policy, and agriculture.

IOs that organize collaboration in a sector or for a policy problem tend also to have a relatively complete contract. The objective of the Organization of Arab Petroleum Export Countries (OAPEC) is clearly specified: "The principal aim of the Organization shall be the co-ordination and unification of the petroleum policies of Member Countries" (1968 OAPEC Agreement), and its rules and regulations are designed to cover all exigencies. Similarly, the World Customs Organization characterizes its mission as one to "improve the effectiveness and the efficiency of its Member Customs administrations across the globe, and to help them fulfill their dual role of facilitating trade whilst ensuring its security" (WCO 2009/10: 1).[9] The 1950 Convention—never amended—uses a few more words in its preamble to express the same goal, and it goes on in Article III to detail the eight tasks delegated to the Council.

Incomplete contracts commit states to broad-ranging cooperation that is only weakly specified. Economic unions would typically fall into this category. An economic union is less specific with regard to its objectives and means than an IO limited to customs cooperation or free trade. The central goal of Benelux was to establish an economic union (1958 Treaty establishing the Benelux Economic Union). Its preamble translates this into three broadly worded purposes: "to strengthen the economic ties between their countries by means of free movement of persons, goods, capital and services"; "to co-ordinate their policies in the economic, financial and social fields in order to attain the most satisfactory level of employment and the highest standard of living"; "to pursue a joint trade policy...by means of the freeest possible trade."

The Shanghai Cooperation Organization (SCO) has broad-ranging goals that range from the purpose to "facilitate comprehensive and balanced economic growth, social and cultural development in the region through joint action on the basis of equal partnership" to "consolidate multidisciplinary cooperation in the maintenance and strengthening of peace, security and stability in the region" (SCO Charter, Art. 1).

Incomplete contracts usually engage people as well as governments. They commit states to a vague purpose—e.g. a "community of peoples" or "ever closer union"—though the means are left open. Cooperation is framed as an evolutionary process that is revealed only over time. The idiomatic case is the European Union along with its predecessors. Successive treaties state the EU's purpose as open-ended. The preamble to the ECSC Treaty reads as follows: "RESOLVED to substitute for historic rivalries a fusion of their essential interests; to establish, by creating an economic community, the foundation of a broad and independent community among peoples long divided by bloody conflicts; and to lay the bases of institutions capable of giving direction to their future common destiny." The latter phrase was refined as "an ever closer union" with the 1957 Rome Treaty. The 2009 Lisbon Treaty reads as follows: "RESOLVED to continue the process of creating an ever closer union among the peoples of Europe, in

---

[9] WCO (2009/10). "World Customs Organization: Mission, Objectives, Activities." Brussels: WCO. Available at http://www.wcoomd.org/en/about-us/what-is-the-wco.aspx (accessed February 20, 2019).

Appendix

which decisions are taken as closely as possible to the citizen in accordance with the principle of subsidiarity."

A lexicon of key terms is applied to categorize the contract of an IO. These are normally found in the preamble and in the first sections of the IO contract.

We applied the coding schema initially to the foundational treaties of thirty-five regional organizations (Marks et al. 2014) and then compared these scores with those of two independent researchers familiar with the study's concepts who each coded thirteen randomly chosen IOs. They agreed on all but one score, producing a Krippendorff's alpha of 0.78.[10] We then implemented the coding, using the same lexicon, to all seventy-six IOs. An online Appendix contains text supporting our estimates.

IOs tend to have stable contracts, but it is not impossible for an IO to redraw its contract. Three IOs moved from a relatively complete to an incomplete contract. The Benelux's original contract, the Customs Convention of 1944 was short, concise in language, and focused on a single goal: a customs union. Its successor, the Benelux Economic Union of 1958, opened the door for broader interstate collaboration by linking economic and social goals: "believing economic progress, forming the principal aim of their union, must lead to the advancement of the individual and social welfare of their peoples" (1958 Treaty Establishing the Benelux Economic Union, preamble). CARICOM began in 1965 as a free trade association (CARIFTA) with a relatively complete contract, but in 1973 the member states upgraded the purpose to a common market, broadened collaboration to social, cultural, educational, and technological fields, and tellingly, renamed the IO into the Caribbean Community. And finally, the Intergovernmental Authority on Drought and Development (IGADD) began life as an IO for combating drought and desertification in the Sahel. In 1996, it became the Intergovernmental Authority on Development (IGAD) with an incomplete contract that sets out diffuse goals for economic, social, and political cooperation (Art. 7).

Politicization

Politicization is a function of the salience and divisiveness of debate concerning an IO. We adapt Tallberg et al. (2014) who tap media coverage in the LexisNexis database for protests and demonstrations directed at an IO. The estimate is the annual raw count of mentions that combine "PROTESTOR" or "DEMONSTRATOR" with the IO name. We use a three-year equally weighted moving average for the raw count at t, t_{-1}, and t_{-2} to smooth the series.[11]

The base line search segment in the "Build Your Own Segment Search" in LexisNexis, reads

"organization name" OR "organization acronym" w/p demonstrator OR protestor OR protester

---

[10] Krippendorff's alpha measures agreement among coders and ranges from 0, which indicates no agreement beyond chance, to 1, which indicates agreement without exceptions.
[11] We use LexisNexis' default "Major World Publications" going back to 1948. The moving average is divided by 100 for ease of interpretation.

153

Appendix

There are several possible sources of measurement error. One is when a valid reference may refer only to a protest involving a constituent body of an IO. Here we descend a level of analysis to the component bodies and modify the baseline search segment to include an IO's component bodies. An additional issue is that some IOs have acronyms that can also refer to something other than the organization. There are also more general concerns related to the fact that the newspapers covered in LexisNexis vary over time and appear biased to those in the West, particularly in the early years.

This measure is correlated at 0.75 with an estimate of the salience of an IO, which was derived from a count of references to the IO in Google scholar. To minimize error, the search was set to cover publications dated between 2000 and 2014, and to search the organization's official name and acronyms with the "exact phrase" algorithm. Miscategorized references were removed after a manual check of each reference.[12]

Discussion

Politicization is highly skewed towards a small number of IOs as Tables A.12 and A.13 reveal. For the 3,292 IO-years in our sample, the median observation is zero. While all but twenty-three IOs have been subject to protests or demonstrations that are picked up in the data, 96.6 percent of all references are skewed to twenty-four IOs. Figure A.2 plots politicization for fifty-three IOs that have a positive score on a log10 scale. It shows that politicization exceeds five references annually for ten IOs, in descending order: WTO, UN, APEC, EU, NATO, IMF, World Bank, International Criminal Court, ASEAN, and NAFTA.

Figure A.3 shows that politicization picks up from the early 1990s, peaks around 2000, then declines to a level that is still three times higher than in the 1990s. The data series underestimates politicization prior to 1980 when LexisNexis newspaper coverage was spottier. Even granting this, it is clear that there has been a sharp upward shift in recent decades. It is interesting to note that the age of an IO is a weak predictor of its politicization ($r = 0.11$). The average age of IOs without politicization is not much lower than that for IOs with very frequent politicization.

Table A.12. Descriptives for politicization

Indicator	Mean	Median	Coefficient of variation	Min	Max	Q25	Q75	N
Politicization (annual)	6.83	0	6.56	0	746	0	0	3292
Politicization (moving average)	6.47	0	5.91	0	565	0	0	3288

Note: annual observations or three-year moving averages for 76 IOs from 1950 to 2010. Raw counts of mentions in LexisNexis.

---

[12] For IOs with a large number of references, the first hundred and last hundred cites were manually examined to calculate the proportion of valid references. The total number of references for this IO was weighted with this proportion to estimate the total number of valid references for this IO.

Appendix

Table A.13. Incidence of politicization

Incidence of politicization	# IOs	Average age of IO (years)	Average politicization (moving average)	Median politicization (moving average)
No politicization	23	43.7	0	0
Infrequent (1 to 4 years in an IO's existence)	13	39.8	0.04	0.03
Relatively frequent (5 to 14 years in an IO's existence)	16	35.9	1.13	0.23
Very frequent (15 years or more in an IO's existence)	24	50.8	22.57	2.24
Total	76	43.6	7.37	0.08

Note: three-year moving averages for 76 IOs from 1950 to 2010. Raw counts on politicization.

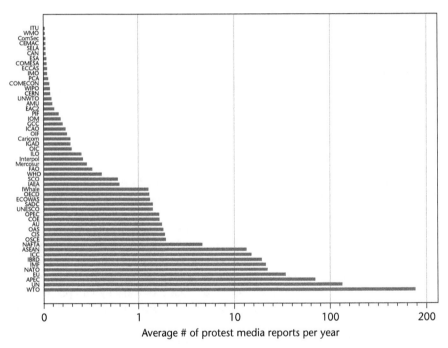

Figure A.2 Average annual politicization by IO

Note: 53 IOs with non-zero politicization (1950–2010). Average annual politicization is estimated as politicization divided by the number of years in the dataset. The X-axis is a log-scale.

Appendix

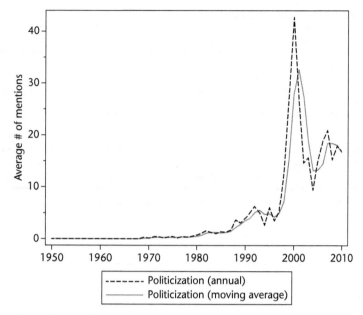

Figure A.3 Trends in politicization

Note: annual observations or three-year moving averages for 76 IOs for 1950–2010. Raw counts of references in LexisNexis.

Trade Interdependence

The literature on trade refers to several measures of trade interdependence. We use three commonly used measures which cover a reasonably long period for all IO member states: intra-IO trade share, trade intensity, and trade introversion. Intra-IO trade share is the simplest and serves as the building block for the remaining indices.

Bilateral trade data and data for some regional trade organizations are regularly published by international organizations. The most comprehensive data come from the UN COMTRADE Database. We begin the series from 1970, when trade data become reasonably complete. We use algorithms kindly made available by Philippe de Lombaerde at the Institute on Comparative Regional Integration Studies of the United Nations University in Bruges (UNU-CRIS).

Intra-IO trade share is calculated using the following formula:

$$ITS_{i,t} = \frac{IT_{i,t}}{T_{i,t}} \times 100$$

where:
$IT_{i,t}$ denotes an IO i's intra-IO trade in year t,
$T_{i,t}$ denotes an IO i's total trade in year t (i's total imports plus total exports).
The value ranges from 0 to 100. This indicator reflects the importance of intra-IO trade (i.e. trade interdependence among member states) of a particular international organization in its overall trade.

Appendix

Trade intensity relates intra-IO trade share to the size of world trade. In its simplest form, it is equal to the ratio of an IO's intra-IO trade share and its share of world trade. It is calculated using the following formula:

$$ITII_{i,t} = \frac{\left(\frac{IT_{i,t}}{T_{i,t}}\right)}{\left(\frac{T_{i,t}}{T_{w,t}}\right)}$$

where:
$IT_{i,t}$ denotes IO i's intra-IO trade in year t,
$T_{i,t}$ denotes IO i's total trade in year t (i's total imports plus total exports),
$T_{w,t}$ denotes the world's total trade in year t (world's total imports plus total exports).

The value ranges from 0 to $\frac{T_{w,t}}{T_{i,t}}$.
This value is:

- equal to zero in the case of no intra-IO trade;
- equal to 1 if the organization's weight in its own trade is equal to its weight in world trade (geographic neutrality);
- higher than 1 if intra-IO trade is relatively more important than trade flows with the rest of the world;
- equal to the reciprocal of the organization's share in world trade when all trade is intra-IO (no extra-IO trade)—that is, the maximum value of the ITII index is the higher the smaller the organization's total trade.

Trade intensity's minimum value is zero, and there is no set maximum value.

Trade introversion compares the relative size an IO's internal trade and its external trade, and it rises (falls) only if the intensity of intra-IO trade grows more (less) rapidly than the intensity of extra-IO trade. It is defined as follows:

$$STJ_{i,t} = \frac{\frac{HITI_{i,t}}{HETI_{i,t}} - 1}{\frac{HITI_{i,t}}{HETI_{i,t}} + 1} = \left(HITI_{i,t} - HETI_{i,t}\right) \Big/ \left(HITI_{i,t} + HETI_{i,t}\right)$$

with $HITI_{i,t}$ a homogeneous version of the intra-IO trade intensity index, the maximum value of which is independent from the IO i's trade size. Its denominator is not the organization i's share in world trade, but its share in the trade of the rest of the world:

$$HITI_{i,t} = \frac{\left(\frac{IT_{i,t}}{T_{i,t}}\right)}{\left(\frac{ET_{i,t}}{T_{w,t} - IT_{i,t}}\right)}$$

HETI (homogeneous extra-IO trade intensity index) is the complementary indicator of HITI. It is defined for IO i as:

$$HETI_{i,t} = \frac{1 - \left(\frac{IT_{i,t}}{T_{i,t}}\right)}{1 - \left(\frac{ET_{i,t}}{T_{w,t} - IT_{i,t}}\right)}$$

where:
$IT_{i,t}$ denotes organization i's intra-IO trade in year t,
$ET_{i,t}$ denotes organization i's extra-IO trade in year t,

Appendix

Table A.14. Correlations among measures of trade interdependence

	Intra-IO trade share	Trade intensity
Trade intensity	−0.025	
	(p = 0.433)	
Trade introversion	0.136	0.216
	(p = 0.000)	(p = 0.000)

Note: N = 34 IOs from 1970 to 2010 (1,013 IO-years).

Table A.15. Descriptives for trade interdependence

Indicator	Mean	Median	Coefficient of variation	Min	Max	Q25	Q75
Intra-IO trade	15.92	9.93	1.06	0.04	72.12	5.18	18.18
Trade intensity	56.47	5.13	4.73	0.25	5228.30	2.21	18.19
Trade introversion	0.68	0.76	0.52	−0.60	1.00	0.62	0.92

Note: N = 34 IOs from 1970 to 2010 (1,013 IO-years).

$T_{i,t}$ denotes organization i's total trade in year t (i's total imports plus total exports), $T_{w,t}$ denotes the world's total trade in year t (the world's total imports plus total exports).

The index for *Trade introversion* is:

- equal to −1 in the case of no intra-IO trade;
- equal to zero if the organization's weight in its own trade is equal to its weight in the trade of the rest of the world (geographic neutrality);
- equal to 1 in the case of no extra-IO trade.

The value for *Trade introversion* ranges from −1 to +1.

In theory, it is possible to calculate these indices for each international organization, but it makes most sense to estimate them for organizations that have a mandate in trade. Furthermore, a comparison of indices across IOs is substantively meaningful only for IOs that have comparable membership sizes short of the globe as a whole.

Each index has strengths and weaknesses (Iapadre and Plummer 2011). The most commonly used index is intra-IO trade share, though it is sensitive to the economic cycle, which expands or contracts an IO's intra-trade value irrespective of whether there has been trade integration. The trade intensity index avoids this problem though it has limitations that complicate comparison across IOs. Its maximum value is a decreasing function of an IO's total trade, which implies that a given value stands for different things for different-sized IOs, and it is characterized by range asymmetry, in that the range below unity is much smaller than above, which can bias comparison of IOs with values on either side of unity. The trade introversion index is the most complex and least intuitive of the three, but avoids these problems (Iapadre and Plummer 2011: 108).

The three measures approach trade interdependence quite differently, as is apparent in Table A.14 which reveals weak associations among the three indices for the thirty-four IOs for which we have data. Table A.15 provides descriptives.

References

Abbott, Kenneth W. and Duncan Snidal. 2000. "Hard and Soft Law in International Governance." *International Organization*, 54(3): 421–56.
Abbott, Kenneth W. and Duncan Snidal. 2004. "Pathways to International Cooperation." In Eyal Benvenisti and Moshe Hirsch (eds.), *The Impact of International Law on International Cooperation: Theoretical Perspectives*, 50–84. Cambridge: Cambridge University Press.
Abbott, Kenneth. W., Philipp Genschel, Duncan Snidal, and Bernhard Zangl. 2015. "Orchestration: Global Governance Through Intermediaries." In Kenneth W. Abbott, Philipp Genschel, Duncan Snidal, and Bernhard Zangl (eds.), *International Organizations as Orchestrators*, 3–36. Cambridge: Cambridge University Press.
Abbott, Kenneth. W., Philipp Genschel, Duncan Snidal, and Bernhard Zangl. 2016. "Two Logics of Indirect Governance: Delegation and Orchestration." *British Journal of Political Science*, 46(4): 719–29.
Acharya, Amitav. 2001. *Constructing a Security Community in Southeast Asia: ASEAN and the Problem of Regional Order*. New York: Routledge.
Achiume, Tendayi. 2018. "The SADC Tribunal: Sociopolitical Dissonance and the Authority of International Courts." In Karen J. Alter, Laurence R. Helfer, and Mikael Rask Madsen (eds.), *International Court Authority*, 124–46. Oxford: Oxford University Press.
Adcock, Robert and David Collier. 2001. "Measurement Validity: A Shared Standard for Qualitative and Quantitative Research." *American Political Science Review*, 5(3): 529–46.
Adler, Emanuel. 2013. "Constructivism in International Relations: Sources, Contributions, and Debates." In Walter Carlsnaes, Thomas Risse, and Beth A. Simmons (eds.), *Handbook of International Relations*, 112–44. Oxford: Oxford University Press.
Aksoy, Deniz. 2012. "Institutional Arrangements and Logrolling: Evidence from the European Union." *American Journal of Political Science*, 56(3): 538–52.
Allee, Todd and Manfred Elsig. 2016. "Why do Some International Institutions Contain Strong Dispute Settlement Provisions? New Evidence from Preferential Trade Agreements." *Review of International Organizations*, 11(1): 89–120.
Alter, Karen J. 2008. "Delegating to International Courts: Self-Binding vs. Other-Binding Delegation." *Law and Contemporary Problems*, 71(1): 37–76.
Alter, Karen J. 2012. "The Global Spread of European Style International Courts." *West European Politics*, 35(1): 135–54.
Alter, Karen J. 2014. *The New Terrain of International Law: Courts, Politics, Rights*. Princeton, NJ: Princeton University Press.

References

Alter, Karen J. and Liesbet Hooghe. 2016. "Regional Dispute Settlement." In Tanja Börzel and Thomas Risse (eds.), *The Oxford Handbook of Comparative Regionalism*, 538–58. Oxford: Oxford University Press.

Alter, Karen J. and Sophie Meunier. 2009. "The Politics of International Regime Complexity." *Perspectives on Politics*, 7(1): 13–24.

Alter, Karen J., James T. Gathii, and Laurence R. Helfer. 2016. "Backlash against International Courts in West, East and Southern Africa: Causes and Consequences." *The European Journal of International Law*, 27(2): 293–328.

Appleman Williams, William. 1972. *The Tragedy of American Diplomacy*. New York: W.W. Norton.

Aristotle. N.d. [1912]. *Politeia*. London: MacMillan.

Arnold, Christian and Berthold Rittberger. 2013. "The Legalization of Dispute Resolution in Mercosur." *Journal of Politics in Latin America*, 5(3): 97–132.

Arrow, Kenneth J. 1974. *The Limits of Organization*. New York: W.W. Norton.

ASEAN. 1967. "Founding Document of ASEAN." Bangkok, August 8.

ASEAN. 1976a. "Treaty of Amity and Cooperation." Bali, February 24.

ASEAN. 1976b. "Agreement on the Establishment of the ASEAN Secretariat." February 24.

ASEAN. 1992. "Protocol Amending the Agreement on the Establishment of the ASEAN Secretariat." Manila, July 22.

ASEAN. 1996. "The Protocol on Dispute Settlement Mechanism." Manila, November 20.

ASEAN. 2004. "ASEAN Protocol on Enhanced Dispute Settlement Mechanism." Vientiane, November 29.

Avant, Deborah and Oliver Westerwinter (eds.) 2016. *The New Power Politics: Networks and Transnational Security Governance*. Oxford: Oxford University Press.

Awoumou, Come Damien Georges. 2008. "ECCAS or CEMAC? Which Regional Economic Community for Central Africa?" In Chrysantus Ayangafac (ed.), *Political Economy of Regionalisation in Central Africa*, 109–49. Pretoria: Institute of Security Studies.

Axelrod, Robert. 1984. *The Evolution of Cooperation*. New York: Basic Books.

Aziz, Shaukat, Luisa Dias Diogo, and Jens Stoltenberg. 2006. *Delivering as One: Report of the High-Level Panel on United Nations System-Wide Coherence in the Areas of Development, Humanitarian Assistance and the Environment*. New York: United Nations.

Baccini, Leonardo. 2010. "Explaining Formation and Design of EU Trade Agreements: The Role of Transparency and Flexibility." *European Union Politics*, 11(2): 195–217.

Baccini, Leonardo and Andreas Dür. 2012. "The New Regionalism and Policy Interdependency." *British Journal of Political Science*, 42(1): 57–79.

Baccini, Leonardo, Andreas Dür, and Manfred Elsig. 2015. "The Politics of Trade Agreement Design: Revisiting the Depth-Flexibility Nexus." *International Studies Quarterly*, 59(4): 765–75.

Bailey, Michael A., Anton Strezhnev, and Erik Voeten. 2017. "Estimating Dynamic State Preferences from United Nations Voting Data." *Journal of Conflict Resolution*, 61(2): 430–56.

Balassa, Bela. 1961. *The Theory of Economic Integration*. Homewood, IL: Richard D. Irwin.

Barker, Ernest. 2010 [1918]. *Greek Political Theory*. London: Routledge.

Barnett, Michael and Liv Coleman. 2005. "Designing Police: Interpol and the Study of Change in International Organizations." *International Studies Quarterly*, 49(4): 593–620.

References

Barnett, Michael and Martha Finnemore. 2004. *Rules for the World: International Organizations in Global Politics*. Ithaca, NY: Cornell University Press.

Bartels, Larry M. 1991. "Instrumental and 'Quasi-Instrumental' Variables." *American Journal of Political Science*, 35(3): 777–800.

Bartolini, Stefano. 2005. *Restructuring Europe: Centre Formation, System Building, and Political Structuring Between the Nation State and the European Union*. Oxford: Oxford University Press.

Beck, Hans and Peter Funke (eds.). 2015. *Federalism in Greek Antiquity*. Cambridge: Cambridge University Press.

Beck, Nathaniel and Jonathan N. Katz. 2011. "Modeling Dynamics in Time-Series-Cross-Section Political Economy Data." *Annual Review of Political Science*, 14: 331–52.

Becker, Sascha O., Thiemo Fetzer, and Dennis Novy. 2017. "Who Voted for Brexit? A Comprehensive District-Level Analysis." *Economic Policy*, 32(92): 601–51.

Beckert, Jens. 1996. "What Is Sociological About Economic Sociology? Uncertainty and the Embeddedness of Economic Action." *Theory and Society*, 25(6): 803–40.

Beckert, Jens. 2003. "Economic Sociology and Embeddedness: How Shall We Conceptualize Economic Action?" *Journal of Economic Issues*, 37(3): 769–87.

Berger-Eforo, Judith. 1996. "Sanctuary for the Whales: Will This Be the Demise of the International Whaling Commission or a Viable Strategy for the Twenty-First Century?" *Pace International Law Review*, 8(2): 439–83.

Bernauer, Thomas. 1995. "The Effect of International Environmental Institutions: How We Might Learn More." *International Organization*, 49(2): 351–77.

Bernhard, Helen, Urs Fischbacher, and Ernst Fehr. 2006. "Parochial Altruism in Humans." *Nature*, 442: 912–5.

Beyeler, Michelle and Hanspeter Kriesi. 2005. "Transnational Protest and the Public Sphere." *Mobilization*, 10(1): 95–109.

Beyers, Jan and Jarle Trondal. 2004. "How Nation-States 'Hit' Europe: Ambiguity and Representation in the European Union." *West European Politics*, 27(5): 919–42.

Bezuijen, Jeanine. (2015). "Exploring the Causes for Change in Regional Third Party Dispute Settlement." *World Trade Review*, 14(S1): 59–81.

Bianculli, Andrea C. 2016. "Latin America." In Tanja Börzel and Thomas Risse (eds.), *The Oxford Handbook of Comparative Regionalism*, 154–77. Oxford: Oxford University Press.

Bickerton, Christopher J., Dermot Hodson, and Uwe Puetter. 2015. "The New Intergovernmentalism and the Study of European Integration." In Christopher J. Bickerton, Dermot Hodson, and Uwe Puetter (eds.), *The New Intergovernmentalism: States and Supranational Actors in the Post-Maastricht Era*, 1–50. Oxford: Oxford University Press.

Biermann, Frank and Bernd Siebenhüner (eds.). 2009. *Managers of Global Change: The Influence of International Environmental Bureaucracies*. Cambridge, MA: MIT Press.

Biermann, Frank, Bernd Siebenhüner, Steffen Bauer, Per-Olof Busch, Sabine Campe, Klaus Dingwerth, Torsten Grothmann, Robert Marschinski, and Mireia Tarradell. 2009. "Studying the Influence of International Bureaucracies: A Conceptual Framework." In Frank Biermann and Bernd Siebenhüner (eds.), *Managers of Global Change: The Influence of International Environmental Bureaucracies*, 37–74. Cambridge, MA: MIT Press.

References

Bingham, Tom. 2011. *The Rule of Law*. London: Penguin.

Blake, Daniel J. and Autumn Lockwood Payton. 2009. "Decision Making in International Organizations: An Interest Based Approach to Voting Rule Selection." Unpublished manuscript.

Blake, Daniel J. and Autumn Lockwood Payton. 2015. "Balancing Design Objectives: Analyzing New Data on Voting Rules in Intergovernmental Organizations." *Review of International Organizations*, 10(3): 377–402.

Boak, A.E.R. 1921. "Greek Interstate Associations and the League of Nations." *American Journal of International Law*, 15: 375–83.

Boehmer, Charles, Erik Gartzke, and Timothy Nordstrom. 2004. "Do Intergovernmental Organizations Promote Peace?" *World Politics*, 57(1): 1–38.

Boekestijn, A.J. 1994. "Soevereiniteit en integratie: de Benelux 1945-1958." In A. Postma, H. Balthazar, L.J. Brinkhorst, Michel Dumoulin, and Norbert von Kunitzki (eds.), *Benelux in de kijker: Vijftig jaar samenwerking*, 99–124. Tielt: Memorial Books.

Bollen, Kenneth and Pamela Paxton. 2000. "Subjective Measures of Liberal Democracy." *Comparative Political Studies*, 33(1): 58–86.

Bolt, Jutta and Jan Luiten van Zanden. 2014. "The Maddison Project: Collaborative Research on Historical National Accounts." *The Economic History Review*, 67(3): 627–51.

Bond, Martyn. 2012. *The Council of Europe: Structure, History and Issues in European Politics*. New York: Routledge.

Bornschier, Simon. 2018. "Globalization, Cleavages, and the Radical Right." In Jens Rydgren (ed.), *The Oxford Handbook of the Radical Right*, 212–38. Oxford: Oxford University Press.

Börzel, Tanja. 2016. "From EU Governance of Crisis to Crisis of EU Governance: Regulatory Failure, Redistributive Conflict and Euroskeptic Publics." *Journal of Common Market Studies*, 54(S1): 8–31.

Börzel, Tanja and Thomas Risse. 2018. "From the Euro to the Schengen Crises: European Integration Theories, Politicization, and Identity Politics." *Journal of European Public Policy*, 25(1): 83–108.

Bow, Brian. 2015. "Legitimacy, Politicization, and Regional Integration in North America." In Achim Hurrelmann and Steffen Schneider (eds.), *The Legitimacy of Regional Integration in Europe and the Americas*, 33–56. Basingstoke: Palgrave Macmillan.

Bradley, Curtis A. and Judith G. Kelley. 2008. "The Concept of International Delegation." *Law and Contemporary Problems*, 71(1): 1–36.

Brazys, Samuel, Adrian O'Hagan, Diana Panke, and Oliver Westerwinter. 2017. "Can't Buy Me Love? Specific and Diffuse Reciprocity in International Relations." Unpublished manuscript.

Brosig, Malte. 2011. "Overlap and Interplay between International Organisations: Theories and Approaches." *South African Journal of International Affairs*, 18(2): 147–67.

Brown, Robert L. 2010. "Measuring Delegation." *Review of International Organizations*, 5(2): 141–75.

Buchanan, James M. and Gordon Tullock. 1962. *The Calculus of Consent: Logical Foundations of Constitutional Democracy*. Ann Arbor: University of Michigan Press.

References

Buchanan, Patrick J. 1993. "America First, NAFTA Never." *Washington Post*, November 7. Available at https://www.washingtonpost.com/archive/opinions/1993/11/07/america-first-nafta-never/c8450c08-b14b-4a25-abe8-0b7cfc992e11/?noredirect=on&utm_term=.64316b5dec3a (accessed September 3, 2018).

Bulmer-Thomas, Victor. 1998. "The Central American Common Market: From Closed to Open Regionalism." *World Development*, 26(2): 313–22.

Büthe, Tim and Helen V. Milner. 2014. "Institutional Diversity in Trade Agreements and Foreign Direct Investment: Credibility, Commitment, and Economic Flows in the Developing World, 1970–2007." *World Politics*, 66(1): 88–122.

Caldentey del Pozo, Pedro. 2014. "El Sistema de la Integración Centroamericana y la Cooperación Sur-Sur." In Bruno Ayllón, Tahina Ojeda, and Javier Surasky (eds.), *Cooperación Sur-Sur: Regionalismos e Integración en América Latina*, 108–27. Madrid: Instituto Universitario de Desarrollo y Cooperación.

Cameron, Maxwell and Brian Tomlin. 2001. *The Making of NAFTA: How the Deal Was Done*. Ithaca, NY: Cornell University Press.

Carnegie, Allison. 2014. "States Held Hostage: Political Hold-Up Problems and the Effects of International Institutions." *American Political Science Review*, 108(1): 54–70.

Carroll, Lewis. 1895. "What the Tortoise Said to Achilles." *Mind*, 104(416): 691–3. Reprinted 1982 in *The Penguin Complete Lewis Carroll*. Penguin: Harmondsworth, 1104–8.

Carrubba, Clifford J. and Matthew Gabel. 2017. "International Courts: A Theoretical Assessment." *Annual Review of Political Science*, 20: 55–73.

Cary, M. 1923. "A Constitution of the United States of Greece." *The Classical Quarterly*, 17(3/4): 137–48.

Cavallaro, James L. and Stephanie Erin Brewer. 2008. "Reevaluating Regional Human Rights Litigation in the Twenty-First Century: The Case of the Inter-American Court." *American Journal of International Law*, 102(4): 768–827.

Chayes, Abram and Antonia Handler Chayes. 1993. "On Compliance." *International Organization*, 48(2): 175–205.

Checkel, Jeffrey. 2001. "Why Comply? Social Learning and European Identity Change." *International Organization*, 55(3): 553–88.

Childers, Erskine and Brian Urquhart. 1999. *Renewing the United Nations System*. Uppsala: Dag Hammarskjöld Foundation.

Chinaka, Cris. 2009. "Mugabe Says Zimbabwe Land Seizures Will Continue." *Mail&Guardian*, February 28. Available at https://mg.co.za/article/2009-02-28-mugabe-says-zimbabwe-land-seizures-will-continue (accessed April 27, 2019).

Chomsky, Noam. 2015. *The Minimalist Program*. Cambridge, MA: MIT Press.

CIA World Factbook. Available at https://www.cia.gov/library/publications/the-world-factbook/, regularly updated (2011–12 values used in dataset).

Clapham, Andrew. 2012. *Brierly's Law of Nations: An Introduction to the Role of International Law in International Relations*. 7th edn. Oxford: Oxford University Press.

Claude, Inis L. 1956. *From Swords to Plowshares*. New York: Random House.

Cockerham, Geoffrey. 2007. "The Delegation of Dispute Settlement Authority to Conventional International Governmental Organizations." *International Politics*, 44: 732–52.

References

Comisión de Juristas para la Integración Regional. 2019. "Declaración sobre la eventual suspensión de la elección directa de los parlamentarios argentinos ante el Parlamente del Mercosur." Declaración No. 01/2019, Buenos Aires, February 27.

Commission of the European Communities. 1992. "Europe and the Challenge of Enlargement. Prepared for the European Council, Lisbon, 26–27 June 1992." *Bulletin of the European Communities*, 6–1992, Supplement 3/92.

Commonwealth CMAG. 2016. "Concluding Statement of the Commonwealth Ministerial Action Group." New York, September 23.

Commonwealth COMSEC. 2004. "Harare Commonwealth Declaration 1991."

Conceição-Heldt, Eugénia da. 2013. "Two-Level Games and Trade Cooperation: What Do We Now Know?" *International Politics*, 50(4): 579–99.

Cooley, Alexander and Hendrik Spruyt. 2009. *Contracting States: Sovereign Transfer in International Relations*. Princeton, NJ: Princeton University Press.

Copelovitch, Mark, Jeffry Frieden, and Stefanie Walter. 2016. "The Political Economy of the Euro Crisis." *Comparative Political Studies*, 49(7): 811–40.

Council of Europe (CoE). 1949. "Statute of the Council of Europe." May 5.

Council of Ministers. 1966. "Extraordinary Session of the Council, Luxembourg, 17 to 18 and 28 to 29 January 1966." *Bulletin of the European Communities*, 3–1966.

Cram, Laura. 2012. "Does the EU Need a Navel? Implicit and Explicit Identification with the European Union." *Journal of Common Market Studies*, 50(1): 71–86.

Curtice, John. 2017. "Why Leave Won the UK's EU Referendum." *Journal of Common Market Studies*, 55(Annual Review): 19–37.

Dahl, Robert A. 1957. "The Concept of Power." *Behavioral Science*, 2(3): 201–15.

Dahl, Robert A. 1967. "The City in the Future of Democracy." *American Political Science Review*, 61(4): 953–70.

Dahl, Robert A. 1968. "Power." In David L. Sills (ed.), *The International Encyclopedia of the Social Sciences*, Vol. 12, 405–15. New York: Macmillan.

Davis, Christina. 2012. *Why Adjudicate? Enforcing Trade Rules in the WTO*. Princeton, NJ: Princeton University Press.

Davis, Christina. 2016. "More than Just a Rich Country Club: Membership Conditionality and Institutional Reform in the OECD." Working paper.

Davis, Christina and Meredith Wilf. 2017. "Joining the Club: Accession to the GATT/WTO." *Journal of Politics*, 79(3): 964–78.

De Vries, Catherine E. 2018a. "The Cosmopolitan-Parochial Divide: Changing Patterns of Party and Electoral Competition in the Netherlands and Beyond." *Journal of European Public Policy*, 25(11): 1541–65.

De Vries, Catherine E. 2018b. *Euroscepticism and the Future of European Integration*. Oxford: Oxford University Press.

De Vries, Catherine E. and Sara B. Hobolt. 2018. "*Challenger Parties*." Book manuscript.

de Wilde, Pieter, Anna Leupold, and Henning Schmidtke. 2016. "Introduction: The Differentiated Politicisation of European Governance." *West European Politics*, 39(1): 3–22.

de Wilde, Pieter, Anna Leupold, and Henning Schmidke (eds.) 2017. *The Differentiated Politicisation of European Governance*. Abingdon: Routledge.

References

de Wilde, Pieter, Ruud Koopmans, Wolfgang Merkel, Oliver Strijbis, Michael Zürn (eds.) 2019. *The Struggle Over Borders: Cosmopolitanism and Communitarianism*. Cambridge: Cambridge University Press.

Deflem, Mathieu. 2002. "The Logic of Nazification: The Case of the International Criminal Police Commission ('Interpol')." *International Journal of Comparative Sociology*, 43(1): 21–44.

Delors, Jacques. 1985. "Speech by Jacques Delors, Luxembourg, 9 September 1985." *Bulletin of the European Communities*, 9–1985.

Dennison, James and Andrew Geddes. 2018. "Brexit and the Perils of 'Europeanised' Migration." *Journal of European Public Policy*, 25(8): 1137–53.

Deutsch, Karl W. 1957. *Political Community and the North Atlantic Area: International Organization in the Light of Historical Experience*. New York: Greenwood Press.

Deutsch, Karl W. 1966 [1953]. *Nationalism and Social Communication: An Inquiry in the Foundations of Nationality*. Cambridge, MA: Massachusetts Institute of Technology Press.

Díez-Medrano, Juan. 2003. *Framing Europe: Attitudes to European Integration in Germany, Spain, and the United Kingdom*. Princeton, NJ: Princeton University Press.

Díez Medrano, Juan and P. Gutiérrez. 2001. "Nested Identities: National and European Identities in Spain." *Journal of Ethnic and Migration Studies*, 24(5): 753–78.

Dingwerth, Klaus, Ina Lehmann, Ellen Reichel, Tobias Weise, and Antonia Witt. 2015. "Many Pipers, Many Tunes? Die Legitimationskommunikation internationaler Organisationen in komplexen Umwelten." *Politische Vierteljahresschrift*, 49: 186–212.

Dooge Committee. 1985. "Report from the Ad Hoc Committee on Institutional Affairs." *Bulletin of the European Communities*, 3–1985.

Drezner, Daniel. 2007. *All Politics is Global*. Princeton, NJ: Princeton University Press.

Duina, Francesco and Tobias Lenz. 2016. "Regionalism and Diffusion Revisited: From Final Design Towards Stages of Decision-Making." *Review of International Studies*, 42(4): 773–97.

Dür, Andreas, Leonardo Baccini, and Manfred Elsig. 2014. "The Design of International Trade Agreements: Introducing a New Dataset." *Review of International Organizations*, 9(3): 353–75.

Dworkin, Ronald. 1988. *Law's Empire*. Cambridge, MA: Belknap Press.

Ecker-Ehrhardt, Matthias. 2014. "Why Parties Politicise International Institutions: On Globalisation Backlash and Authority Contestation." *Review of International Political Economy*, 21(6): 1275–312.

Ecker-Ehrhardt, Matthias. 2018. "Self-Legitimation in the Face of Politicization: Why International Organizations Centralized Public Communication." *Review of International Organizations*, 13(4): 519–46.

Egeberg, Morten. 1999. "Transcending Intergovernmentalism? Identity and Role Perceptions of National Officials in EU Decision-Making." *Journal of European Public Policy*, 6(3): 456–74.

El-Affendi, Abdelwahab. 2009. "The Perils of Regionalism: Integration as a Source of Instability in the Horn of Africa?" *Journal of Intervention and Statebuilding*, 3(1): 1–19.

Elias, T.O. 1965. "The Charter of the Organization of African Unity." *American Journal of International Law*, 59(2): 243–67.

References

Elliott, Larry. 2018. "Trump's WTO threats matter – especially to a post-Brexit Britain." *The Guardian*, September 2. Available at https://www.theguardian.com/business/2018/sep/02/trumps-world-trade-wto-threat-threat-matters-especially-britain (accessed September 3, 2018).

Ellis, Charles Howard. 1929. *The Origin, Structure & Working of the League of Nations*. Boston, MA: Houghton Mifflin.

Ellis, David. 2009. "On the Possibility of 'International Community'." *International Studies Review*, 11(1): 1–26.

Elsig, Manfred and Jappe Eckhardt. 2015. "The Creation of the Multilateral Trade Court: Design and Experiential Learning." *World Trade Review*, 14(S1): S13–S32.

European Council. 2001. "Laeken Declaration on the Future of the European Union of 15 December 2001." *Bulletin of the European Union*, 12–2001.

Evans, Geoffrey. 1999. "Europe: A New Cleavage?" In Geoffrey Evans and Pippa Norris (eds.), *Critical Elections: British Parties and Voters in Long-Term Perspective*, 207–22. London: Sage.

Evans, Geoffrey and James Tilley. 2017. *The New Politics of Class: The Political Exclusion of the British Working Class*. Oxford: Oxford University Press.

Evans, Geoffrey, Noah Carl, and James Dennison. 2017. "Brexit: The Causes and Consequences of the UK's Decision to Leave the EU." In Manuel Castells, Olivier Bouin, Joao Caraça, Gustavo Cardoso, John Thompson, and Michel Wieviorka (eds.), *Europe's Crises*, 380–404. Cambridge: Polity.

Fawcett, Louise. 2012. "The History and Concept of Regionalism." European Society of International Law Conference Paper 4/2012, Valencia.

Feenstra, Robert C., Robert Inklaar, and Marcel Timmer. 2013. "The Next Generation of the Penn World Table." *NBER Working Paper*, No. 19255.

Finnemore, Martha. 1993. "International Organizations as Teachers of Norms: The United Nations Educational, Scientific, and Cultural Organization and Science Policy." *International Organization*, 47(4): 565–97.

Fooner, Michael. 1973. *Interpol: The Inside Story of the International Crime-Fighting Organization*. Chicago, IL: Henry Regnery Company.

Franck, Thomas. 1988. "Legitimacy in the International System." *American Journal of International Law*, 82(4): 705–59.

Fredland, Richard A. 1973. "The OAU after Ten Years: Can it Survive?" *African Affairs*, 72(288): 309–16.

Gardini, Gian Luca. 2015. "Towards Modular Regionalism: The Proliferation of Latin American Cooperation." *Revista Brasileira de Politica Internacional*, 58(1): 210–29.

Genschel, Philipp and Markus Jachtenfuchs. 2016. "More Integration, Less Federation: The European Integration of Core State Powers." *Journal of European Public Policy*, 23(1): 42–59.

Genschel, Philipp and Markus Jachtenfuchs. 2018. "From Market Integration to Core State Powers: The Eurozone Crisis, the Refugee Crisis and Integration Theory." *Journal of Common Market Studies*, 56(1): 178–96.

Gibbons, Robert and Rebecca Henderson. 2012. "Relational Contracts and Organizational Capabilities." *Organization Science*, 23(5): 1350–64.

Glasius, Marlies. 2008. "Global Justice Meets Local Civil Society: The International Criminal Court's Investigation of the Central African Republic." *Alternatives*, 33: 413–33.

Godwin Bongyu, Moye. 2009. "The Economic and Monetary Community of Central Africa (CEMAC) and the Decline of Sovereignty." *Journal of Asian and African Studies*, 44(4): 389–406.

Goetze, Stefan and Berthold Rittberger. 2010. "A Matter of Habit? The Sociological Foundations of Empowering the European Parliament." *Comparative European Politics*, 8(1): 37–54.

Goldstein, Judith, Miles Kahler, Robert Keohane, and Anne-Marie Slaughter. 2000. "Introduction: Legalization and World Politics." *International Organization*, 54(3): 385–99.

Graham, Kennedy. 2012. "The Regional Input for Delivering as One." In Philippe Lombaerde, Francis Baert, and Tania Felício (eds.), *The United Nations and the Regions*, 189–213. Berlin: Springer.

Graham, Kennedy and Tania Felício. 2006. *Regional Security and Global Governance: A Study of Interaction between Regional Agencies and the UN Security Council with a Proposal for a Regional-Global Security Mechanism*. Brussels: VUB Press.

Grande, Edgar and Swen Hutter. 2016. "Beyond Authority Transfer: Explaining the Politicization of Europe." *West European Politics* 39(1): 23–43.

Grande, Edgar and Hanspeter Kriesi. 2016. "Conclusions: The Postfunctionalists Were (Almost) Right." In Swen Hutter, Edgar Grande, and Hanspeter Kriesi (eds.), *Politicizing Europe: Integration and Mass Politics*, 279–300. Cambridge: Cambridge University Press.

Grande, Edgar and Tobias Schwarzbözl. 2017. "Politicizing Europe in the UK. Dynamics of Inter-Party Competition and Intra-Party Conflict." Paper prepared for the Conference "Rejected Europe. Beloved Europe. Cleavage Europe" at the European University Institute, Florence, May 18–19.

Gray, Julia. 2014. "Domestic Capacity and the Implementation Gap in Regional Trade Agreements." *Comparative Political Studies*, 47(1): 55–87.

Gray, Julia. 2018. "Life, Death, or Zombie? The Vitality of International Organizations." *International Studies Quarterly*, 62(1): 1–13.

Gray, Julia and Jonathan B. Slapin. 2012. "How Effective Are Preferential Trade Agreements? Ask the Experts." *Review of International Organizations*, 7(3): 309–33.

Green-Pedersen, Christoffer. 2012. "A Giant Fast Asleep? Party Incentives and the Politicisation of European Integration." *Political Studies*, 60(1): 115–30.

Greif, Avner and David Laitin. 2004. "A Theory of Endogenous Institutional Change." *American Political Science Review*, 98(4): 633–52.

Grieco, Joseph. 1990. *Cooperation Among Nations: Europe, America and Non-Tariff Barriers to Trade*. Ithaca, NY: Cornell University Press.

Grigorescu, Alexandru. 2015. *Democratic Intergovernmental Organizations? Normative Pressures and Decision-Making Rules*. Cambridge: Cambridge University Press.

Grosbois, Th. 1994. "De onderhandelingen van London voor een Benelux douane-unie (1941–1944)." In A. Postma, H. Balthazar, L.J. Brinkhorst, Michel Dumoulin, and Norbert von Kunitzki (eds.), *Benelux in de kijker: Vijftig jaar samenwerking*, 39–69. Tielt: Memorial Books.

References

Haas, Ernst B. 1958. *The Uniting of Europe: Political, Social, and Economical Forces, 1950–1957*. Stanford, CA: Stanford University Press.

Haas, Ernst B. 1980. "Why Cooperate? Issue-Linkage and International Regimes." *World Politics*, 32(3): 357–405.

Haas, Peter. 1992. "Introduction: Epistemic Communities and International Policy Coordination." *International Organization*, 46(1): 1–35.

Habermas, Jürgen. 1981. *Theorie des kommunikativen Handelns*, Vols. I and II. Frankfurt am Main: Suhrkamp.

Hafner-Burton, Emilie. 2005. "Trading Human Rights: How Preferential Trade Agreements Influence Government Repression." *International Organization*, 59: 593–629.

Haftel, Yoram. 2011. *Regional Economic Institutions and Conflict Mitigation: Design, Implementation and the Promise of Peace*. Ann Arbor, MI: University of Michigan Press.

Haftel, Yoram. 2013. "Commerce and Institutions: Trade, Scope, and the Design of Regional Economic Organizations." *Review of International Organizations*, 8(3): 389–414.

Haftel, Yoram and Stephanie Hofmann. 2017. "Institutional Authority and Security Cooperation within Regional Economic Organizations." *Journal of Peace Research*, 54(4): 484–98.

Haftel, Yoram and Alexander Thompson. 2006. "The Independence of International Organizations: Concept and Applications." *Journal of Conflict Resolution*, 50(2): 253–75.

Hammarskjöld, Dag. 1955. "United Nations: World on Trial – Interview with Dag Hammarskjöld." *Time Magazine*, 65(26): June 27.

Hanhimäki, Jussi M. 2015. *The United Nations: A Very Short Introduction*. Oxford: Oxford University Press.

Hansen, Mogens Herman. 2006. *An Introduction to the Ancient Greek City-State*. Oxford: Oxford University Press.

Hart, Oliver and John Moore. 2008. "Contracts as Reference Points." *Quarterly Journal of Economics*, 123(1): 1–48.

Hartigan, J.A. and P.M. Hartigan. 1985. "The Dip Test of Unimodality." *Annals of Statistics*, 13: 70–84.

Häusermann, Silja and Hanspeter Kriesi. 2015. "What Do Voters Want? Dimensions and Configurations in Individual-Level Preferences and Party Choice." In Pablo Beramendi, Silja Häusermann, Herbert Kitschelt, and Hanspeter Kriesi (eds.), *The Politics of Advanced Capitalism*, 202–30. Cambridge: Cambridge University Press.

Hawkins, Darren G., David A. Lake, Daniel L. Nielson, and Michael J. Tierney. 2006a. "Delegation under Anarchy: States, International Organizations, and Principal-Agent Theory." In David A. Lake, Daniel L. Nielson, and Michael J. Tierney (eds.), *Delegation and Agency in International Organizations*, 3–38. Cambridge: Cambridge University Press.

Hawkins, Darren G., David A. Lake, Daniel L. Nielson, and Michael J. Tierney (eds.) 2006b. *Delegation and Agency in International Organizations*. Cambridge: Cambridge University Press.

Hayes-Renshaw, Fiona, Wim van Aken, and Helen Wallace. 2006. "When and Why the EU Council of Ministers Votes Explicitly." *Journal of Common Market Studies*, 44(1): 161–94.

Hebel, Kai and Tobias Lenz. 2016. "The Identity/Policy Nexus in European Foreign Policy." *Journal of European Public Policy*, 23(4): 473–91.

References

Heisenberg, Dorothée. 2005. "The Institution of 'Consensus' in the European Union: Formal versus Informal Decision-Making in the Council." *European Journal of Political Research*, 44(1): 65–90.

Henrikson, Alan K. 1996. "The United Nations and Regional Organizations: 'King-Links' of a 'Global Chain'." *Duke Journal of Comparative and International Law*, 7: 35–70.

Herman, Lawrence L. 2010. *NAFTA Disputes After Fifteen Years*. Backgrounder: International Policy Series, No. 133, July. Toronto: C.D. Howe Institute.

Herrmann, Richard K. and Marilynn B. Brewer. 2004. "Identities and Institutions: Becoming European in the EU." In Richard K. Herrmann, Marilynn B. Brewer, and Thomas Risse (eds.), *Becoming European in the EU*, 1–22. Lanham, MD: Rowman and Littlefield.

Hetherington, Marc and Jonathan Weiler. 2018. *Prius or Pickup? How the Answers to Four Simple Questions Explain America's Great Divide*. New York: Houghton Mifflin Harcourt Publishing Company.

Hilderbrand, Robert C. 1990. *Dumbarton Oaks: The Origins of the United Nations and the Search for Postwar Security*. Chapel Hill: University of North Carolina Press.

Hinsley, F. H. 1966. *Sovereignty*. New York: Basic Books.

Hobbes, Thomas. 2001 [1651]. *Leviathan*. South Bend, IN: Infomotions.

Hobolt, Sara B. 2016. "The Brexit Vote: A Divided Nation, a Divided Continent." *Journal of European Public Policy*, 23(9): 1259–77.

Hobolt, Sara B. 2018. "Brexit and the 2017 UK General Election." *Journal of Common Market Studies*, 56(S1): 39–50.

Hobolt, Sara B. and James Tilley. 2016. "Fleeing the Centre: The Rise of Challenger Parties in the Aftermath of the Euro Crisis." *West European Politics*, 39(5): 971–91.

Hobolt, Sara B., Thomas J. Leeper, and James Tilley. 2018. "Divided by the Vote: Affective Polarization in the Wake of Brexit." Paper presented at the American Political Science Association, Boston, August 30-September 2.

Hoffmann, Andrea Ribeiro. 2015. "Politicization and Legitimacy in Mercosur." In Achim Hurrelmann and Steffen Schneider (eds.), *The Legitimacy of Regional Integration in Europe and the Americas*, 57–72. Basingstoke: Palgrave Macmillan.

Hofmann, Stephanie. 2013. *European Security in NATO's Shadow: Party Ideologies and Institution Building*. Cambridge: Cambridge University Press.

Hofmann, Stephanie and Frédéric Mérand. 2012. "Regional Organizations à la Carte: The Effects of Institutional Elasticity." In T.V. Paul (ed.), *International Relations Theory and Regional Transformation*, 133–57. Cambridge: Cambridge University Press.

Höglinger, Dominic. 2016. *Politicizing European Integration: Struggling with the Awakening Giant*. Basingstoke: Palgrave Macmillan.

Hooghe, Liesbet (ed.) 1996. *Cohesion Policy and European Integration: Building Multilevel Governance*. Oxford: Oxford University Press.

Hooghe, Liesbet. 2005. "Many Roads Lead to International Norms, But Few Via International Socialization: A Case Study of the European Commission." *International Organization*, 59(4): 861–98.

Hooghe, Liesbet and Gary Marks. 1999. "Making of A Polity: The Struggle over European Integration." In Herbert Kitschelt, Gary Marks, Peter Lange, and John Stephens (eds.), *Continuity and Change in Contemporary Capitalism*, 70–97. Cambridge: Cambridge University Press.

References

Hooghe, Liesbet and Gary Marks. 2001. *Multi-Level Governance and European Integration*. Lanham, MD: Rowman & Littlefield.

Hooghe, Liesbet and Gary Marks. 2003. "Unraveling the Central State, but How? Types of Multi-Level Governance." *American Political Science Review*, 97(2): 233–43.

Hooghe, Liesbet and Gary Marks. 2005. "Calculation, Community, and Cues: Public Opinion on European Integration." *European Union Politics*, 6(4): 419–43.

Hooghe, Liesbet and Gary Marks. 2009a. "Does Efficiency Shape the Territorial Structure of Government?" *Annual Review of Political Science*, 12: 225–41.

Hooghe, Liesbet and Gary Marks. 2009b. "A Postfunctionalist Theory of European Integration: From Permissive Consensus to Constraining Dissensus." *British Journal of Political Science*, 39(1): 1–23.

Hooghe, Liesbet and Gary Marks. 2015. "Delegation and Pooling in International Organizations." *Review of International Organizations*, 10(3): 305–28.

Hooghe, Liesbet and Gary Marks. 2016. *Community, Scale, and Regional Governance*, Vol. II. Oxford: Oxford University Press.

Hooghe, Liesbet and Gary Marks. 2018. "Cleavage Theory and Europe's Crises: Lipset, Rokkan and the Transnational Cleavage." *Journal of European Public Policy*, 25(1): 109–35.

Hooghe, Liesbet and Gary Marks. 2019. "Grand Theories of European Integration in the Twenty-first Century." *Journal of European Public Policy*, published online: https://doi=10.1080/13501763.2019.1569711.

Hooghe, Liesbet, Tobias Lenz, and Gary Marks. 2018. "Contested World Order: The Delegitimation of International Governance." *Review of International Organizations*, published online: https://doi.org/10.1007/s11558-018-9334-3.

Hooghe, Liesbet, Gary Marks, Arjan H. Schakel, Sara Niedzwiecki, Sandra Chapman Osterkatz, and Sarah Shair-Rosenfield. 2016. *Measuring Regional Authority: A Postfunctionalist Theory of Governance*, Vol. I. Oxford: Oxford University Press.

Hooghe, Liesbet, Gary Marks, Tobias Lenz, Jeanine Bezuijen, Besir Ceka, and Svet Derderyan. 2017. *Measuring International Authority: A Postfunctionalist Theory of Governance*, Vol. III. Oxford: Oxford University Press.

Hoopes, Townsend and Douglas Brinkley. 1997. *FDR and the Creation of the U.N.* New Haven, CT: Yale University Press.

Hosli, Madeleine O., Mikko Mattila, and Marc Uriot. 2011. "Voting in the Council of the European Union after the 2004 Enlargement: A Comparison of Old and New Member States." *Journal of Common Market Studies*, 49(6): 1249–70.

Hug, Simon and Thomas König. 2002. "In View of Ratification: Governmental Preferences and Domestic Constraints at the Amsterdam Intergovernmental Conference." *International Organization*, 56(2): 447–76.

Hume, David. 1896 [1739]. *Treatise of Human Nature, Book 2, Part III, Section 3*. Reprinted from L.A. Selby-Bigge. *Original Edition in Three Volumes and Edited, with an Analytical Index*. Oxford: Clarendon Press.

Huntington, Samuel P. 1996. *The Clash of Civilizations and the Remaking of World Order*. New York: Simon & Schuster.

Hurrell, Andrew. 1993. "International Society and the Study of Regimes: A Reflective Approach." In Volker Rittberger (ed.), *Regime Theory and International Relations*, 49–63. Oxford: Oxford University Press.

Hurrelmann, Achim and Steffen Schneider (eds.) 2015. *The Legitimacy of Regional Integration in Europe and the Americas*. Basingstoke: Palgrave Macmillan.

Hurrelmann, Achim, Anna Gora, and Andrea Wagner. 2015. "The Politicization of European Integration: More than an Élite Affair?" *Political Studies*, 63(1): 43–59.

Hutter, Swen. 2014. *Protesting Culture and Economics in Western Europe: New Cleavages in Left and Right Politics*. Minneapolis: University of Minnesota Press.

Hutter, Swen and Edgar Grande. 2014. "Politicizing Europe in the National Electoral Arena: A Comparative Analysis of Five West European Countries, 1970–2010." *Journal of Common Market Studies*, 52(5): 1002–18.

Hutter, Swen and Hanspeter Kriesi. 2018. "Restructuring the Party Systems in North-Western Europe: Six Countries Compared." Paper presented at the conference "2017: Europe's Bumper Year of Elections," RSCAS, EUI Florence, March 8–9.

Hutter, Swen, Edgar Grande, and Hanspeter Kriesi (eds.) 2016. *Politicising Europe: Integration and Mass Politics*. Cambridge: Cambridge University Press.

Iapadre, P. Lelio and Michael Plummer. 2011. "Statistical Measures of Regional Trade Integration." In Philippe de Lombaerde, Ronato G. Flores, P. Lelio Iapadre, and Michael Schulz (eds.), *The Regional Integration Manual*, 98–123. London: Routledge.

Ikenberry, G. John. 2001. *After Victory: Institutions, Strategic Restraint, and the Rebuilding of Order after Major Wars*. Princeton, NJ: Princeton University Press.

Ikenberry, G. John. 2011. *Liberal Leviathan: The Origins, Crisis, and Transformation of the American World Order*. Princeton, NJ: Princeton University Press.

Ikenberry, G. John. 2018. "The End of Liberal International Order?" *International Affairs*, 94(1): 7–23.

Inglehart, Ronald. 1970. "Public Opinion and Regional Integration." In Leon Lindberg and Stuart Scheingold (eds.), *Regional Integration: Theory and Research*, 160–91. Cambridge, MA: Harvard University Press.

Inglehart, Ronald F. and Pippa Norris. 2016. "Trump, Brexit, and the Rise of Populism: Economic Have-Nots and Cultural Backlash." Paper presented at the Annual Meeting of the American Political Science Association, Philadelphia, September 1–4.

Jackson, Robert. 2000. *The Global Covenant: Human Conduct in a World of States*. New York: Oxford University Press.

Jacobson, Harold K. 1998. *International Governmental Organizations: Memberships and Characteristics, 1981 and 1992* (ICPSR 6737).

Jefferson, Thomas. 1790. "Opinion on the Constitutionality of the Residence Bill, 15 July 1790." *Founders Online*, National Archives. Available at https://founders.archives.gov/documents/Jefferson/01-17-02-0018-0007 (accessed March 30, 2018).

Jetschke, Anja. 2012. "ASEAN." In Mark Beeson and Richard Stubbs (eds.), *Routledge Handbook of Asian Regionalism*, 327–37. New York: Routledge.

Jetschke, Anja and Saori N. Katada. 2016. "Asia." In Tanja Börzel and Thomas Risse (eds.), *The Oxford Handbook of Comparative Regionalism*, 225–48. Oxford: Oxford University Press.

Jiménez, Edgard Moncayo. 2010. "The Contribution of the Regional UN Economic Commissions to Regional Integration Processes: The Case of ECLAC." *UNU-CRIS Working Paper*, W-2010/8.

References

Jo, Hyeran and Hyun Namgung. 2012. "Dispute Settlement Mechanisms in Preferential Trade Agreements: Democracy, Boilerplates, and the Multilateral Trade Regime." *Journal of Conflict Resolution*, 56(6): 1041–68.

Johns, Leslie. 2015. *Strengthening International Courts: The Hidden Costs of Legalization*. Ann Arbor: University of Michigan Press.

Johnson, Tana. 2013. "Institutional Design and Bureaucrats' Impact on Political Control." *Journal of Politics*, 75(1): 183–97.

Johnson, Tana. 2014. *Organizational Progeny: Why Governments are Losing Control over the Proliferating Structures of Global Governance*. Oxford: Oxford University Press.

Johnstone, Ian. 2005. "The Power of Interpretive Communities." In Michael Barnett and Raymond Duvall (eds.), *Power in Global Governance*, 185–204. Cambridge: Cambridge University Press.

Jones, Erik, R. Daniel Kelemen, and Sophie Meunier. 2016. "Failing Forward? The Euro Crisis and the Incomplete Nature of European Integration." *Comparative Political Studies*, 49(7): 1010–34.

Joris, Tony and Jan Vandenberghe. 2008. "The Council of Europe and the European Union: Natural Partners or Uneasy Bedfellows?" *Columbia Journal of European Law*, 15: 1–41.

Jupille, Joseph, Duncan Snidal, and Walter Mattli. 2013. *Institutional Choice and Global Commerce*. Cambridge: Cambridge University Press.

Kahler, Miles. 1995. *International Institutions and the Political Economy of Integration*. Washington, DC: Brookings Institution Press.

Kahler, Miles. 2000. "Legalization as Strategy: The Asia-Pacific Case." *International Organization*, 54(3): 549–71.

Kahler, Miles and David A. Lake. 2009. "Economic Integration and Global Governance: Why So Little Supranationalism?" In Walter Mattli and Ngaire Woods (eds.), *The Politics of Global Regulation*, 42–75. Princeton, NJ: Princeton University Press.

Kant, Immanuel. 2010 [1795]. *Perpetual Peace: A Philosophical Essay*. New York: Cosimo Classics.

Karns, Margaret P. and Karen Mingst. 2010. *International Organizations: The Politics and Processes of Global Governance*. Boulder, CO: Lynne Rienner.

Kay, Tamara. 2015. "New Challenges, New Alliances: Union Politicization in a Post-NAFTA Era." *Labor History*, 56(3): 246–69.

Keck, Margaret E. and Kathryn Sikkink. 1998. *Activists Beyond Borders: Advocacy Networks in International Politics*. Ithaca, NY: Cornell University Press.

Kelley, Judith. 2007. "Who Keeps International Commitments and Why? The International Criminal Court and Bilateral Nonsurrender Agreements." *American Political Science Review*, 101(3): 573–89.

Kennedy, Paul. 2007. *The Parliament of Man: The Past, Present and Future of the United Nations*. New York: Random House.

Keohane, Robert. 1982. "The Demand for International Regimes." *International Organization*, 36(2): 325–55.

Keohane, Robert O. 1984. *After Hegemony: Cooperation and Discord in the World Political Economy*. Princeton, NJ: Princeton University Press.

Keohane, Robert O. 1986. "Reciprocity in International Relations." *International Organization*, 40(1): 1–27.

Keohane, Robert O. and Stanley Hoffmann. 1991. "Institutional Change in Europe in the 1980s." In Robert O. Keohane and Stanley Hoffmann (eds.), *The New European Community: Decision Making and Institutional Change*, 1–40. Boulder, CO: Westview Press.

Keohane, Robert O. and Joseph S. Nye. 1993. *Power and Interdependence*. London: Longman.

Keohane, Robert O. and Elinor Ostrom (eds.) 1995. *Local Commons and Global Interdependence*. London: Sage.

Kersten, A.E. 1994. "Politieke aspecten van de Benelux-samenwerking: wisselwerking tussen interne opbouw and international machtsvorming, 1944–1958." In A. Postma, H. Balthazar, L.J. Brinkhorst, Michel Dumoulin, and Norbert von Kunitzki (eds.), *Benelux in de kijker: Vijftig jaar samenwerking*, 79–90. Tielt: Memorial Books.

Khong, Yuen Foong and Helen E.S. Nesadurai. 2007. "Hanging Together, Institutional Design, and Cooperation in Southeast Asia." In Amitav Acharya and Alastair Iain Johnston (eds.), *Crafting Cooperation: Regional Institutions in Comparative Perspective*, 32–82. Cambridge: Cambridge University Press.

Kindleberger, Charles. 1973. *The World in Depression*. Boston, MA: Little, Brown.

Kirsch, Werner and Jessica Langner. 2011. "Invariably Suboptimal: An Attempt to Improve the Voting Rules of the Treaties of Nice and Lisbon." *Journal of Common Market Studies*, 49(6): 1317–38.

Kleider, Hanna and Florian Stoeckel. 2019. "The Politics of International Redistribution: Explaining Public Support for Fiscal Transfers in the EU." *European Journal of Political Research*, 58(1): 4–29.

Kleine, Mareike. 2013. *Informal Governance in the European Union*. Ithaca, NY: Cornell University Press.

Klingemann, Hans-Dieter and Steven Weldon. 2013. "A Crisis of Integration? The Development of Transnational Dyadic Trust in the European Union, 1954–2004." *European Journal of Political Research*, 52(4): 457–82.

Knack, Stephen. 2001. "Trust, Associational Life and Economic Performance." Paper presented at the HRDC-OECD International Symposium on The Contribution of Investment in Human and Social Capital to Sustained Economic Growth and Well-Being, Canada, Château Frontenac, Québec City, March 19–21.

Kono, Daniel Y. 2007. "Making Anarchy Work: International Legal Institutions and Trade Cooperation." *Journal of Politics*, 69(3): 746–59.

Koremenos, Barbara. 2005. "Contracting around International Uncertainty." *American Political Science Review*, 99(4): 549–65.

Koremenos, Barbara. 2008. "When, What and Why Do States Choose to Delegate?" *Law and Contemporary Problems*, 71(1): 151–92.

Koremenos, Barbara. 2016. *The Continent of International Law: Explaining Agreement Design*. Cambridge: Cambridge University Press.

Koremenos, Barbara and Michael Lerner. 2017. "Membership Matters: Membership Provisions in International Agreements." Paper presented at the Annual Meeting of the American Political Science Association, San Francisco, August 31–September 3.

References

Koremenos, Barbara, Charles Lipson, and Duncan Snidal. 2001. "The Rational Design of International Institutions." *International Organization*, 54(4): 761–99.

Krasner, Stephen D. 1976. "State Power and the Structure of International Trade." *World Politics*, 28(3): 317–47.

Krehbiel, Keith. 1988. "Spatial Models of Legislative Choice." *Legislative Studies Quarterly*, 13(3): 259–319.

Kriesi, Hanspeter, Edgar Grande, Romain Lachat, Martin Dolezal, Simon Bornschier, and Timotheos Frey. 2006. "Globalization and the Transformation of the National Political Space: Six European Countries." *European Journal of Political Research*, 45(6): 921–56.

Kriesi, Hanspeter, Edgar Grande, Romain Lachat, Martin Dolezal, Simon Bornschier, and Timotheos Frey. 2008. *West European Politics in the Age of Globalization*. Cambridge: Cambridge University Press.

Kucik, Jeffrey and Eric Reinhardt. 2008. "Does Flexibility Promote Cooperation? An Application to the Global Trade Regime." *International Organization*, 62(3): 477–505.

Kuhn, Theresa. 2015. *Experiencing European Integration: Transnational Lives and European Identity*. Oxford: Oxford University Press.

Kuhn, Theresa and Florian Stoeckel. 2014. "When European Integration Becomes Costly: The Euro Crisis and Public Support for European Economic Governance." *Journal of European Public Policy*, 21(4): 624–41.

Kuhn, Theresa, Erika van Elsas, Armen Hakhverdian, and Wouter van der Brug. 2016. "An Ever Wider Gap in an Ever Closer Union: Rising Inequalities and Euroscepticism in 12 West European Democracies, 1976–2008." *Socio-Economic Review*, 14(1): 27–35.

Laffan, Brigid. 1992. *Integration and Co-Operation in Europe*. London: Routledge.

Laffan, Brigid. 2016a. "Europe's Union in Crisis: Tested and Contested." *West European Politics*, 39(5): 915–32.

Laffan, Brigid. 2016b. "Core-Periphery Dynamics in the Euro Area: From Conflict to Cleavage?" In Jose M. Magone, Brigid Laffan, and Christian Schweiger (eds.), *Power and Conflict in a Dualist Economy*, 19–35. London: Routledge.

Laffont, Jean-Jacques and David Martimort. 2002. *The Theory of Incentives: The Principal-Agent Model*. Princeton, NJ: Princeton University Press.

Lakatos, Imre. 1970. "Falsification and the Methodology of Scientific Research Programmes." In Imre Lakatos and Alan Musgrave (eds.), *Criticism and the Growth of Knowledge*, 91–196. Cambridge: Cambridge University Press.

Lake, David. 2018. "International Legitimacy Lost? Rule and Resistance When America Is First." *Perspectives on Politics* 16(1): 6–21.

Lake, David. 2009. *Hierarchy in International Relations*. Ithaca, NY: Cornell University Press.

Lake, David A. 2007. "Delegating Divisible Sovereignty: Sweeping a Conceptual Minefield." *Review of International Organizations*, 2(3): 219–37.

Lake, David A. and Mathew McCubbins. 2006. "The Logic of Delegation to International Organizations." In Darren G. Hawkins, David A. Lake, Daniel L. Nielson, and Michael L. Tierney (eds.), *Delegation and Agency in International Organizations*, 341–68. Cambridge: Cambridge University Press.

Lee, Matthew. 2018. "The International Criminal Court unacceptably threatens American sovereignty and U.S. national security interests." *Washington Post*, September 11.

Lenz, Tobias. 2012. "Spurred Emulation: The EU and Regional Integration in Mercosur and SADC." *West European Politics*, 35(1): 155–74.

Lenz, Tobias and Alexandr Burilkov. 2017. "Institutional Pioneers in World Politics: Regional Institution Building and the Influence of the European Union." *European Journal of International Relations*, 23(3): 654–80.

Lenz, Tobias and Lora Viola. 2017. "Legitimacy and Institutional Change in International Organizations: A Cognitive Approach." *Review of International Studies*, 43(5): 939–61.

Lenz, Tobias, Alexandr Burilkov, and Lora Viola. 2019. "Legitimacy and the Cognitive Sources of International Institutional Change: The Case of Regional Parliamentarization." *International Studies Quarterly* (forthcoming).

Lenz, Tobias, Jeanine Bezuijen, Liesbet Hooghe, and Gary Marks. 2015. "Patterns of International Authority: Task-Specific vs. General-Purpose." *Politische Vierteljahresschrift*, 49: 107–32.

Liddell, George and Robert Scott. 1940. *A Greek-English Lexicon*. Oxford: Clarendon Press.

Lindberg, Leon and Stuart Scheingold. 1970. *Europe's Would-Be Polity*. Englewood Cliffs, NJ: Prentice-Hall.

Linos, Katerina and Tom Pegram. 2016. "The Language of Compromise in International Agreements." *International Organization*, 70(3): 587–621.

Lipset, Seymour Martin. 1960. *Political Man: The Social Bases of Politics*. London: Heinemann.

Lipson, Charles. 1991. "Why Are Some International Agreements Informal?" *International Organization*, 45(4): 495–538.

Locke, John. 1728 [1690]. *Two Treatises of Government: Book II: An Essay Concerning the True Original, Extent, and End of Civil Government*. London: A. Bettesworth.

Lombaerde, Philippe, Francis Baert, and Tania Felício (eds.). 2012. *The United Nations and the Regions*. Berlin: Springer.

Lubin, Asaf. 2017. "Politics, Power Dynamics, and the Limits of Existing Self-Regulation and Oversight in ICC Preliminary Examinations." In Morten Bergsmo and Carsten Stahn (eds.), *Quality Control in Preliminary Examination: Reviewing Impact, Policies and Practices*. https://ssrn.com/abstract=2978551.

Lundgren, Magnus, Theresa Squatrito, and Jonas Tallberg. 2018. "Stability and Change in International Policy-Making: A Punctuated Equilibrium Approach." *Review of International Organizations*, 13(4): 547–72.

McCabe, Kevin, Daniel Houser, Lee Ryan, Vernon Smith, and Theodore Trouard. 2001. "A Functional Imagining Study of Cooperation in Two-Person Reciprocal Exchange." *Proceedings of the National Academy of Sciences*, 98(20): 11832–5.

McCall Smith, James. 2000. "The Politics of Dispute Settlement Design: Explaining Legalism in Regional Trade Pacts." *International Organization*, 54(1): 137–80.

MacKenzie, David Clarke. 2010. *A World Beyond Borders: An Introduction to the History of International Organizations*. Toronto: University of Toronto Press.

McKinnon, Don. 2005. "The Commonwealth Secretariat: Looking Forward to the Next 40 Years." *The Round Table*, 94(380): 293–300.

References

McNamara, Kathleen. 2015. *The Politics of Everyday Europe: Constructing Authority in the European Union*. Oxford: Oxford University Press.

Maggi, Giovanni and Massimo Morelli. 2006. "Self-Enforcing Voting in International Organizations." *American Economic Review*, 96(4): 1137–58.

Magliveras, Konstantinos D. 1999. *Exclusion from Participation in International Organisations: The Law and Practice Behind Member States' Expulsion and Suspension of Membership*. The Hague: Kluwer Law International.

Makinda, Samuel M. and F. Wafula Okumu. 2008. *The African Union: Challenges of Globalization, Security, and Governance*. London: Routledge.

Malinowski, W.R. 1962. "Centralization and Decentralization in the United Nations Economic and Social Activities." *International Organization*, 16(3): 521–41.

Mann, Michael. 1986. *The Sources of Social Power: Volume 1: A History of Power from the Beginning to AD 1760*. Cambridge: Cambridge University Press.

Mansergh, Nicholas. 2013 [1968]. *Survey of British Commonwealth Affairs: Problems of Wartime Cooperation and Post-War Change 1939–1952*. London: Routledge.

Mansfield, Edward D. 1998. "The Proliferation of Preferential Trading Agreements." *Journal of Conflict Resolution*, 42(5): 523–43.

Mansfield, Edward D. and Helen Milner. 2012. *Votes, Vetoes, and the Political Economy of International Trade Agreements*. Princeton, NJ: Princeton University Press.

Mansfield, Edward D. and Diana C. Mutz. 2012. "Support for Free Trade: Self-Interest, Socio-Tropic Politics, and Out-Group Anxiety." *International Organization*, 63(3): 425–57.

Mansfield, Edward D., Helen Milner, and Jon Pevehouse. 2008. "Democracy, Veto Players and the Depth of Regional Integration." *The World Economy*, 31(1): 67–96.

Manulak, Michael. 2017. "Leading by Design: Informal Influence and International Secretariats." *Review of International Organizations*, 12(4): 497–522.

Marks, Gary. 1999. "Territorial Identities in the European Union." In Jeffrey J. Anderson (ed.), *Regional Integration and Democracy: Expanding on the European Experience*, 69–91. Boulder, CO: Rowman & Littlefield.

Marks, Gary. 2012. "Europe and Its Empires: From Rome to the European Union." *Journal of Common Market Studies*, 50(1): 1–20.

Marks, Gary and Marco Steenbergen (eds.). 2004. *European Integration and Political Conflict: Citizens, Parties, Groups*. Cambridge: Cambridge University Press.

Marks, Gary and Carole Wilson. 2000. "The Past in the Present: A Theory of Party Response to European Integration." *British Journal of Political Science*, 30(3): 433–59.

Marks, Gary, David Attewell, Jan Rovny, and Liesbet Hooghe. 2018. "The Social Basis of the Transnational Cleavage." Unpublished manuscript.

Marks, Gary, Tobias Lenz, Besir Ceka, and Brian Burgoon. 2014. "Discovering Cooperation: A Contractual Approach to Institutional Change in Regional International Organizations." *EUI Working Paper RSCAS 2014/65*, Florence: Robert Schuman Centre for Advanced Studies.

Marshall, Monty G., Ted Robert Gurr, and Keith Jaggers. 2017. *Polity IV Project: Political Regime Characteristics and Transitions, 1800–2016*. Center for Systemic Peace.

Martin, Lisa. 1992. "Interests, Power, and Multilateralism." *International Organization*, 46(4): 762–92.

Martin, Lisa. 1995. "Heterogeneity, Linkage, and Commons Problems." In Robert O. Keohane and Elinor Ostrom (eds.), *Local Commons and Global Interdependence*, 71–91. Thousand Oaks, CA: Sage.

Martin, Lisa. 2006. "Distribution, Information, and Delegation to International Organizations: The Case of IMF Conditionality." In Darren G. Hawkins, David A. Lake, Daniel L. Nielson, and Michael J. Tierney (eds.), *Delegation and Agency in International Organizations*, 140–64. Cambridge: Cambridge University Press.

Mattila, Mikko. 2009. "Roll Call Analysis of Voting in the European Council of Ministers after the 2004 Enlargement." *European Journal of Political Research*, 48(6): 840–57.

Mattli, Walter. 1999. *The Logic of Regional Integration: Europe and Beyond*. Cambridge: Cambridge University Press.

Maxwell, Rahsaan. 2019. "Cosmopolitan Immigration Attitudes in Large European Cities: Contextual or Compositional Effects?" *American Political Science Review*, published online: https://doi:10.1017/S0003055418000898.

Mayer, Frederick W. 1998. *Interpreting NAFTA: The Science and Art of Political Analysis*. New York: Columbia University Press.

Mearsheimer, John J. 1995. "The False Promise of International Institutions." *International Security*, 19(3): 5–49.

Merrills, J. G. 2011. *International Dispute Settlement*. Cambridge: Cambridge University Press.

Meyer, Jan-Henrik. 2017. "From Nature to Environment: International Organizations and Environmental Protection before Stockholm." In Wolfram Kaiser and Jan-Henrik Meyer (eds.), *International Organizations and Environmental Protection: Globalization and Conservation in the Twentieth Century*, 31–74. New York: Berghahn Books.

Meyer, Peter J. 2014. *Organization of American States: Background and Issues for Congress*. Washington, DC: Congressional Research Service 7–5700.

Mikesell, Raymond F. 1958. "The Lessons of Benelux and the European Coal and Steel Community for the European Economic Community." *The American Economic Review*, 48(2): 428–41.

Milewicz, Karolina, James Hollway, Claire Peacock, and Duncan Snidal. 2018. "Beyond Trade: The Expanding Scope of the Nontrade Agenda in Trade Agreements." *Journal of Conflict Resolution*, 62(4): 743–73.

Miller, Luis and Christoph Vanberg. 2013. "Decision Costs in Legislative Bargaining: An Experimental Analysis." *Public Choice*, 155(3–4): 373–94.

Mills, Kurt and Alan Bloomfield. 2018. "African Resistance to the International Criminal Court: Halting the Advance of the Anti-Impunity Norm." *Review of International Studies*, 44(1): 101–27.

Milner, Helen. 1991. "The Assumption of Anarchy in International Relations Theory: A Critique." *Review of International Studies*, 17(1): 67–85.

Mitchell, Sara McLaughlin and Emilia Justyna Powell. 2009. "Legal Systems and Variance in the Design of Commitments to the International Court of Justice." *Conflict Management and Peace Science*, 26(2): 164–90.

Mitchell, Sara McLaughlin and Emilia Justyna Powell. 2011. *Domestic Law Goes Global: Legal Traditions and International Courts*. Cambridge: Cambridge University Press.

References

Mitrany, David. 1948. "The Functional Approach to World Organization." *International Affairs*, 24(3): 350–63.

Mitrany, David. 1966. *A Working Peace System*. Chicago, IL: Quadrangle Books.

Moe, Terry. 2005. "Power and Political Institutions." *Perspectives on Politics*, 3(2): 215–33.

Moe, Terry M. 2012. "Delegation, Control, and the Study of Public Bureaucracy." In Robert Gibbons and John Roberts (eds.), *Handbook of Organizational Economics*, 1148–82. Princeton, NJ: Princeton University Press.

Moravcsik, Andrew. 1993. "Preferences and Power in the European Community: A Liberal Intergovernmentalist Approach." *Journal of Common Market Studies*, 31(4): 473–524.

Morgan, Catherine. 2003. *Early Greek States Beyond the Polis*. New York: Routledge.

Morgenstern, Scott, Arturo Borja Tamayo, Philippe Faucher, and Daniel Nielson. 2007. "Scope and Trade Agreements." *Canadian Journal of Political Research*, 40(1): 157–83.

Morgenthau, Hans. 1948. *Politics Among Nations: The Struggle for Power and Peace*. New York: Knopf.

Morrow, James. 2014. *Order within Anarchy: The Laws of War as an International Institution*. Cambridge: Cambridge University Press.

Morse, Julia C. and Robert O. Keohane. 2014. "Contested Multilateralism." *Review of International Organizations*, 9(4): 385–412.

Müller, Wolfgang C., Torbjörn Bergman, and Kaare Strøm. 2003. "Parliamentary Democracy: Promise and Problems." In Kaare Strøm, Wolfgang C. Müller, and Torbjörn Bergman (eds.), *Delegation and Accountability in Parliamentary Democracies*, 3–33. Oxford: Oxford University Press.

Munck, Ronaldo. 2007. *Globalization and Contestation: The New Great Counter-Movement*. New York: Routledge.

Mutz, Diana C. 2018. "Status Threat, Not Economic Hardship, Explains the 2016 Presidential Vote." *Proceedings of the National Academy of Sciences of the United States of America*. Available at https://www.pnas.org/cgi/doi/10.1073/pnas.1718155115.

Mutz, Diana C. and Eunji Kim. 2017. "The Impact of In-Group Favoritism on Trade Preferences." *International Organization*, 71(4): 827–50.

Mwale, Siteke. 2001. "An Historical Background to the Formation of COMESA." In Victor Murinde (ed.), *The Free Trade Area of the Common Market for Eastern and Southern Africa*, 31–40. Burlington, VT: Ashgate.

Mytelka, Lynn. 1974. "A Genealogy of Francophone West and Equatorial African Regional Organizations." *Journal of Modern African Studies*, 12(2): 297–320.

Nathan, Laurie. 2013. "The Disbanding of the SADC Tribunal: A Cautionary Tale." *Human Rights Quarterly*, 35(4): 870–92.

Nelson, Stephen and Peter Katzenstein. 2014. "Uncertainty, Risk, and the Financial Crisis of 2008." *International Organization*, 68(2): 361–92.

Nkrumah, Kwame. 1963. *Africa Must Unite*. New York: Praeger.

North, Douglass. 1990. *Institutions, Institutional Change and Economic Performance*. Cambridge: Cambridge University Press.

Novak, Stephanie. 2013. "The Silence of Ministers: Consensus and Blame Avoidance in the Council of the European Union." *Journal of Common Market Studies*, 51(6): 1091–107.

References

Nye, Joseph S. 1967. "Central American Regional Integration." *International Conciliation*, 36(572): 3–66.

Ostrom, Elinor. 1990. *Governing the Commons: The Evolution of Institutions for Collective Action*. Cambridge: Cambridge University Press.

Ostrom, Elinor. 1998. "A Behavioral Approach to the Rational Choice Theory of Collective Action: Presidential Address." *American Political Science Review*, 92(1): 1–22.

Ostrom, Elinor. 2005. *Understanding Institutional Diversity*. Princeton, NJ: Princeton University Press.

Ostrom, Vincent. 1979. "Federal Principles of Organization and Ethnic Communities." In Daniel J. Elazar (ed.), *Federalism and Political Integration*, 73–86. Ramat Gan: Turtledove Publishing.

Packer, Corinne and Donald Rukare. 2002. "The New African Union and its Constitutive Act." *American Journal of International Law*, 96(2): 365–79.

Panke, Diana and Sören Stapel. 2018. "Overlapping Regionalism in Europe: Patterns and Effects." *British Journal of Politics and International Relations*, 20(1): 239–58.

Patel, Kiran Klaus. 2013. "Provincialising European Union: Co-Operation and Integration in Europe in a Historical Perspective." *Contemporary European History*, 22(4): 649–73.

Patel, Kiran Klaus and Oriane Calligaro. 2017. "The True 'Euresco'? The Council of Europe, Transnational Networking and the Emergence of European Community Cultural Policies, 1970–90." *European Review of History*, 24(3): 399–422.

Patrick, Stewart M. 2017. *The Sovereignty Wars: Reconciling America with the World*. Washington DC: Brookings Institution Press.

Pearce, Neil and Debbie A. Lawlor. 2016. "Causal Inference—So Much More Than Statistics." *International Journal of Epidemiology*, 45(6): 1895–903.

Pearl, Judea. 2009. *Causality: Models, Reasoning, and Inference*. New York: Cambridge University Press.

Pearl, Judea, Madelyn Glymour, and Nicholas P. Jewell. 2016. *Causal Inference in Statistics: A Primer*. Chichester: Wiley.

Pelc, Krzysztof. 2016. *Making and Bending International Rules: The Design of Exceptions and Escape Clauses in Trade Law*. Cambridge: Cambridge University Press.

Peralta, Gabriel Aguilera. 2016. "El Regionalismo Centroamericano: Entre la Unión y la Integración." *OASIS*, 24: 89–105.

Pevehouse, Jon C., Timothy Nordstrom, and Kevin Warnke. 2004. "The COW-2 International Organizations Dataset Version 2.0." *Conflict Management and Peace Science*, 21(2): 101–19.

Piattoni, Simona. 2010. *The Theory of Multi-Level Governance: Conceptual, Empirical, and Normative Challenges*. Oxford: Oxford University Press.

Pierson, Paul. 2000. "The Limits of Design: Explaining Institutional Origins and Change." *Governance*, 13(4): 475–99.

Polk, Jonathan and Jan Rovny. 2017. "Anti-Elite/Establishment Rhetoric and Party Positioning on European Integration." *Chinese Political Science Review*, 2(3): 356–71.

Pollack, Mark A. 2003. *The Engines of European Integration: Delegation, Agency, and Agenda Setting in the EU*. Oxford: Oxford University Press.

References

Pollack, Mark A. and Gregory M. Shaffer. 2012. "The Interaction of Formal and Informal Lawmaking." In Joost Pauwelyn, Ramses A. Wessel, and Jan Wouters (eds.), *Informal International Lawmaking*, 241–70. Oxford: Oxford University Press.

Polyakova, Alina and Neil Fligstein. 2016. "Is European Integration Causing Europe to Become More Nationalist? Evidence from the 2007–9 Financial Crisis." *Journal of European Public Policy*, 23(1): 60–83.

Posner, Eric A. and Alan O. Sykes. 2014. "Voting Rules in International Organizations." *Coase-Sandor Working Paper Series in Law and Economics*, No. 673.

Posner, Eric A. and John Yoo. 2005. "Judicial Independence in International Tribunals." *California Law Review*, 93(1): 1–74.

Posner, Richard A. 2004. "The Law and Economics of Contract Interpretation." *Texas Law Review*, 83(6): 1581–614.

Prosser, Christopher. 2016. "Dimensionality, Ideology and Party Positions towards European Integration." *West European Politics*, 39(4): 731–54.

Rae, Douglas. 1967. *The Political Consequences of Electoral Laws*. New Haven, CT: Yale University Press.

Rathbun, Brian C. 2007. "Uncertain About Uncertainty: Understanding the Multiple Meanings of a Crucial Concept in International Relations Theory." *International Studies Quarterly*, 51(3): 533–57.

Rathbun, Brian C. 2012. *Trust in International Cooperation: International Security Institutions, Domestic Politics, and American Multilateralism*. Cambridge: Cambridge University Press.

Rawls, John. 1971. *A Theory of Justice*. Cambridge, MA: Harvard University Press.

Rawls, John. 1999. *The Law of Peoples, with "The Idea of Public Reason Revisited."* Cambridge, MA: Harvard University Press.

Rennie, Kriston R. 2013. *The Foundations of Medieval Papal Legation*. New York: Palgrave Macmillan.

Renou, Ludovic. 2011. "Group Formation and Governance." *Journal of Public Economic Theory*, 13(4): 595–630.

Riches, Cromwell A. 1933. *Unanimity Rule and the League of Nations*. Baltimore, MD: Johns Hopkins University Press.

Riches, Cromwell A. 1940. *Majority Rule in International Organization: A Study of the Trend from Unanimity to Majority Decision*. Baltimore, MD: Johns Hopkins University Press.

Riggirozzi, Pia. 2015. "The Social Turn and Contentious Politics in Latin American Post-Neoliberal Regionalism." In Achim Hurrelmann and Steffen Schneider (eds.), *The Legitimacy of Regional Integration in Europe and the Americas*, 229–50. Basingstoke: Palgrave Macmillan.

Riker, William H. 1964. *Federalism: Origin, Operation, Significance*. Boston, MA: Little, Brown.

Risse, Thomas. 1999. "International Norms and Domestic Change: Arguing and Strategic Adaptation in the Human Rights Area." *Politics and Society*, 27(4): 526–56.

Risse, Thomas. 2000. "Let's Argue! Communicative Action in World Politics." *International Organization*, 54(1): 1–39.

Risse, Thomas. 2010. *A Community of Europeans? Transnational Identities and Public Spheres*. Ithaca, NY: Cornell University Press.

Risse, Thomas. 2017. "De-Centering the European Union: Policy Diffusion among European Regional Organizations – A Comment." *European Review of History*, 24(3): 472–83.

Risse, Thomas, Stephen C. Ropp, and Kathryn Sikkink (eds.) 1999. *The Power of Human Rights: International Norms and Domestic Change*. Cambridge: Cambridge University Press.

Risse-Kappen, Thomas. 1995. *Cooperation Among Democracies: The European Influence on U.S. Foreign Policy*. Princeton, NJ: Princeton University Press.

Rittberger, Berthold. 2005. *Building Europe's Parliament: Democratic Representation Beyond the Nation State*. Oxford: Oxford University Press.

Rittberger, Berthold. 2012. "Institutionalizing Representative Democracy in the European Union: The Case of the European Parliament." *Journal of Common Market Studies*, 50(2): 18–37.

Rixen, Thomas and Bernhard Zangl. 2013. "The Politicization of International Economic Institutions in US Public Debates." *Review of International Organizations*, 8(3): 363–87.

Rocabert, Jofre, Frank Schimmelfennig, Thomas Winzen, and Loriana Crasnic. 2018. "The Rise of International Parliamentary Institutions: Purpose and Legitimation." *Review of International Organizations*, doi: /10.1007/s11558-018-9326-3.

Rohrschneider, Robert and Stephen Whitefield. 2016. "Responding to Growing European Union-Skepticism? The Stances of Political Parties Toward European Integration in Western and Eastern Europe Following the Financial Crisis." *European Union Politics*, 17(1): 138–61.

Romano, Cesare. 2011. "A Taxonomy of International Rule of Law Institutions." *Journal of International Dispute Settlement*, 2(1): 241–77.

Romano, Cesare, Karen J. Alter, and Yuval Shany. 2014. "Mapping International Adjudicative Bodies, Issues, and Players." In Cesare Romano, Karen J. Alter, and Yuval Shany (eds.), *The Oxford Handbook of International Adjudication*, 3–26. Oxford: Oxford University Press.

Rosendorff, B. Peter. 2005. "Stability and Rigidity: Politics and the Design of the WTO's Dispute Resolution Procedure." *American Political Science Review*, 99(3): 389–400.

Rosendorff, Peter and Helen Milner. 2001. "The Optimal Design of International Trade Institutions: Uncertainty and Escape." *International Organization*, 55(4): 829–57.

Ruggie, John G. 1982. "International Regimes, Transactions, and Change: Embedded Liberalism in the Postwar Economic Order." *International Organization*, 36(2): 379–415.

Ruggie, John G. 2003. "The United Nations and Globalization: Patterns and Limits of Institutional Adaptation." *Global Governance*, 9: 301–21.

Russett, Bruce M. 1967. *International Regions and International System: Study in Political Ecology*. Chicago, IL: Rand McNally and Company.

Russett, Bruce M., John R. Oneal, and M. Michaelene Cox. 2000. "Clash of Civilizations, or Realism and Liberalism Déjà Vu? Some Evidence." *Journal of Peace Research*, 37(5): 583–608.

Rydgren, Jens (ed.). 2013. *Class Politics and the Radical Right*. London: Routledge.

SADC. 2001a. "Protocol on Tribunal and the Rules of Procedure Thereof." August 7.

References

SADC. 2001b. "The Treaty of the Southern African Development Community as Amended." August 14.

SADC. 2014. "Protocol on the Tribunal in the Southern African Development Community." August 18.

Sandel, Michael. 1998. *Liberalism and the Limits of Justice.* Cambridge: Cambridge University Press.

Sandholtz, Wayne and John Zysman. 1989. "1992: Recasting the European Bargain." *World Politics*, 42(1): 95–128.

Sandler, Todd. 2004. *Global Collective Action.* Cambridge: Cambridge University Press.

Saurugger, Sabine. 2016. "Politicisation and Integration through Law: Whither Integration Theory?" *West European Politics*, 39(5): 933–52.

Schedler, Andreas. 2012. "Judgment and Measurement in Political Science." *Perspectives on Politics*, 10(1): 21–36.

Schimmelfennig, Frank. 2002. "Goffman Meets IR: Dramaturgical Action in International Community." *International Review of Sociology*, 12(3): 417–37.

Schimmelfennig, Frank. 2010. "The Normative Origins of Democracy in the European Union: Toward a Transformationalist Theory of Democratization." *European Political Science Review*, 2(2): 211–33.

Schimmelfennig, Frank. 2014. "European Integration in the Euro Crisis: The Limits of Postfunctionalism." *Journal of European Integration*, 36(3): 321–37.

Schimmelfennig, Frank. 2018a. "European Integration (Theory) in Times of Crisis: A Comparison of the Euro and Schengen Crises." *Journal of European Public Policy*, 25(7): 969–89.

Schimmelfennig, Frank. 2018b. "Brexit: Differentiated Integration in the European Union." *Journal of European Public Policy*, 25(8): 1154–73.

Schmitter, Philippe C. 1969. "Three Neo-Functional Hypotheses about International Integration." *International Organization*, 23(1): 161–6.

Schmitter, Philippe C. 1970a. "A Revised Theory of Regional Integration." *International Organization*, 24(4): 836–68.

Schmitter, Philippe C. 1970b. "Central American Integration: Spill-Over, Spill-Around or Encapsulation?" *Journal of Common Market Studies*, 9(1): 1–48.

Schmitter, Philippe C. 1996. "Examining the Present Euro-Polity with the Help of Past Theories." In Gary Marks, Fritz W. Scharpf, Philippe C Schmitter, and Wolfgang Streeck (eds.), *Governance in the European Union*, 121–50. London and Thousand Oaks, CA: Sage.

Schuman, Frederick L. 1951. "The Council of Europe." *American Political Science Review*, 45(3): 724–40.

Sewell, James P. 1975. *UNESCO and World Politics: Engaging in International Relations.* Princeton, NJ: Princeton University Press.

Sexton, Jay. 2011. *The Monroe Doctrine: Empire and Nation in Nineteenth Century America.* New York: Hill and Wang.

Shanks, Cheryl, Harold K. Jacobson, and Jeffrey H. Kaplan. 1996. "Inertia and Change in the Constellation of International Governmental Organizations, 1981–1992." *International Organization*, 50(4): 593–627.

Shaw, Timothy. 2005. "Four Decades of Commonwealth Secretariat and Foundation: Continuing Contributions to Global Governance?" *The Round Table*, 94(380): 359–65.

Shaw, Timothy. 2008. *Commonwealth: Inter- and Non-State Contributions to Global Governance*. New York: Routledge.

Shelton, Dinah (ed.) 2000. *Commitment and Compliance: The Role of Non-Binding Norms in the International Legal System*. Oxford: Oxford University Press.

Shubik, Martin. 1982. *Game Theory in the Social Sciences, Vol. 1: Concepts and Solutions*. Cambridge, MA: MIT Press.

Sidanius, Jim, Hillary Haley, Ludwin Molina, and Felicia Pratto. 2007. "Vladimir's Choice and the Distribution of Social Resources: A Group Dominance Perspective." *Group Processes and Intergroup Relations*, 10(2): 257–65.

Sikkink, Kathryn and Carrie Booth Walling. 2007. "The Impact of Human Rights Trials in Latin America." *Journal of Peace Research*, 44(4): 427–45.

Simmons, Beth and Allison Danner. 2010. "Credible Commitments and the International Criminal Court." *International Organization*, 64(2): 225–56.

Simmons, Beth A. 2009. *Mobilizing for Human Rights: International Law in Domestic Politics*. Cambridge: Cambridge University Press.

Simon, Herbert. 1981. *The Sciences of the Artificial*. Cambridge, MA: MIT Press.

Singer, J. David. 1987. "Reconstructing the Correlates of War Dataset on Material Capabilities of States, 1816–1985." *International Interactions*, 14: 115–32.

Singer, J. David, Stuart Bremer, and John Stuckey. 1972. "Capability Distribution, Uncertainty, and Major Power War, 1820–1965." In Bruce Russett (ed.), *Peace, War, and Numbers*, 19–48. Beverly Hills, CA: Sage.

Slater, Jerome. 1969. "The Limits of Legitimization in International Organizations: The Organization of American States and the Dominican Crisis." *International Organization*, 23(1): 48–72.

Smith, Vernon L. 2010. "Theory and Experiment: What Are the Questions?" *Journal of Economic Behavior and Organization*, 73: 3–15.

Snidal, Duncan. 1985. "Coordination Versus Prisoners' Dilemma: Implications for International Cooperation and Regimes." *American Political Science Review*, 79(4): 923–42.

Snidal, Duncan. 1994. "The Politics of Scope: Endogenous Actors, Heterogeneity and Institutions." *Journal of Theoretical Politics*, 6(4): 449–72.

Solingen, Etel. 2008. "The Genesis, Design and Effects of Regional Institutions: Lessons from East Asia and the Middle East." *International Studies Quarterly*, 52: 261–94.

Solingen, Etel and Joshua Malnight. 2016. "Globalization, Domestic Politics, and Regionalism." In Tanja Börzel and Thomas Risse (eds.), *The Oxford Handbook of Comparative Regionalism*, 64–86. Oxford: Oxford University Press.

Soriano, Víctor Fernández. 2017. "Facing the Greek Junta: The European Community, the Council of Europe and the Rise of Human-Rights Politics in Europe." *European Review of History*, 24(3): 358–76.

Spierenburg, Dirk. 1994. "Gesprek met Dirk Spierenburg." In A. Postma, H. Balthazar, L.J. Brinkhorst, Michel Dumoulin, and Norbert von Kunitzki (eds.), *Benelux in de kijker: Vijftig jaar samenwerking*, 92–7. Tielt: Memorial Books.

References

Stein, Arthur. 1982. "Cooperation and Collaboration: Regimes in an Anarchic World." *International Organization*, 36(2): 299–324.

Stock, James H. and Mark W. Watson. 2008. "Heteroskedasticity-Robust Standard Errors for Fixed Effects Regression." *Econometrica*, 76: 155–74.

Stone, Randall. 2011. *Controlling Institutions: International Organizations and the Global Economy*. Cambridge: Cambridge University Press.

Stone Sweet, Alec and Thomas Brunell. 1998. "Constructing a Supranational Constitution: Dispute Resolution and Governance in the European Community." *American Political Science Review*, 92(1): 63–80.

Stubager, Rune. 2010. "The Development of the Education Cleavage: Denmark as a Critical Case." *West European Politics*, 33(3): 505–33.

Sugden, Robert. 1986. *The Economics of Rights, Cooperation and Welfare*. Oxford: Blackwell.

Tajfel, Henri. 1981. *Human Groups and Social Categories: Studies in Social Psychology*. Cambridge: Cambridge University Press.

Tajfel, Henri and John C. Turner. 1986. "The Social Identity Theory of Intergroup Behavior." In Stephen Worchel and William G. Austin (eds.), *Psychology of Intergroup Relations*, 7–24. Chicago, IL: Nelson-Hall.

Tallberg, Jonas. 2002. "Delegation to Supranational Institutions: Why, How, and with What Consequences?" *West European Politics*, 25(1): 23–46.

Tallberg, Jonas, Thomas Sommerer, Theresa Squatrito, and Christer Jönsson. 2013. *The Opening up of International Organizations: Transnational Access in Global Governance*. Cambridge: Cambridge University Press.

Tallberg, Jonas, Thomas Sommerer, Theresa Squatrito, and Christer Jönsson. 2014. "Explaining the Transnational Design of International Organizations." *International Organization*, 68(4): 741–74.

Tarrow, Sidney. 2005. *The New Transnational Activism*. Cambridge: Cambridge University Press.

Teasdale, Anthony. 1993. "The Life and Death of the Luxembourg Compromise." *Journal of Common Market Studies*, 31(4): 567–79.

Teney, Céline, Onawa P. Lacewell, and Pieter de Wilde. 2013. "Winners and Losers of Globalization in Europe: Attitudes and Ideologies." *European Political Science Review*, 6(4): 575–95.

Thatcher, Margaret. 1989. "House of Commons PQs." *Hansard IIC* [153/162 66].

Thomas, Christopher and Juliana T. Magloire. 2000. *Regionalism versus Multilateralism: The Organization of American States in a Global Changing Environment*. Boston, MA: Kluwer Academic Publishers.

Thompson, James D. 2003. *Organizations in Action*. New Brunswick, NJ: Transaction Publishers.

Thomson, Robert. 2011. *Resolving Controversy in the European Union*. Cambridge: Cambridge University Press.

Trubek, David M. and Louise G. Trubek. 2005. "Hard and Soft Law in the Construction of Social Europe: The Role of the Open Method of Co-Ordination." *European Law Journal*, 11: 343–64.

Tsebelis, George. 2002. *Veto Players: How Political Institutions Work*. Princeton, NJ: Princeton University Press.

Tsebelis, George and Hyeonho Hahm. 2014. "Suspending Vetoes: How the Euro Countries Achieved Unanimity in the Fiscal Compact." *Journal of European Public Policy*, 21(10): 1388–411.

Tuomela, Raimo. 2007. *The Philosophy of Sociality: The Shared Point of View*. Oxford: Oxford University Press.

UNESCO. 1946. *Constitution of the United Nations Educational, Scientific and Cultural Organization*. London, November 16.

Vabulas, Felicity. 2017. "Withdrawing from Intergovernmental Organizations: Understanding When and Why States Exit." Paper presented at the Annual Meeting of the American Political Science Association, San Francisco, August 31–September 3.

Vabulas, Felicity and Duncan Snidal. 2013. "Organization without Delegation: Informal Intergovernmental Organizations (IIGOs) and the Spectrum of Intergovernmental Arrangements." *Review of International Organizations*, 8(2): 193–220.

Van Aken, Wim. 2012. "Voting the Council of the European Union." *SIEPS Report No. 2*. Stockholm: Swedish Institute for European Policy Studies.

Van Elsas, Erika J., Armen Hakhverdian, and Wouter van der Brug. 2016. "United Against a Common Foe? The Nature and Origins of Euroscepticism among Left-Wing and Right-Wing Citizens." *West European Politics*, 39(6): 1181–204.

Van Kersbergen, Kees, and Catherine E. De Vries. 2007. "Interests, Identity and Political Allegiance in the European Union. *Acta Politica*, 42(2): 307–28.

van Roon, G. 1994. "Toenadering in golven: de voorgeschiedenis van de Benelux." In A. Postma, H. Balthazar, L.J. Brinkhorst, Michel Dumoulin, and Norbert von Kunitzki (eds.), *Benelux in de kijker: Vijftig jaar samenwerking*, 11–37. Tielt: Memorial Books.

Van Wynen Thomas, Ann and A.J. Thomas Jr. 1970. "The Organization of American States and the Monroe Doctrine: Legal Implications." *Louisiana Law Review*, 30(4): 541–81.

Verdier, Daniel. 2015. "The Dilemma of Informal Governance with Outside Option as Solution." *International Theory*, 7: 195–229.

Vernon, Raymond. 1971. *Sovereignty at Bay: The Multinational Spread of U.S. Enterprises*. New York: Basic Books.

Voeten, Erik. 2007. "The Politics of International Judicial Appointments: Evidence from the European Court of Human Rights." *International Organization*, 61(4): 669–701.

Waltz, Kenneth. 1979. *Theory of International Politics*. Reading, MA: Addison-Wesley.

Wassenberg, Birte. 2017. "Between Cooperation and Competitive Bargaining: The Council of Europe, Local and Regional Networking, and the Shaping of the European Community's Regional Policies, 1970s–90s." *European Review of History*, 24(3): 423–44.

WCO. 2009/10. *World Customs Organization: Mission, Objectives, Activities*. Brussels: World Customs Organization.

Webber, Douglas. 2019. *European Disintegration? The Politics of Crisis in the European Union*. London: Red Globe Press.

Weber, Max. 1958. "The Three Types of Legitimate Rule." Translated by Hans Gerth. *Berkeley Publications in Society and Institutions*, 4(1): 1–11.

Weber, Max. 1968. *Economy and Society*. Edited by Günther Roth and Claus Wittich. Berkeley: University of California Press.

References

Weisglas, M. 1994. "Gesprek met Prof. dr. M. Weisglas." In A. Postma, H. Balthazar, L.J. Brinkhorst, Michel Dumoulin, and Norbert von Kunitzki (eds.), *Benelux in de kijker: Vijftig jaar samenwerking*, 71–6. Tielt: Memorial Books.

Welz, Martin. 2013. *Integrating Africa: Decolonization's Legacies, Sovereignty and the African Union*. London: Routledge.

Westerwinter, Oliver. 2016. "The Politics of Informal Governance." Unpublished manuscript.

White, Nigel David. 2000. "The United Nations System: Conference, Contract or Constitutional Order?" *Singapore Journal of International and Comparative Law*, 4: 281–99.

Williams, Paul D. 2007. "From Non-Intervention to Non-Indifference: The Origins and Development of the African Union's Security Culture." *African Affairs*, 106(423): 253–79.

Williamson, Oliver. 1975. *Markets and Hierarchies: Analysis and Antitrust Implications*. New York: Free Press.

Wooldridge, Jeffrey. 2002. *Econometric Analysis of Cross Section and Panel Data*. Cambridge, MA: MIT Press.

Yack, Bernard. 1993. *The Problems of a Political Animal*. Berkeley: University of California Press.

Zafar, Ali and Keiko Kubota. 2003. "Regional Integration in Central Africa: Key Issues." *Africa Region Working Paper Series No. 52*. Washington, DC: The World Bank.

Zamora, Stephen. 1980. "Voting in International Economic Organizations." *American Journal of International Law*, 74: 566–608.

Zürn, Michael. 1992. *Interessen und Institutionen in der internationalen Politik: Grundlegung und Anwendung des situationsstrukturellen Ansatzes*. Opladen: Leske and Budrich.

Zürn, Michael. 2004. "Global Governance and Legitimacy Problems." *Government and Opposition*, 39(2): 260–87.

Zürn, Michael. 2012. "The Politicization of World Politics and Its Effects: Eight Propositions." *European Political Science Review*, 6(1): 47–71.

Zürn, Michael. 2018. *A Theory of Global Governance: Authority, Legitimacy, and Contestation*. Oxford: Oxford University Press.

Zürn, Michael, Martin Binder, and Matthias Ecker-Ehrhardt. 2012. "International Authority and Its Politicization." *International Theory*, 4(1): 69–106.

Index

Abbott, Kenneth W. 97, 125–6
Acharya, Amitav 100
Achiume, Tendayi 102
Adcock, Robert 26
Affluence 66–7, 69, 71, 73, 97–8, 110, 131, 135, 138
African Union (AU) 55, 58, 68, 73, 81–3, 151; Organization of African Unity (OAU) 55, 81
Agenda setting 7, 34–6, 39, 86–7, 99, 101, 109, 125, 131, 136–7, 141–2, 144
Aksoy, Deniz 87, 159
Allee, Todd 44, 159
Alter, Karen J. 44, 74, 80, 88, 101–2
Anarchy 3–4, 6, 12, 123, 126, 128
Andean Community (CAN) 46, 49, 80, 90, 94
Angola 81
Appleman Williams, William 80
Arab Maghreb Union (AMU) 49, 150
Argentina 94
Aristotle 14, 17, 21, 123
Arnold, Christian 44
Arrow, Kenneth J. 87
Association of Southeast Asian Nations (ASEAN) 30, 40, 64, 100–1, 146, 154
Attewell, David ix
Austria 24
Authority 38, 41–3, 45, 49, 67, 74, 76–7, 84–7, 89, 91, 94, 97–9, 103–11, 113, 115, 117, 119–21, 126–9, 131–3, 136–7, 139–42, 150–1, 153, 159; International authority ix, 3–4, 7, 26–7, 29, 31–3, 35, 37–9, 41, 43, 84–5, 87–9, 91, 95, 97–101, 103, 119, 121, 130, 140–1, 145; Legal authority 28, 31; Measure of International Authority (MIA) viii, ix, 38, 43, 140–1
Avant, Deborah 126
Awoumou, Come Damien Georges 116
Axelrod, Robert 15
Aziz, Shaukat 78

Baccini, Leonardo 44, 72
Baert, Francis 78
Bailey, Michael A. 113, 137

Balassa, Bela 145
Bank for International Settlements (BIS) 55, 64, 112, 139
Barker, Ernest 21
Barnett, Michael 44, 112
Bartels, Larry M. 100
Bartolini, Stefano 89
Bauer, Steffen *see* Biermann et al. 2009 30
Beck, Hans 22
Beck, Nathaniel 69
Becker, Sascha O. 133
Beckert, Jens 16
Benelux Union (BENELUX) 150, 152–3
Berger-Eforo, Judith 57
Bergman, Torbjörn 87
Bernauer, Thomas 44
Bernhard, Helen 130
Beyeler, Michelle 97
Beyers, Jan 88
Bezuijen, Jeanine iii, viii, 3, 58
Bianculli, Andrea C. 79
Bickerton, Christopher J. 23
Biermann, Frank ix, 30, 44
Binder, Martin 85, 133
Bindingness 7, 35–6, 94–6, 111, 140, 142
Bingham, Tom 123
Blake, Daniel J. 44, 109
Bloomfield, Alan 57
Boak, A.E.R. 21–2
Boehmer, Charles 138, 145
Boekestijn, A.J. 70
Bollen, Kenneth 37
Bolt, Jutta 135
Booth Walling, Carrie 80
Bond, Martyn 74
Borja Tamayo, Arturo *see* Morgenstern et al. 2007 85
Bornschier, Simon 89; *see* Kriesi et al. 2006 19, 133; *see* Kriesi et al. 2008 23, 85, 89
Börzel, Tanja viii, 23, 64, 89–90
Bow, Brian 90
Bradley, Curtis A. 33, 87
Brazys, Samuel 14

Index

Bremer, Stuart *see* Singer, J. David et al. 1972 138
Brewer, Marilynn B. 130
Brewer, Stephanie Erin 80
Brinkley, Douglas 107, 114
Brosig, Malte 74
Brown, Robert L. 33
Brunell, Thomas 66, 70
Buchanan, James M. 105–6
Buchanan, Patrick J. 90
Bulmer-Thomas, Victor 29
Burgoon, Brian viii, 70
Burilkov, Alexandr 11, 44, 94
Burundi 81
Busch, Per-Olof *see* Biermann et al. 2009 30
Büthe, Tim 71

Caldentey del Pozo, Pedro 29
Calligaro, Oriane 74
Cameron, Maxwell 90
Campe, Sabine see Biermann et al. 2009 30
Canada 60–1, 80
Caribbean Community (CARICOM) 29, 64–5, 80, 90, 139, 150, 153; Caribbean Free Trade Association (CARIFTA) 29, 151, 153
Carl, Noah 89
Carnegie, Allison 66, 70, 97
Carroll, Lewis 78, 123
Carrubba, Clifford J. 88
Cary, M. 22
Cavallaro, James L. 80
Ceka, Besir iii, viii, 3, 70
Central African Customs and Economic Union (UDEAC) 116
Central American Integration System (SICA) 29, 90, 139, 150; Organization of Central American States (ODECA) 29
Central Commission for the Navigation of the Rhine (CCNR) 40, 45, 49, 139
Centre for Agriculture and Bioscience International (CABI) 55, 139, 150
Chad 82
Chapman Osterkatz, Sandra 3
Chayes, Abram 16, 62
Checkel, Jeffrey ix, 62
Childers, Erskine 76
Chinaka, Cris 102
Chomsky, Noam 46
CIA World Factbook 135, 148
Clapham, Andrew 124
Claude, Inis L. 114, 115
Cockerham, Geoffrey 44
Coleman, Liv 44, 112
Collier, David 26–7
Commission of the European Communities 118

Common Market for Eastern and Southern Africa (COMESA) 29, 55, 139, 150; Preferential Trade Area for Eastern and Southern Africa (PTA-ESA) 29
Commonwealth Ministerial Action Group (CMAG) 79
Commonwealth of Nations 68, 78, 83, 139, 150
Commonwealth Secretariat (ComSec) 79; Commonwealth Ministerial Action Group (CMAG) 79
Community i–iii, 2–3, 5–6, 9–10, 12–19, 21–5, 20, 40, 44, 46–59, 61–83, 85–6, 88, 99–100, 112, 116–17, 121, 125, 130–6, 139, 148–52; Epistemic community 99, 113, 136; Overarching community 5, 11, 51, 124–5; Transnational community 7, 18–19, 25, 45, 47–8, 105, 130–1
Community of Latin American and Caribbean States (CELAC) 79–80
Compliance 94–5, 101, 136–7, 140–1, 151; Financial compliance 96, 109, 115–16, 142–4
Conceição-Heldt, Eugénia da ix, 84
Consensus 15, 31, 39, 59, 80, 94, 99–101, 103, 109, 118, 133
Constructivism 5
Contract vii, 4, 6–7, 10–15, 20, 29, 44–6, 48–50, 53, 58–71, 73, 83, 85, 88, 93, 100, 103, 105, 121–4, 127–8, 130–1, 135–6, 138, 146, 151, 153; Complete contract 4, 53, 61, 65, 68, 91, 136, 151–3; Contractual basis 2, 7, 44, 61, 65; Incomplete contract 2, 4, 6, 14–15, 22, 25, 48, 53, 58, 60–2, 64–5, 68, 70, 73–5, 78, 83, 92, 122, 125, 151–3; Incomplete contracting vii, 14, 60, 67, 72–3, 83, 85–6, 122, 125, 131, 151; Social contract 6, 12, 20; Social contract theory vii, 3, 6, 11, 128
Cooley, Alexander 49
Copelovitch, Mark 64, 90
Core policy 74, 136, 138, 146; Policy portfolio i, vii, 1–2, 5, 7, 25, 30, 44–50, 52–3, 56, 58–63, 65–7, 69–75, 77, 79, 81, 83–8, 92, 96, 98–9, 103, 105, 109, 121–2, 129, 131, 133, 145–6, 148, 151; Policy scope 29, 44, 53, 56, 60, 62–3, 66, 69–71, 73, 83, 85–7, 91, 96, 98–100, 110, 113, 135–8, 145–7
Core state powers 97–9, 110, 136, 138
Council for Mutual Economic Assistance (COMECON) 29
Council of Europe (CoE) 58, 73–5, 112, 151
Council of Ministers 116–17
Cox, M. Michaelene 135, 148
Cram, Laura 130
Crasnic, Loriana *see* Rocabert et al. 2018 44
Curtice, John 89

Index

Dahl, Robert 24, 28
Danner, Allison 57
Davis, Christina ii, 44, 58
De Lombaerde, Philippe 138, 156
De Vries, Catherine E. 24, 89, 133
de Wilde, Pieter 18, 24, 84, 88–9, 133
Deflem, Mathieu 112
Delegation vii, 7, 2–7, 32–4, 36–44, 84–6, 90–4, 97–102, 117, 121, 129, 131, 135–6, 138, 140–4
Delors, Jacques 117
Democracy 66–7, 69–71, 73, 79, 91, 94, 97–8, 102, 110, 131, 136, 138, 145
Denmark 51, 89, 150
Dennison, James 24, 89
Derderyan, Svet iii, viii, 3
Deutsch, Karl W. 17, 21, 47, 148
Díez Medrano, Juan ix, 130
Dingwerth, Klaus 133; *see* Biermann et al. 2009 30
Diogo, Luisa Dias 78
Dolezal, Martin *see* Kriesi et al. 2006 19, 133; *see* Kriesi et al. 2008 23, 85, 89
Dooge Committee 117
Drezner, Daniel 23
Duina, Francesco 44
Dür, Andreas 44, 72
Dworkin, Ronald 88

East African Community (EAC) 29, 40, 64, 125, 150
Ecker-Ehrhardt, Matthias 85, 91, 133
Eckhardt, Jappe 44
Economic and Monetary Community of Central African States (CEMAC) 116, 150
Economic Community of West African States (ECOWAS) 49, 68
Economic interdependence 72
Economies of scale 12, 20, 47, 119
Egeberg, Morten 88
Egypt 77
El-Affendi, Abdelwahab 54
Elias, T.O. ix, 81
Elliott, Larry 91
Ellis, Charles Howard 115
Ellis, David 48
Elsig, Manfred 44, 72
Enlargement 117–18, 136, 138
Epistemic community 99, 113, 136
Estonia 51
European Central Bank (ECB) 23, 90
European Coal and Steel Community (ECSC) 9–10, 22, 29–30, 74, 125, 152
European Council 118
European Court of Justice 102
European Economic Area (EEA) 40
European Economic Community (EEC) 29–30

European Organization for Nuclear Research (CERN) 46, 63
European Parliament 48, 94
European Space Agency (ESA) 46
European Union (EU) vii, 9–10, 21–2, 29–30, 46, 48–9, 51, 54, 60, 64, 68, 73–4, 82, 86, 89–90, 94, 116, 119, 121, 125, 127, 151–2; Commission of the European Communities 118; Dooge Committee 117; European Central Bank (ECB) 23, 90; European Coal and Steel Community (ECSC) 9–10, 22, 29–30, 74, 125, 152; European Council 118; European Court of Justice 102; European Economic Area (EEA) 40; European Economic Community (EEC) 29–30; European Parliament 48, 94
Evans, Geoffrey 133

Faucher, Philippe *see* Morgenstern et al. 2007 85
Fawcett, Louise 78
Federalism iii, 4, 20–1, 74
Feenstra, Robert C. 135, 137
Fehr, Ernst 130
Felício, Tania 78
Fetzer, Thiemo 133
Fiji 79
Financial compliance 7, 34, 96, 109, 115–16, 142–4
Finland 51, 150
Finnemore, Martha 44, 91
Fischbacher, Urs 130
Fligstein, Neil 89
Fooner, Michael 112
France 10, 89, 117, 126
Franck, Thomas 88
Fredland, Richard A. 81
Frey, Timotheos *see* Kriesi et al. 2006 19, 133; *see* Kriesi et al. 2008 23, 85, 89
Frieden, Jeffry 64, 90
Functionalist theory 2, 4, 12, 103, 128; Postfunctionalist theory 1, 6–7, 9, 11, 13, 15, 17, 19, 21, 23, 25, 103, 121, 124
Funke, Peter 22

Gabel, Matthew 88
Gardini, Gian Luca 80
Gartzke, Erik 138, 145
Gathii, James T. 102
Geddes, Andrew 24
General purpose governance 4, 7, 11, 14, 47, 49, 57, 61, 73, 75, 78, 82, 131, 151
Genschel, Philipp ix, 23, 90, 97, 136; *see* Abbott et al. 2015 125; *see* Abbott et al. 2016 126
Germany i, 10, 112
Ghana 81

189

Index

Gibbons, Robert 48
Glymour, Madelyn 50
Godwin Bongyu, Moye 116
Goetze, Stefan 94
Goldstein, Judith 44
Gora, Anna 89
Governance iii, v, vii, ix, 1–8, 10–25, 28, 32–3, 45, 47–8, 50, 52–3, 58–9, 61, 73, 75–6, 79, 85, 94, 99, 104–5, 114, 121–32; General purpose governance 4, 7, 11, 14, 47, 49, 57, 61, 73, 75, 78, 82, 131, 151; International governance i–ii, vii, 2–6, 8, 10–11, 13–14, 17–20, 22, 25, 33, 38, 47, 49, 59, 67, 82, 84–5, 89–90, 99, 103–4, 120–5, 127–34; Task-specific governance 7, 48–50, 52, 57, 122, 124
Graham, Kennedy 77–8
Grande, Edgar ix, 23, 85, 88–9; see Kriesi et al. 2006 19, 133; see Kriesi et al. 2008 23, 85, 89
Gray, Julia viii, 26–7, 29, 37, 72, 93
Green-Pedersen, Christoffer 89
Greif, Avner 62
Grieco, Joseph 97
Grigorescu, Alexandru 44, 74
Grosbois, Th. 70
Grothmann, Torsten see Biermann et al. 2009 30
Gurr, Ted Robert 136, 149
Gutiérrez, P. 130

Haas, Ernst B. 48
Haas, Peter 99
Habermas, Jürgen 15
Hafner-Burton, Emilie 44
Haftel, Yoram viii, 109, 145
Hahm, Hyeonho 87
Hakhverdian, Armen 89, 133
Haley, Hillary see Sidanius et al. 2007 130
Hammarskjöld, Dag 77
Handler Chayes, Antonia 16, 63
Hanhimäki, Jussi M. 76
Hansen, Mogens Herman 21
Hart, Oliver 14–15, 61, 124
Hartigan, J.A. 55–6
Hartigan, P.M. 55–6
Häusermann, Silja 133
Hawkins, Darren G. 32, 44, 66, 87–8, 97
Hayes-Renshaw, Fiona 32, 118
Hebel, Kai 19
Heisenberg, Dorothée 32
Helfer, Laurence R. 102
Henderson, Rebecca 48
Henrikson, Alan K. 78
Herman, Lawrence L. 61
Herrmann, Richard K. 130

Hetherington, Marc 24
Hilderbrand, Robert C. 107
Hinsley, F. H. 127
Historical ties 66–7, 137–8, 150–1; Historical ties extended 137–8, 151
Hobbes, Thomas 3, 12, 20, 127
Hobolt, Sara B. 24, 32, 89, 133
Hoffmann, Andrea Ribeiro 90
Hoffmann, Stanley 117
Hofmann, Stephanie 80, 145
Höglinger, Dominic 89
Hollway, James see Milewicz et al. 2018 70
Hooghe, Liesbet i–iii, v–vi, viii, 3, 19, 23–4, 26, 29, 32–5, 38–9, 47, 63, 75, 84–5, 88–90, 101, 121, 127–8, 130, 132–3, 136–7, 141, 147
Hoopes, Townsend 107, 115
Hosli, Madeleine O. 118
Houser, Daniel see Mccabe et al. 2001 16
Hug, Simon 87
Hume, David 15
Huntington, Samuel P. 135, 148
Hurrell, Andrew 76
Hurrelmann, Achim 23, 85, 89–90
Hutter, Swen 24, 85, 88–9

Iapadre, P. Lelio 138, 158
Iceland 51, 150
Ideal points 70, 113, 137–8, 148
Ikenberry, G. John 38, 78
Implementation 118, 140
Indonesia 100
Inglehart, Ronald 89, 133
Inklaar, Robert 135, 137
Inter-American Court of Human Rights (IACHR) 80
Inter-American Development Bank (IADB) 79
Interdependence 4, 6, 16, 70–3, 83, 99, 128; Economic interdependence 72; Trade interdependence 72–3, 83, 99, 131, 135, 138, 148, 156, 158
Intergovernmental Authority on Development (IGAD) 65, 150, 153
Intergovernmental Organization for International Carriage by Rail (OTIF) 42, 49, 55
International Atomic Energy Agency (IAEA) 40, 112
International authority 41, 43, 84–5, 87–9, 91, 93, 95, 97–101, 103, 119, 121, 130, 140, 141, 145, 159
International Civil Aviation Organization (ICAO) 40, 84, 94
International Court of Justice 37, 57
International Criminal Court (ICC) 57, 132, 140, 155

International Criminal Police Organization (Interpol) 111–12
International Labour Organization (ILO) 112, 114
International Monetary Fund (IMF) 45, 91–2, 94–5, 111, 132, 140
International Organization for Migration (IOM) 57
International scale 45
International Telecommunications Union 75
International Whaling Commission (IWhale) 46, 57
Iran 132
Iraq 126

Jachtenfuchs, Markus ix, 23, 90, 97, 136
Jackson, Robert 48
Jacobson, Harold K. 135, 149
Jaggers, Keith 136, 149
Jefferson, Thomas 18
Jetschke, Anja 100–1
Jewell, Nicholas P. 50
Jiménez, Edgard Moncayo 77
Jo, Hyeran 44
Johns, Leslie 44
Johnson, Tana 31, 76, 99
Johnstone, Ian 16
Jones, Erik R. 90
Jönsson, Christer *see* Tallberg et al. 2013 44; *see* Tallberg et al. 2014 87, 94, 97, 153
Joris, Tony 74–5
Jupille, Joseph 61
Jurisdiction 6, 12, 18, 25, 28, 45, 47, 88–9, 102, 128

Kahler, Miles 33, 70, 101
Kant, Immanuel 3, 20
Kaplan, Jeffrey H. 135, 149
Karns, Margaret P. 77
Katada, Saori N. 100
Katz, Jonathan N. 69
Katzenstein, Peter 16
Kay, Tamara 85
Keck, Margaret E. 19
Kelemen, Daniel 90
Kelley, Judith G. 33, 57, 87
Kennedy, Paul 77
Keohane, Robert O. 117, 128
Kersten, A.E. 70
Khong, Yuen Foong 101
Kim, Eunji 130
Kindleberger, Charles 66
Kirsch, Werner 118
Kleider, Hanna 89
Kleine, Mareike 32, 125
Klingemann, Hans-Dieter 23
Knack, Stephen 14, 62

König, Thomas 87
Kono, Daniel Y. 88, 97
Koopmans, Ruud *see* De Wilde et al. 2019 18, 24, 84, 88–9, 133
Koremenos, Barbara ix, 16, 32, 44, 66, 87–8, 97, 107, 123, 128
Krasner, Stephen D. ix, 97
Krehbiel, Keith 87
Kriesi, Hanspeter ix, 19, 23–4, 85, 88–9, 97, 133
Kubota, Keiko 116
Kucik, Jeffrey 44
Kuhn, Theresa 23, 89

La Francophonie (OIF) 55, 68
Lacewell, Onawa P. 133
Lachat, Romain *see* Kriesi et al. 2006 19, 133; *see* Kriesi et al. 2008 23, 85, 89
Laffan, Brigid ix, 74, 89
Laffont, Jean-Jacques 16
Laitin, David 62
Lakatos, Imre 46
Lake, David A. 132
Langner, Jessica 118
Latin American and Caribbean Economic System (SELA) 79
Latin American Integration Association (ALADI) 79
Lawlor, Debbie A. 50
League of Arab States (LOAS) 58, 151
Lee, Matthew 132
Leeper, Thomas J. 24, 133
Legal authority 28, 31
Lehmann, Ina *see* Dingwerth et al. 2015 133
Lenz, Tobias i–iii, v–vi, 3, 11, 19, 26, 33, 38, 44, 47, 70, 94, 102, 128, 132
Lerner, Michael 44
Leupold, Anna 84, 88–9
Liberal institutionalism 4
Liddell, George 14
Lindberg, Leon 63, 137
Linos, Katerina 125
Lipset, Seymour Martin 21
Lipson, Charles 16, 44, 66, 97, 107, 125, 128
Locke, John 3, 12, 123
Lockwood Payton, Autumn 44, 109
Lombaerde, Philippe 78, 138, 156
Lundgren, Magnus 145
Luxembourg 70, 117–18

MacKenzie, David Clarke 76
Maggi, Giovanni 108
Magloire, Juliana T. 80
Magliveras, Konstantinos D. 112
Majoritarianism 4, 107–8, 118; Simple majority 39, 96, 99, 105–6, 109–10, 112, 114–15, 142; Supermajority 39, 96, 109–10, 112, 115–16, 118

191

Index

Makinda, Samuel M. 81
Malaysia 100
Maldives 79
Malinowski, W.R. 77
Malnight, Joshua 90
Mann, Michael 17
Mansergh, Nicholas 78
Mansfield, Edward D. 44, 66, 85
Manulak, Michael 44
Marks, Gary i–iii, v–vi, ix, 3, 12, 17, 19, 23–4, 26, 32–3, 38, 47, 63, 70, 84–5, 89–90, 127–8, 130, 132–3, 137, 153
Marschinski, Robert *see* Biermann et al. 2009 30
Marshall, Monty G. 136, 149
Martimort, David 16
Martin, Lisa 66, 97
Mattila, Mikko 32, 118
Mattli, Walter iii, 61, 66, 70, 97, 116
Maxwell, Rahsaan 133
Mayer, Frederick W. 90
McCabe, Kevin 16
McCall Smith, James 35, 44
McCubbins, Mathew 33
McKinnon, Don 78
McNamara, Kathleen 89
Mearsheimer, John J. 4
Measure of International Authority (MIA) viii, ix, 38, 43, 140–1
Measurement viii, 26, 27, 32, 37, 154
Membership 2, 5, 7, 17, 24, 29, 44–5, 49–59, 66, 68–9, 71, 73–5, 78, 80, 82, 97, 104–11, 113–17, 119–22, 128–9, 135–7, 142, 150, 158; Membership accession 7, 43, 52, 95, 109, 136–7, 141–2, 144; Membership suspension 109, 136–7, 141–2, 144
Mérand, Frédéric 80
Mercosur Parliament 94
Merkel, Wolfgang *see* De Wilde et al. 2019 18, 24, 84, 88–9, 133
Merrills, J. G. 35
Meunier, Sophie 74, 90
Mexico 60
Meyer, Jan-Henrik 74
Meyer, Peter J. 80
Mikesell, Raymond F. 70
Milewicz, Karolina 70
Miller, Luis 105–6
Mills, Kurt 57
Milner, Helen 4, 44, 66, 71
Mingst, Karen 77
Mitchell, Sara McLaughlin 44, 136, 149
Mitrany, David 18
Moe, Terry M. 86, 123
Molina, Ludwin *see* Sidanius et al. 2007 130
Moore, John 14–15, 61, 124

Morelli, Massimo 108
Morgan, Catherine 22
Morgenstern, Scott 85
Morgenthau, Hans 127
Morrow, James 16
Mozambique 81
Müller, Wolfgang C. 87
Munck, Ronaldo 91
Mutz, Diana C. 85, 130, 133
Mwale, Siteke 55
Mytelka, Lynn 116

Namgung, Hyun 44
Namibia 81
Nathan, Laurie 102
National sovereignty 1, 5, 9, 18–19, 25, 59, 81, 84, 91, 104–5, 117, 119–20, 123, 126–7, 133, 144–5
National veto 4, 7, 26, 33, 36, 39, 43, 87, 104–5, 108, 115–17, 119–20, 129, 131, 142
Nelson, Stephen 16
Nesadurai, Helen E.S. 101
Netherlands 51
Niedzwiecki, Sara 3
Nielson, Daniel L. *see* Morgenstern et al. 2007 85; *see* Hawkins et al. 2006a 87–8, 97; *see* Hawkins et al. 2006b 32, 44, 66
Nigeria 79
Nkrumah, Kwame 81
Nordic Council (NORDIC) 51, 150
Nordstrom, Timothy 29, 136–8, 145
Norm 2, 5, 7, 16–19, 25, 47, 94–5, 141; Normative commonality 45, 47, 53, 65, 68; Shared norm 2, 7, 11, 49, 59–60, 62, 67, 78, 83, 86, 112, 130, 150
Normative commonality 45, 47, 53, 65, 68
Norris, Pippa 133
North American Free Trade Agreement (NAFTA) 23, 46, 55, 60–1, 68, 90, 121, 132, 139, 151, 154; United States-Mexico-Canada Agreement (USMCA) 60
North Atlantic Treaty Organization (NATO) 68, 72, 102, 126, 154
North, Douglass 31
Norway 51, 150
Novak, Stephanie 32, 118–19
Novy, Dennis 133
Nye, Joseph S. 29, 70

O'Hagan, Adrian 162
Okumu, F. Wafula 81
Oneal, John R. 135, 148
Organization of African Unity (OAU) 55, 81; African Union (AU) 55, 58, 68, 73, 81–3, 151

Organization for Economic Co-Operation and Development (OECD) 58; Organization for European Economic Cooperation (OEEC) 74
Organization for European Economic Cooperation (OEEC) 74
Organization for Security and Cooperation in Europe (OSCE) 55
Organization of American States (OAS) 58, 68, 73, 79–80, 82–3, 151; Inter-American Court of Human Rights (IACHR) 80; Inter-American Development Bank (IADB) 79
Organization of Arab Petroleum Export Countries (OAPEC) 152
Organization of Central American States (ODECA) 29;Central American Integration System (SICA) 29, 80, 90, 94, 150
Organization of Islamic Cooperation (OIC) 55, 121
Organization of Petroleum-Exporting Countries (OPEC) 49
Ostrom, Elinor 5, 14–17, 48, 62, 70, 151
Ostrom, Vincent 21

Packer, Corinne 81
Pakistan 79
Pan American Health Organization (PAHO) 79
Panke, Diana 74
Paraguay 94
Patel, Kiran Klaus 74–5
Patrick, Stewart M. 126
Paxton, Pamela 37
Peacock, Claire see Milewicz et al. 2018 70
Pearce, Neil 50
Pearl, Judea 50, 111
Pegram, Tom 125
Pelc, Krzysztof 44
Peralta, Gabriela Aguilera 29
Permanent Court of Arbitration (PCA) 57, 115–16, 143
Pevehouse, Jon 29, 66, 136–7
Philippines 100
Piattoni, Simona 89
Pierson, Paul 86
Plummer, Michael 138, 158
Policy iii, 5–6, 12, 28, 37, 39, 45–7, 52, 58, 60, 63, 66, 70–1, 74–5, 80–8, 91–2, 94, 99–101, 113, 115–16, 118, 124, 126, 136, 146; Policy making 7, 34, 43, 92, 94–6, 109, 115–16, 136–7, 141–4;Policy portfolio i, vii, 1–2, 5, 7, 25, 30, 44–50, 52–3, 56, 58–63, 65–7, 69–75, 77, 79, 81, 83–8, 92, 96, 98–9, 103, 105, 109, 121–2, 129, 131, 133, 145–6, 148, 151; Policy scope 29, 44, 53, 56, 60, 62–3, 66, 69–71, 73, 83, 85–7, 91, 96, 98–100, 110, 113, 135–8, 145–7

Politicization 7–8, 18–19, 23, 84–5, 88–91, 97–103, 110, 127, 133–5, 137–8, 153–6
Polk, Jonathan 89
Pollack, Mark A. 32, 87, 97, 126
Polyakova, Alina 89
Pooling i, 7, 10, 23, 25–7, 32–4, 36–43, 69, 84–7, 91, 94–5, 97–101, 104–5, 107, 109–13, 116, 119–21, 129, 131, 135, 137–8, 140–4
Portfolio 52, 63–4, 74, 83, 103, 128, 145–6; Policy portfolio i, vii, 1–2, 5, 7, 25, 30, 44–50, 52–3, 56, 58–63, 65–7, 69–75, 77, 79, 81, 83–8, 92, 96, 98–9, 103, 105, 109, 121–2, 129, 131, 133, 145–6, 148, 151; Portfolio change 65, 99, 137–8
Posner, Eric A. 105, 116
Posner, Richard A. 62
Postfunctionalist theory 1, 6–7, 9, 11, 13, 15, 17, 19, 21, 23, 25, 103, 121, 124; Postfunctionalism 2–3, 6, 121–2
Powell, Emilia Justyna 44, 136, 149
Power asymmetry 66–7, 69–71, 73, 83, 97–9, 110, 131, 137–8
Pratto, Felicia see Sidanius et al. 2007 130
Preferential Trade Area for Eastern and Southern Africa (PTA-ESA) 29; Common Market for Eastern and Southern Africa (COMESA) 29, 54–5, 150
Prosser, Christopher 89
Public goods 1–2, 7–8, 12, 16–17, 19–20, 24, 45, 47–9, 66, 127–8, 130–2
Puetter, Uwe 23

Rae, Douglas 149
Rathbun, Brian C. 16, 85
Rawls, John 3, 12–13, 21, 127
Realism 3
Reichel, Ellen see Dingwerth et al. 2015 133
Reinhardt, Eric 44
Rennie, Kriston R. 32
Renou, Ludovic 108
Rhodesia 81
Riches, Cromwell A. 114–15
Riggirozzi, Pia 80, 91
Riker, William H. 4
Risse, Thomas ii, viii, 15, 19, 64, 75, 89–90, 97, 130
Risse-Kappen, Thomas 97
Rittberger, Berthold 44, 94
Rixen, Thomas 85
Rocabert, Jofre 44
Rohrschneider, Robert 89
Romano, Cesare 35, 116
Ropp, Stephen C. 19
Rosendorff, B. Peter 44
Rovny, Jan 89
Ruggie, John G. 76, 132
Rukare, Donald 81

193

Index

Russett, Bruce M. 77, 135, 148
Ryan, Lee *see* McCabe et al. 2001 16
Rydgren, Jens 133

SADC Tribunal 102
Sandel, Michael 14
Sandholtz, Wayne 87, 117
Sandler, Todd 128
Saurugger, Sabine 89
Scale i–iii, 3–4, 6–7, 12, 17, 19–20, 22, 24–5, 35, 37, 39, 44, 46–7, 49–52, 54–7, 59, 68, 75, 82–4, 88–91, 93–4, 99, 103–11, 114, 116, 119, 128–9, 132, 136–7, 141, 143, 154–5; International scale 45; Territorial scale 1
Schakel, Arjan H. 3
Schedler, Andreas 37
Scheingold, Stuart 63, 137
Schimmelfennig, Frank ix, 48, 89–90, 94 see Rocabert et al. 2018 44
Schmidtke, Henning 84, 89
Schmitter, Philippe C. 29, 48, 63, 85, 89, 137
Schneider, Steffen 23, 85, 90
Schuman, Frederick L. 74
Schwarzbözl, Tobias 89
Scott, Robert 14
Security 1, 12, 20, 44, 55, 75–7, 80–1, 89, 91, 97, 100, 104, 107, 115, 132, 136, 138–9, 145, 152
Self-rule i, vii, 2, 5, 11, 18–22, 24, 85, 89, 102–3; Shared rule i, 2, 4–5, 18–19, 22, 24, 47, 85, 89, 124, 127, 132
Senegal 82
Sewell, James P. 91
Sexton, Jay 80
Shaffer, Gregory M. 126
Shair-Rosenfield, Sarah 3, 76
Shared norm 2, 7, 11, 49, 59–60, 62, 67, 78, 83, 86, 112, 130, 150
Shared rule i, 2, 4–5, 18–19, 22, 24, 47, 85, 89, 124, 127, 132
Shanghai Cooperation Organization (SCO) 152
Shanks, Cheryl 135, 149
Shany, Yuval 35
Shaw, Timothy 79, 118
Shelton, Dinah 126
Shubik, Martin 107
Sidanius, Jim 130
Siebenhüner, Bernd 44; *see* Biermann et al. 2009 30
Sikkink, Kathryn 19, 80
Simmons, Beth ii, 19, 44, 57, 66, 97
Simon, Herbert 49
Simple majority 39, 96, 99, 105–6, 109–10, 112, 114–15, 142
Singapore 100
Singer, J. David 138

Slapin, Jonathan B. 72
Slater, Jerome 80
Slaughter, Anne-Marie *see* Goldstein et al. 2000 44
Smith, Vernon 16, 35, 44; *see* Mccabe et al. 2001 16
Snidal, Duncan ix, 15–16, 44, 50, 61, 66, 97, 107, 125–6, 128; *see* Milewicz et al. 2018 70; *see* Abbott et al. 2015 125; *see* Abbott et al. 2016 126
Social contract vii, 3, 6, 11–12, 20, 128
Sociality 2, 5, 11, 12–14, 16, 19, 21, 45, 50, 59, 105, 130–1
Solingen, Etel ii, 85, 90
Somalia 81
Sommerer, Thomas viii; *see* Tallberg et al. 2013 44; *see* Tallberg et al. 2014 87, 94, 97, 153
Soriano, Víctor Fernández 75
South Africa 79
South Sudan 81
Southern African Customs Union (SACU) 40, 46
Southern African Development Community (SADC) 46, 102; SADC Tribunal 102
Southern Common Market (Mercosur) 30, 45, 80, 90, 94; Mercosur Parliament 94
Sovereignty 9–10, 18, 78, 114, 125–7, 132; National sovereignty 1, 5, 9, 18–19, 25, 59, 81, 84, 91, 104–5, 117, 119–20, 123, 126–7, 133, 144–5
Spierenburg, Dirk 70
Spruyt, Hendrik 49
Squatrito, Theresa ix, 145; *see* Tallberg et al. 2013 44; *see* Tallberg et al. 2014 87, 94, 97, 153
Stapel, Sören 74
Steenbergen, Marco viii, 89
Stein, Arthur 97
Stock, James H. 69
Stoeckel, Florian 89
Stoltenberg, Jens 78
Stone, Randall 125
Stone Sweet, Alec 66, 70
Strezhnev, Anton 113, 137
Strijbis, Oliver *see* De Wilde et al. 2019 18, 24, 84, 88–9, 133
Strøm, Kaare 87
Stubager, Rune 133
Stuckey, John *see* Singer et al. 1972 138
Sudan 81
Sugden, Robert 31
Supermajority 39, 96, 109–10, 112, 115–16, 118
Supranationalism 37, 84–5, 89, 99, 103
Sweden 24, 51, 150
Sykes, Alan O. 105

Index

Tajfel, Henri 130
Tallberg, Jonas ii, ix, 32, 44, 87, 94, 97, 145, 153
Tarradell, Mireia *see* Biermann et al. 2009 30
Tarrow, Sidney 19, 97
Task-specific governance 7, 48–50, 52, 57, 122, 124
Teasdale, Anthony 117
Teney, Céline 133
Territorial scale 1
Thailand 100
Thatcher, Margaret 117
Thomas Jr., A.J. 80
Thomas, Christopher 80
Thompson, Alexander 109
Thompson, James D. 61
Thomson, Robert 32
Tierney, Michael J. *see* Hawkins et al. 2006a 87–8, 97; *see* Hawkins et al. 2006b 32, 44, 66
Tilley, James 24, 89, 133
Timmer, Marcel 135, 137
Tomlin, Brian 90
Trade 12, 30, 44, 49, 55, 60–1, 64, 67, 70–3, 83–4, 99, 112, 116–17, 126, 132–3, 138–41, 145, 151–3, 156–8; Trade interdependence 6, 71–3, 83, 99, 131, 135, 138, 148, 156, 158; Trade policy 71–2, 138, 152
Trade interdependence 6, 71–3, 83, 99, 131, 135, 138, 148, 156, 158
Trade policy 71–2, 138, 152
Transnational community 7, 18–19, 25, 45, 47–8, 105, 130–1
Transnationalism 132–4
Trondal, Jarle 88
Trouard, Theodore *see* McCabe at al. 2001 16
Trubek, David M. 126
Trubek, Louise G. 126
Tsebelis, George 87, 107
Tullock, Gordon 105–6
Tuomela, Raimo 17
Turkey 24
Turner, John C. 130

UN Economic and Social Council (ECOSOC) 77
UN Educational, Scientific and Cultural Organization (UNESCO) 40, 91, 112, 132
UN General Assembly 77, 137
UN Industrial Development Organization (UNIDO) 112
Unanimity 1, 58, 86–7, 94, 101, 104–9, 113–19; Consensus 15, 31, 39, 59, 80, 94, 99–101, 103, 109, 118, 133
Union of South American Nations (UNASUR) 80
United Kingdom 51, 116
United Nations (UN) iii, vii, 18, 30, 46, 54–5, 58, 68, 70–1, 73, 75–8, 81–3, 102, 107, 112–13, 115, 121, 137–8, 148, 154, 156; Commonwealth of Nations 68, 78, 83, 139, 150; UN Economic and Social Council (ECOSOC) 77; UN Educational, Scientific and Cultural Organization (UNESCO) 40, 91, 112, 132; UN General Assembly 77, 137; UN Industrial Development Organization (UNIDO) 112
United States 23, 80, 90, 107, 126, 132–3
United States-Mexico-Canada Agreement (USMCA) 60; North American Free Trade Agreement (NAFTA) 23, 46, 55, 60–1, 68, 90, 121, 132, 139, 151
Universal Postal Union (UPU) 112, 114
Uriot, Marc 118
Urquhart, Brian 76

Vabulas, Felicity 125
Van Aken, Wim 32, 118
Van der Brug, Wouter 89, 133
Van Elsas, Erika J. 89, 133
Van Kersbergen, Kees 89
Van Roon, G. 70
Van Wynen Thomas, Ann 80
Van Zanden, Jan Luiten 135, 137
Verdier, Daniel 125
Vernon, Raymond 127
Veto 77, 86–7, 95–6, 103, 107, 109–10, 115, 117–18; National veto 4, 7, 26, 33, 36, 39, 43, 87, 104–5, 108, 115–17, 119–20, 129, 131, 142; Veto player 7, 86, 107, 119
Viola, Lora viii, 11, 44, 94
Voeten, Erik ix, 44, 113, 137

Wagner, Andrea 89
Walter, Stefanie 90
Waltz, Kenneth 4, 128
Warnke, Kevin 29, 136–7
Wassenberg, Birte 75
Watson, Mark W. 69
Webber, Douglas 89
Weber, Max ix, 28
Weiler, Jonathan 24
Weise, Tobias *see* Dingwerth et al. 2015 133
Weisglas, M. 70
Weldon, Steven 23
Welz, Martin 81
Westerwinter, Oliver 125–6
White, Nigel David 76
Whitefield, Stephen 89
Wilf, Meredith 44
Williams, Paul D. 82
Williamson, Oliver 15, 124
Wilson, Carole 89

195

Index

Winzen, Thomas 181; *see* Rocabert et al. 2018 44
Witt, Antonia *see* Dingwerth et al. 2015 133
Wooldridge, Jeffrey 69
World Bank (IBRD) 30, 91, 132, 154
World Customs Organization (WCO) 46, 152
World Health Organization (WHO) 30, 45, 75, 94
World Trade Organization (WTO) 91, 102, 112, 154

Yack, Bernard 17
Yoo, John 116

Zafar, Ali 116
Zamora, Stephen 113–14
Zangl, Bernhard 85; *see* Abbott et al. 2015 125; *see* Abbott et al. 2016 126
Zimbabwe 79, 102
Zürn, Michael 85, 89, 97, 133
Zysman, John 87, 117